CELTIC SACRED
LANDSCAPES

CELTIC SACRED LANDSCAPES

NIGEL PENNICK

with 64 illustrations

Thames & Hudson

Frontispiece: The Celtic cross at Ballaugh, Isle of Man, carved by the Manx runemaster Gaut Björnsson, reproduces in stone the wintry solar phenomenon of the sun-wheel.

Illustrations and text © 1996 Nigel Pennick

First published in hardcover in the United States of America in 1996 by Thames & Hudson Inc., 500 Fifth Avenue, New York, New York 10110

First paperback edition 2000

Library of Congress Catalog Card Number 95-60273
ISBN 0-500-28201-3

Printed and bound in Slovenia

Contents

The Inner and the Outer Landscape

The three principal endeavours of a Bard:
One is to learn and collect sciences;
The second is to teach;
And the third is to make peace
And to put an end to all injury;
For to do contrary to these things
Is not usual or becoming to a Bard.

The Triads of Britain

IF WE LOOK at the landscape through contemporary eyes, our view can be only partial; people in other times, or with other beliefs, have seen things quite differently. The nature of some languages makes it impossible to speak or think in abstract terms, and it was so in pre-modern Celtic tongues. The Celtic bards, in the times before literacy, recorded and remembered everything poetically. Notable events, and their location in the landscape, were recalled in oral aphorisms, ballads, sagas and triads. This poetic vision of the landscape, ensouled with spirits, is a particularly human and therefore humane vision of the world. It describes Carl Jung's enigmatic 'unknown topographical law that rules a man's disposition'. Humans are at one with nature. We are part of it, not separate from it. To the bard, the powers of nature, animals and the human psyche are best personified in anthropomorphic forms that exemplify these qualities. Because they are essential qualities, archetypes and images, and because their existence is implicit rather than explicit in the material world, they are 'otherworldly'. Nevertheless, their existence is real: events, thoughts, ideas, physical objects and places can be understood in terms of these essences.

It is inevitable that everything described by humans must be explained in human terms. These descriptions are interpretations of reality according to the structure and function of human consciousness. We should always bear in mind that, whilst many descriptions render the perceived reality very well, we should never take them literally. For, once they become literal, perceptions take on a life of their own, separate from the reality they once attempted to describe. This important principle is recognized by ancient bardism and modern psychology alike. Homer remarked, 'Harsh are the Gods on him who sees them manifestly', and millennia later Alfred Adler echoed his warning with 'What makes madness is literalism'. In this book, when I write of the psychical and the supernatural, I treat them as recognized realities within the traditional Celtic world-view. Of course, according to one's own preferences or prejudices, any established belief may be questioned and criticized. But, whether or not they appear rational from the standpoint of modern materialism, the beliefs that underlie this book reveal the inner nature of a truly human relationship with the land. For the greater part of human history, such things have been within the very fabric of existence.

The Celtic world-view knows no absolute dividing line between mythology and history. Myths are neither the inventions of archaic poetic imagination, nor the rationalizations of inexplicable phenomena by primitives. They represent primordial truths expressed at the highest level comprehensible to human beings. They should be understood as they live, without any ideological resolution, for there can be no final exegesis. Myths are capable of a number of different interpretations, all of which are equally valid in the circumstances, for they are essentially personal experiences. 'The very tendency to superstition, so marked in Irish nature,' wrote Lady Wilde in her *Ancient Legends of Ireland*, 'arises from an instinctive dislike of the narrow limitations of common sense. It is characterized by a passionate yearning towards the vague, the mystic, the invisible and the boundless infinite of the realms of imagination.'

As human beings, we are rooted in the earth, but modern civilization obscures the fact to the point where many people appear to be unaware of it. Much current human behaviour results from the denial of this reality. Traditional wisdom recognizes and celebrates our relationship with subtle qualities in the land. This is expressed in the relationship between each individual and the land. It manifests its spiritual nature in different places through different spiritual qualities. There is no feature of the landscape that is not associated in local tradition with some event or legend. If we open ourselves to this possibility, we can have a personal spiritual relationship with these qualities. In simple terms, these experiences can be described as our personal relationship with the goddess of the landscape, who is Mother Earth in her local form. Since the eighteenth century this has been described as the *genius loci*, the 'spirit of the place', but it can be described better as the *anima loci*, the 'place-soul'. It can be experienced by anyone anywhere, and it is essentially personal and ineffable. It can be likened to a rainbow: anyone who experiences it sees more or less the same thing, yet in another sense each 'sees' his or her own rainbow, for it is present in that form only within the particular observer.

Modernism recognizes no real spiritual or even physical difference of note between places. Implicit in this view is the tenet that any differences that do exist can be overcome by the power of technology. The effect of this is the innate tendency of modernism to reduce the land to a random series of virtually uninhabitable 'nowheres', brought into being by the denial of place. The impersonal nature of industry means that the local earth as provider is no longer honoured. Nobody knows precisely where anything comes from, or who made it, or how. It is delocalized and depersonalized, identified only by a trade name and perhaps the country from which it comes. Despite this, each thing does have an origin. It has its own personal history. It came into being, then was harvested, processed or made by someone, somehow, somewhere, and transported to where it is now.

In traditional Celtic society, nothing was impersonal. Everything was a subject, not an object, and was spoken of by its own personal name. Every thing, artifact and place was named, reflecting the character of its animated nature. Each name possessed a personal quality that had meaning both with regard to the thing itself and to those who lived with and related to it. With the rise of manufacturing industry, this personal contact was lost; most artifacts became anonymous products. Their essential character no longer reflected the character of its maker, use and users. Trade became the main consideration. Today, the naming of the animated world survives in truncated form in the names of private and public houses, hotels, aircraft and ships, and occasionally other personal possessions such as cars, knives, guns and guitars.

Even in antiquity, the Celts were renowned for their reverence for the spoken word: bards received the highest honours, and druids perpetuated their wisdom by means of a highly developed art of memory. Bardic knowledge utilized a sophisticated system of metaphor, allegory and symbolism, giving access to the invisible inner nature of things. In the first century BCE, when the Celts in Cisalpine Gaul were conquered by Rome, Celtic families produced many outstanding men of letters, *inter alia*, Cato, Catullus, Varro and Virgil. Later, in the north, Irish, British and Breton bards laid the foundations of the medieval literature of Western Europe.

The themes recorded in this Celtic spiritual literature are reflected in the Celtic landscape. They recall the ensouled world of Celtic tradition, in which every place and artifact has its own personality, reflecting multiple meanings in the physical and non-material worlds. When studied knowingly, legends and stories that can be taken literally contain within themselves a deeper symbolic meaning. The interchangeable forms of Celtic art express the plurality of existence, the multifaceted experiences of life, death and rebirth. Each type of artifact expresses its own symbolic qualities, mythic traditions that still exist in contemporary Celtic art and spirituality.

Celtia was never homogeneous. From the earliest times, the Celts were divided into innumerable families, clans and tribes. In the second century of our era, Ptolemy listed thirty-three separate tribes, which today would be called 'ethnic groups', in Britain alone. Since then, ceaseless migrations, wars, conquests and exterminations have destroyed certain parts of Celtia and mixed others, both with one another and with other European ethnic groupings. Today, reflecting their different histories, there are several different aspects of the Celtic landscape. Primarily, this book deals with the sacred landscapes of the countries where Celtic culture is still predominant or acknowledged as being significant: Ireland, Scotland, the Isle of Man, Wales, Cornwall and Brittany. Those where elements of the Celtic sacred landscape remain, but are overlaid with other cultures to a greater extent, include England, parts of France, Belgium, Germany, Switzerland, Austria, Italy and Hungary.

Throughout history there is a continuous process whereby culture develops and changes according to the needs and prevailing beliefs of the times. Celtic culture has been through several stages where new influences have been absorbed and reinterpreted according to the Celtic genius. Celtic culture was modified materially by the introduction of iron technology, contacts with Greek and Etruscan culture, Roman domination, the change from polytheism to monotheism, and finally the development of modern technical civilization. For instance, essences personified as goddesses and gods by polytheism were redefined under monotheism as aspects of godhead, e.g. angels, saints and demons. Their essential natures, however, remained unchanged. Equally, people continued to recognize and celebrate the inherent qualities of sacred places under the aegis of a different theological interpretation. The real disruption of Celtic sanctity was not the result of polytheism's absorption into and transformation by Christianity. Both systems sustained a continuum of the sacred, in which profound religious significance could be found in the seemingly insignificant things of everyday life. Under both the Celtic and the Roman Catholic Churches, the shrines of saints and cults of holy places flourished; only when national Churches were invented were the ancient places abandoned, the stopping-places wrecked and the shrines profaned and robbed. An emphasis on the ascendancy of messianic scripture, and the concomitant doctrine of the unimportance of place, overwhelmed the more gentle devotion to the sacred earth, paving the way for the modern, desacralized world.

Today, there is a real difference between the Celtic landscapes that underwent the Reformation and those that remained Catholic. With a few notable exceptions, the sacred places of England, Wales and Scotland were disempowered and often utterly destroyed. Hereditary or traditional guardians – the coarbs and dewars – were dispossessed, and sometimes imprisoned. In South Uist, Ireland and Brittany, however, the Celtic sacred landscape continues to flourish in a much more traditional form. Local people cherish their shrines and saints; they place flowers and offerings at stopping-places, crosses, stones and holy wells. Wayside shrines and chapels are maintained for the spiritual refreshment of the traveller. Because the *anima loci* is acknowledged, the sacred landscape is also a humane landscape. It is this interactive quality that is appraised in *Celtic Sacred Landscapes*.

The Celtic Symbolic Landscape

*Those ancient sages who sought to obtain the presence of divine
beings by setting up shrines and statues seem to me to have shown
insight into the nature of the universe. They understood that it is
always easy to attract soul and particularly simple to keep it by
constructing an object fashioned so as to be influenced by it
and to receive a share of it.*

Plotinus, *The Soul*, 10

THE CELTIC COSMOS

THE TRADITIONAL cosmology of the bards of Britain, which gives
us an invaluable insight into Celtic beliefs, was nearly lost.
Fortunately, it was pieced together in the sixteenth century by the
Welsh bard Llewellyn Sion who sifted through a chaotic collection of
ancient manuscripts kept at Rhaglan Castle. Although by the standards
of Celtic history it is late, Llewellyn Sion's material gives the most coherent description of the Celtic world-system. According to bardism, the
processes of existence have a threefold nature. Of course, most basically,
all things have a beginning, a middle and an end. But the triadic view has
a much wider application at many levels of existence, as the poetic triads
demonstrate. According to this cosmology, there are three 'circles' or
'worlds'. They are viewed either as concentric circles, or, in keeping with
other traditional cosmologies, ascending planes upon the column of the
world tree. World tree or cosmic axis concepts from different parts of the
world are strikingly similar, stemming from a common origin within the
human psyche. They tell of a vertical axis running through this plane
above and below the earth, linking us to other planes of existence.

Although refuted by the known facts of material existence, this symbolic hierarchical universe is valid psychologically as a model of being. It
contains four 'circles of being'. The outermost circle or the base of the
tree is Annwn, the Abyss. Known also as Anghar (The Loveless Place)

The Cosmic Axis, according to Welsh tradition. Abred (middle earth) stands above the underworld, Annwn, whilst above it are Gwynvyd, the heavenly upperworld, and Ceugant, the ineffable place of Hên Ddihenydd, the 'Ancient and Unoriginated One'.

and Affan (The Invisible Land), these are the unseen roots of the world tree beneath the earth. The realm of the unconscious, Annwn is the incorporeal abode of unformed matter, elementals, wraiths and demonic spirits. Above this is Cylch y Abred, the middle world upon which we walk. Here, good and evil are in equal measure, and hence there is free will, for in Abred every act is one of choice or consent. This is the realm of the ego. Above this earth is Cylch y Gwynvyd, the heavenly realm of enlightened, divine beings and those humans who have transcended the cycle of their earthly lives. This is the realm of the fully conscious mind. The uppermost level, Cylch y Ceugant, is the unattainable sole abode of the transcendent Hên Ddihenydd, assumed to be identical with the God of the monotheistic system.

THE SACRED LAND

The traditional view of the world is expressed wholly in symbolic terms. Whenever we perceive any aspect of nature, symbols are revealed to us. 'In the symbol', wrote Goethe, 'the particular represents the general, not as in a dream, nor as in a shadow, but as a living and instantaneous revelation of the inscrutable.' Every place we experience impresses itself symbolically upon our consciousness, and we express these symbols through religious, poetic or scientific metaphors. A system of symbolic correspondences is the psychological basis of the Celtic approach to landscape.

Traditional teachings inform us that the earth is not a dead body, but is infused by a spirit that is its life and soul. It is a world where the material is a reflection of the spirit, and where the spirit reveals itself in the material. Celtic tradition and beliefs are expressed spiritually through the land: the landscape is filled with places where spirit is present. Every time we experience it, this presence encourages us to make an imaginative act that personifies the place to us. Then we perceive its qualities as a personality. This is the *anima loci*, the place-soul. When this is acknowledged and honoured, ensouled sacred places come into being. Our actions enshrine the *anima loci*, bringing the unseen into physical presence. The *anima loci* is the essential personality of a location. Traditionally, it is viewed as a presence or being that exists beyond the everyday realms of human cognizance, perhaps possessing its own consciousness and personality. It is also open to a modern, psychological interpretation. Whichever view we choose, the presence is really perceived as a feeling or atmosphere which is experienced as a totality.

A state of sanctity exists when the innate, essential spiritual nature of a place is manifested in physical form. Its relationship with our human world begins when its *anima loci* is recognized. Natural places are the most basic sacred places: stones, springs, mountains, islands and trees are locations where the *anima loci* may be best approached. Sacred places come into being when humans recognize and acknowledge them. They are ensouled locations where we can experience elevated consciousness, receive religious inspiration and accept healing. They allow fully developed human beings to become at one with nature. There, we are no longer separated from nature by reflection. As time passes, through repetition and development, the innate qualities of sacred places are intensified on physical and other subtler levels. The latent spirit of place is manifested on the material level. At this point a truly sacred place begins to exist for us; the invisible is made visible. Its significance becomes clear as an indicator of metaphysical realities, for within it there is a revelation of the archetypal qualities of the eternal otherworld, that is, paradise.

In addition, the creation of sanctity is more than the mere acknowledgment or reproduction of some specific perception of a place. It is a unique presentation of its inner qualities that does not act as an intermediate filter, interpretation or representation. Rather, nothing comes between: there is total transparency. Pilgrims can experience the influence of souls without interposing intellectual concepts; the sacred place serves as an accessible gateway to the divine. A truly empowered sacred place transcends space and time, presenting timeless existence. Empowerment is most effective when the essences of the subtle world are brought into tangible form, promoting the evolution of the hitherto unmanifested qualities of the *anima loci*. When people perform acts at a place that are in harmony with its inner qualities, then these qualities are enhanced and increased. These acts include the performance of ceremonies, the creation of pleasing and harmonious artifacts – anything that elicits in humans a comparable response.

Enhancing the *anima loci* is a kind of spiritual gardening. It cannot result from attempts to command and control a place, but comes rather from participating consciously in the qualities already present, from which breathes an ennobling presence. The most important condition that we can establish there is an atmosphere of calm, peace and emotional stability, so enabling us to be receptive to the divine. The mind should not turn towards anything profane: no acts that could damage or destroy the *anima loci* should take place. Ceremonies that enhance the qualities of the place, engendering human communion with the *anima loci*, should be conducted. Rituals present elements of the nature of the *anima loci* in human terms. They ensure harmonious conformity of the visible world with the invisible. The important result of these place-related ceremonies is that the participants will go home afterwards carrying new levels of consciousness.

The common northern European understanding of the *anima loci* is best recorded in Iceland. First discovered by voyaging Irish monks, the uninhabited island was colonized by people from Norway and the Western Isles of Scotland in the ninth and tenth centuries. Their traditional practices were documented in *Landnámabók*, the Icelandic 'Book of Settlement', and other contemporary texts. The first settlers were acutely aware of the personality of places. Certain areas and land-holdings were kept specially for the *landvaettir* – 'land-wights' or earth spirits. As in the Celtic Church three centuries earlier, the sites for Icelandic places of worship were selected by geomantic techniques that recognized the *anima loci*. Sacred places were respected and honoured. People directing prayers towards Helgafell, the holy mountain of Iceland, first washed their faces out of respect. On these sacred lands, no fetid smell might be made and no living thing might be destroyed. Ships' figureheads were removed before land was sighted, lest the *landvaettir* be disturbed. Other sacred places were honoured in a way that appears peculiarly modern. *Landnámabók* records how Thorvald Holbarki 'went up to Surtur's Cave and recited there a poem that he had composed about the giant in the cavern.'

Northern European legends and folk traditions of the landscape elsewhere inform us that spiritual orderliness originates in harmonious care of the land as sacred. It is this nurturing, spiritual awareness that brings peace and plenty, a society of good will, fecundity of flocks and herds, and fruitfulness of fields and orchards. All nature-based religions teach the path of life as a means of unification of the aspirant's life with the divine ideal. Religion also seeks to bring about in those who are not conscious devotees an unconscious observance of the path, presenting a way of life that follows precisely the order of nature.

In ensouled landscapes, natural or human-made features are named after qualities, things or people that have a significant bearing on life. The landscape is living and relevant: it has not been reduced to grid co-ordinates or names imposed from outside by mapmakers and non-local travellers. Place-names are often preserved long after their meanings have

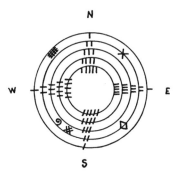

Finn's Shield: an image of the shield of the Irish hero, Finn MacCumhaill, which allocates the letters of the ogham alphabet to the eight directions, as a symbol of wholeness and accomplishment.

faded into oblivion. New languages, brought by incoming settlers or invaders, have superseded the earlier Celtic ones, but many of the names have remained, and so the places' meanings can be recovered. Significant myths and lore relating to places may linger long after they have been desacralized or destroyed. Also, in Ireland, the place-name stories called *Dindsenchas* preserve geomythic tales that express the quality of ensoulment of certain places. Equivalent place-name lore exists in other Celtic-influenced lands.

SPACE AND TIME

At any place on earth, orientation is paramount, for it determines the quality of life there. Hence, traditional societies all over the world have a comprehensive understanding of the interaction between place and direction, often formalized in systems of geomancy appropriate to the local terrain and climate. An ancient Irish adage tells of the most beneficial qualities a place needs for abundance: 'A southern aspect for warmth, a stream across the glebe, choice, prosperous land that would be good for every plant.' Because of their innate nature, the directions have a symbolic quality. The south is equated with warmth and light, whilst the north is the realm of cold and darkness. Sunrise brings to the east the quality of brightness, beginnings and increase, whilst the setting sun of the west indicates decline and closure. In the northern martial arts, the opponents in serious struggles faced each other along the north–south line. It was so in trial by combat. When the fighting was for recreation or practice, such as in tournaments, the combatants fought east–west. When the north faces the south, the opposites of cold and hot, dark and light, face one another. Similarly, in divorces the couples stood north–south, back to back, and walked away from each other. But when east faces west, there is balance.

The sort of weather associated with wind-direction is an important factor that must be taken into account when one decides the placement of a farm or fane. Each *airt* (eighth of the horizon) has its own wind, each possessing its own virtue, an understanding of which is essential in geomancy. Also, traditional cultures throughout the world assert that all existence is pervaded by a subtle 'cosmic breath' which animates all things and empowers their continued existence. This breath is best known in the West as *pneuma*, or the fifth Platonic element, the Quintessence. The Welsh bardic tradition describes it as *anal* or *anadyl*. The breath is what animates the body of animals and also, by analogy, the living body of the earth. A person's life begins when he or she draws the first breath. Although they are never counted, a finite number of breaths measure a life, and death comes with the passing of the final breath. Northern European wind-lore teaches that the quality of the wind at the moment of the first breath determines the character of that life. Because the wind of each airt has its own peculiar attributes, the infant's first inspiration is from the virtue of the prevailing wind. The child's destiny is determined by the winds of the cardinal quarters. Their nature is explained in an old Irish poem, 'The Winds of Fate':

The boy who is born with a westerly wind
Shall have garments, sustenance shall acquire;
He shall have from his lord, assuredly,
Other than food or clothing no more.

The boy who is born with a northerly wind
Will win victory, but shall suffer defeat,
He will be wounded, another shall he wound,
Before ascending to the angelic height.

The boy who is born with the south wind,
Will receive honey, fruit shall obtain.
Bishops and fine musicians
In his house will entertain.

Laden with gold is the east wind,
The best wind of all four that blow;
The boy who is born when that wind blows
In all his days want shall never know.

Whenever the wind does not blow
Over grass or plain or heather,
Whoever is born then,
A fool shall be, boy or girl whether.

When there is no wind, it is a time of danger, and not just for becalmed sailors. A place on land without wind has 'a bad atmosphere' that brings sickness, so a first breath of this 'bad air' was deemed disastrous to the new-born.

In ancient northern Europe, awareness of the cosmos was not just speculative. There was a practical element to everything, and, among other things, Celtic literature gives glimpses of astrological techniques and abilities. In a Welsh poem attributed to Amergin, the author boasts of his astronomical prowess:

> Who telleth the ages of the moon, if not I?
> Who showeth the place where the sun goes to rest, if not I?

Welsh literature preserves lists of asterisms and constellations quite different from the Graeco-Arab ones used in modern astronomy. They are closer to the Norse tradition. In addition, the Irish saga, *The Intoxication of the Ulaid*, records the time-telling at night by the stars, where the hero Cú Chulainn asks his comrade, Lóeg, son of Ríangabur, to go outside 'and look at the stars, and tell me when it is midnight, as you have waited and watched for me often enough at the boundaries of distant lands.' Lóeg goes out, and he waits and watches until midnight comes. At the appropriate moment, he re-enters the house and says: 'It is midnight now, O Cú of the Feats.' There are few alive now who are capable of repeating Lóeg's observation.

Before the less appropriate Mediterranean system of time-telling was introduced by the Church, the northern day cycle was divided into eight tides, each of three hours' duration. Each tide corresponds with one of the eight winds, being the apparent direction of the sun at that time of day. In the Welsh tradition, the parts of the day are named: *Dewaint* (midnight); *Pylgeint* (dawn); *Bore* (morning); *Anterth* (vapourlessness); *Nawn* (noon); *Echwydd* (rest); *Hwyr* or *Gwechwydd* (evening); and *Ucher* (shadow).

To the continental Celts, the year had two halves. It began at Samhain, the most important festival of the year, 1 November in modern reckoning. It marked the end of the grazing season, when the last of the flocks and herds were brought

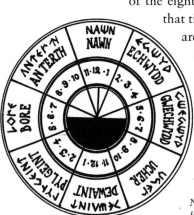

Northern tradition cosmology divides the day into eight tides, here shown in their Welsh form.

to their winter pastures and surplus animals slaughtered. Clans and tribes gathered at their ceremonial centres for a festival of death and renewal, at which the symbolic union of the tribal god with a nature-goddess was celebrated. The summer half of the year began on 1 May with a festival called Beltane or Cétshamhain, when cattle were driven through bonfire smoke to protect them magically in their summer pastures.

In Pagan Ireland the two halves of the year were further subdivided by Imbolc (1 February) and Lughnasa (Lammas, 1 August). These, with the solstices and equinoxes, mark the eightfold division of the year. Like Samhain and Beltane, Imbolc was a pastoral festival, marking the start of lambing, with the first lactation of the ewes. It was sacred to the goddess of creativity and fertility, Brigid, who was later assimilated by the Church into the St Brigid who is still fêted on the same day. The autumnal festival, Lughnasa (Bron Trograin), was probably imported into Ireland at a later date, perhaps by continental devotees of the craftsman-god Lugh. The Irish Lughnasa differs from the other festivals in its agrarian character, celebrating the grain harvest and the baking of the first loaf from it. Through the celebration of these festivals at their sacred places, the ancient sages combined the structure of human life with the eternal cycles of existence, expressing an integrated, holistic world.

As Above, So Below

Nothing in nature is fixed; there is continuous change and flow. Even the most permanent things are subject to gradual alteration. The patterns and forms that typify the art called Celtic are those of the Nwyvre, the mythical dragon that snakes unseen through the earth. They are also based on geometrical criteria that reflect Manred, the underlying matrix of existence. They are ever-changing, fading imperceptibly from one form into another, yet they always express the same essence. Surviving ancient Celtic artifacts express different aspects of this essential continuity, where the forms of this world and the non-material world interpenetrate one another. In the Celtic world-view, the realms of animals and humans, goddesses and gods, and life and death are not separate. They are aspects of a great integrated continuum in which everything is an aspect of the whole, where the principles of self-similarity reflect the basic way that nature is structured. Each torc, ring and metal fitment, however small, is a perfect reflection of this principle. The geometric matrices upon which Celtic tessellations, spirals and knotwork are based are continuous. In their plurality, these patterns are interchangeable. They fade into one another. They are fixed artistic representations of the ever-flowing particles of Manred, for all is flux, and the patterns we see at any one time are the patterns specific to that time, not eternal and unchanging.

According to the bards, the nature of human beings can be understood by studying the relationship between the elements that compose the body and soul. 'There are eight parts in man,' *The Book of Llanrwst* tells us:

> The first is the earth, which is inert and heavy, and from it proceeds the flesh; the second are the stones, which are hard, and the substance of the bones; the third is water, which is moist and cold, and is the substance of the blood; the fourth is the salt, which is briny and sharp, and from it are the nerves, and the temperament of feeling, as regards bodily sense and faculty; the fifth is the firmament or wind, out of which proceeds the breathing; the sixth is the sun, which is clear and fair, and from it proceed the fire, or bodily heat, the light and colour; the seventh is the Holy Ghost, from whom issues the soul and life; and the eighth is Christ, that is, the intellect, wisdom and the light of soul and life.

Attributed to the bard Taliesin, this interpretation of the origin of the soul and life is in accord with that of classical Pagan antiquity. Vitruvius noted: 'Man has been made in both the image of God and the image of the universe.' Similarly, early Christian theorists promoted the same view of the human. Zanchius wrote: 'The body of man is the image of the world, and called therefore *microcosmus*.' He is echoed by Gregory Nazianzene: 'Every creature, both of heaven and earth, is in man.' Thus, the workings of the human body and soul are reflections of the universe.

According to this view, because the human is composed of various elements, the occurrence of these elements in humans reflects nature; so, in turn, nature can be interpreted in terms of the human constitution. Various features of the landscape are reflections of corresponding human parts, so we can relate to them in terms of those parts. This is expressed in ancient legends of a giant who is slain and whose body becomes the earth. It is a motif preserved in northern Europe in the myths of Ymir and Gargantua. A primal giant, he is slain by the gods. His body makes the fabric of the world: his bones become the rocks, his blood the rivers and seas, his hair the plants and his skull the firmament. The giant demonstrates the relationship between the parts of our body and the structure of the world. It is an image of our oneness with the world.

Sacred Trees

No murd'ring Axes let 'em feel,
Nor violate the Groves with impious Steel;
From rude Assaults and Force prophane forbear,
Avenging Deities inhabit there.

R. Rapin, *De Hortorum* (1665)

WHEREVER IT is possible for them to grow, trees are important features of the landscape. They provide people with shelter, materials and fuel and, by their location and shape, express the character of a place. Trees interact dynamically with the environment. Every tree is a living watercourse: its roots, trunk and branches conduct water up from the soil to the leaves, from which it then passes into the atmosphere. Growing, the tree strives towards the light, whilst remaining rooted in the earth. The tree, like the human, is a mediator between the upper and lower worlds, linking with its serpentine watercourses the underworld of the ground, the surface of the ground upon which we live, and the sky and air. Thus, the tree is an image of the cosmic axis, a physical manifestation of the maxim 'as above, so below'. It is a little world in itself, for it provides shelter for many animals, and bears epiphytic and parasitic plants. When dead, it provides fuel and also material for the practitioners of craft. Each species of wood has its own unique characteristics.

As a living being, the tree exists within a limited if indeterminate time-span. It is born from the seed, grows to maturity, reproduces, lives to old age and then dies. Unlike a human being, a tree can be sustained and regenerated by cuttings, or, when cut down, by suckers arising from a living root system. In order to obtain as much light as possible, the branches and leaves are arranged according to precise geometrical laws which reflect the universal order implicit in all things. The shapes that trees take depend primarily upon the genetics encoded within the species; but, as they grow, they are subjected constantly to the prevailing influences of their location. Thus, tree type and shape are good indicators of the physical qualities of a place. The shape of any individual tree depends upon many factors. The basic shape is that which is 'typical' for the species, but, as in most things, the 'ideal' or 'typical' shape is relatively uncommon. Soil conditions, competition from other trees, slope, shade, wind and lightning all affect the way it grows. Also, humans alter trees by accidental or deliberate mutilation. This, too, speaks of the nature of the tree and its environment. In former times, augurs would examine trees to discover the hidden essences and qualities of a place. Water diviners have noted that the forms of trees can indicate the presence of underground water. Where they possess twisted trunks, double forms, and branches that grow back into the trunk, making contorted shapes, they are living indicators of an active place. Traditionally, twisted trees are revered as sacred, and the spiral wands carried today by witches and druids are a reminder of this.

Because they can become charged electrically, trees are frequently struck by lightning. Thunderbolt-damaged trees are readily recognized, for they have a characteristic furrow down one or more of the upper branches which continues down the trunk. Often this furrow takes a spiral pathway down through the middle of the tree, hollowing it out. Although any tree can be struck, there is an enduring tradition that certain kinds of trees 'court the flash' and thus are favourites of the thunder-god. They are trees whose structure and physiology create stronger fields around them. Oaks are particularly prone to lightning damage because they are very deep-rooted, often standing isolated. Because they have rough bark, they conduct the lightning through the woody parts. When wet, smooth-barked trees provide a good pathway for lightning to flow over the surface, but with the oak this is not possible and the current takes the line of least resistance. Travelling through the wood, the lightning explosively vaporizes the water inside, tearing open the trunk and sometimes blowing off branches. Trees struck by lightning often regenerate in a shape known as 'stag-headed', and trees trained artificially to grow in this shape re-create the form of god-chosen trees. Because it is prone to lightning strikes, the oak was especially sacred to the sky-god. Mistletoe, a plant revered by the druids, was reputed to grow there as a result of lightning striking the tree.

The shape of any tree indicates the prevailing local conditions. Isolated groves often have a unified overall canopy shape, where the whole wood resembles an enormous single tree. These groves are most prominent in rolling, hilly country, where they occupy small hill-tops, knolls or ancient burial barrows. Trees growing in very windy places, such as near the sea, have longer and more luxuriant branches on the side sheltered from the prevailing wind. These 'wind-cut' trees look as if they are blowing in the wind like a frozen banner. From a 'wind-cut' tree we can find the prevailing wind direction and estimate its strength.

THE TREE-SPIRIT

The Tree of Life is a symbol present in every human culture. It symbolizes the Great Mother, the nurturer of growth who carries and sustains all life. This is most apparent with 'bleeding' yew trees, from which resin, the tree's 'life blood', issues incessantly, recalling the menstrual blood of women. European myth possesses various versions of the legend that the first human beings were trees transformed by the gods into human form. In *The Aeneid* Virgil tells that the woods 'were first the seat of sylvan powers, of nymphs and fauns, and savage men who took their birth from trunks of trees and stubborn oaks.' Celtic lore tells that the first woman was a rowan tree and the first man an alder. In the light of this myth, when the human being enters a tree at death, it is a return to the origin: part of the soul of the deceased enters a tree planted on the grave. In Wales, Scotland and Ireland there are a number of notable trees that mark the graves of bards and heroes. Similarly, the origin of the wooden coffin comes from burial within a hollowed-out tree trunk. In south

The Celtic tree-spirit appears on buildings as an 'apotropeion', known as the Green Man. This one is from a building in the Andreasplatz in Hildesheim, Germany.

Germany, tree-trunk coffins of the Alamannic period are carved with dragons' heads, signifying the Nwyvre, the corpse-swallowing earth serpent. Tree-burial was customary in Germany until the late Middle Ages.

Celtic beliefs indicate that a tree can be regarded as a deity in its own right and also as the seat of a deity. A tree can serve as a receptacle for an external spirit, what Apollonius of Rhodes calls a 'hamadryad'. Thus, it may be inhabited by individual spirits, fairies or demons. Also, trees may contain certain spirits of humans that have passed into trees, and spirits of the land that have been expelled from their proper dwelling-places and have taken up residence in the nurturing environment of a tree. Like human beings, trees have personal souls, which are manifested as special qualities, strengths and medicinal virtues. In former times, it was customary to give birth beneath certain trees that conferred spiritual support and absorbed some of the pains of labour. In addition, it permitted a human soul residing in the tree between lives to be more readily reincarnated.

A tree may also absorb spirits that might otherwise prove harmful to humans, eliminating harmful influences from its surrounding area. Sometimes the notoriety of an individual tree is so great that it gains widespread fame, and is visited as a tourist attraction. The Nannau Oak near Dolgellau, blown down in 1813, was famed far and wide as a tree haunted by hobgoblins. It became famous throughout Britain when Sir Walter Scott wrote of it in his *Marmion* as 'the Spirit's blasted tree'.

The Wild Wood and Sacred Groves

The natural forest symbolizes the untamed, wild part of the human soul: it is an archetype of wildness. Wildness, however, is not a state of being out of control, rather it signifies innate naturalness existing in balance with natural principles. Eternal, elemental powers reside in the forest, and those who seek may come into contact with them. When people periodically return to the wild, the wild woods give us the possibility of deep psychic healing. The wild wood is the place in which we can restore our conscious link with our inner instincts by contacting the 'wild man' within all of us. When we are supported by the elemental powers of the wood, a rediscovery of forgotten things can take place. Ceremonies of 'Maying' in the woods are a means of doing this. But this can only happen when the untouched wild wood still exists. Once it is destroyed, then the wild part of the human soul is no longer accessible. Reintegration is no longer possible, and the Wasteland comes.

Like the Greeks, the Pagan Celts worshipped in sacred groves called *nemetoi*. These were 'clearings open to the sky', pious enclaves set aside in woodland, dread places held in great awe by the people, entered only by priests and priestesses. In his *Pharsalia* Lucan tells of the Gaulish druids who lived in deep groves and secluded uninhabited woods. The Scholiast remarks that they 'worship the gods in the woods without using temples'. It seems that, like temples, groves were set up or dedicated to specific deities. Dio Cassius writes that the Britons worshipped in sanctuaries where they offered sacrifice to Andraste, goddess of victory. A Gallo-Roman inscription found at Vaison in Vaucluse commemorates the establishment of a nemeton in honour of Belesama. More generally, the goddesses Arnemetia and Nemetona were the deities of the nemeton. Temples came later, following Roman practice.

Although they have long since been abandoned, many nemeton sites are still known. In France, the name of Nanterre recalls the Celtic Nemetodunum. In England there is Vernemeton, 'the especially sacred grove', and in Scotland Medionemeton, 'the middle sanctuary'. An old Irish name for a sacred wood is *Fidnemet*. As centres of native loyalty, they were subject to destruction by conquerors. Lucan describes how Julius Caesar destroyed a nemeton near Marseilles that contained trees fashioned into godly images. During his extirpation of the British druids, Suetonius Paulinus desecrated the Anglesey groves, and in later times St Martin of Tours and St Patrick wielded the axe in the name of their faith. In the eleventh century, the Irish high king Brian Boru spent a month destroying the sacred grove of Thor near Dublin. Paradoxically, other Celtic Christians were planters. The *Liber Landavensis* tells us that in sixth-century Brittany the British monks Teilo and Samson 'planted a great grove of fruit-bearing trees, to the extent of three miles, from Dôl as far as Cai.' To this day, St Teilo is the patron of apple trees. In Wales, all trees growing on land dedicated to St Beuno were once deemed sacred, and could not be cut or damaged in any way.

Some of the great Celtic forests were considered wholly sacred in their own right. Among them were the forests of Brocéliande and Morrois and the Wood of Caledon. Little of them remains today. Deforestation has reduced them to a fraction of their former size. The few remnants of Brocéliande are the Forêt de Huelgoat, the Forêt de Paimpont, and the twin sacred woods called Coat-an-Hay and Coat-an-Noz, the 'Day Wood' and the 'Night Wood' respectively, close to the Breton holy hill of Menez-Bré. In Scotland, the Wood of Caledon once stretched from Glencoe to

Braemar and from Glen Lyon to Glen Affric. In legend, it was destroyed by a monster called Muime, which was brought from Scandinavia to fly over the forest, dropping flaming brands upon it. Historically, however, it was at the hands of people that it fell. Between the ninth and twelfth centuries the forest suffered merciless felling and burning. Warring clans set the woodland alight, either to extirpate their enemies or to eliminate wolves. Later, more trees were felled for shipbuilding, and between the fifteenth and eighteenth centuries ironmasters took timber to stoke their foundries. Yet more destruction was wrought by the two world wars, so that the only significant remains of this once great forest are in the Black Wood of Rannoch at Loch Tulla.

The result of this human carelessness was an ecological catastrophe, commemorated in bardic renderings such as 'What shall we henceforth do without timber? The last of the woods is fallen', or in Aodhagan O Rathaille's lament, 'Woe, your woods are withering away'. The destructive consequences of this deforestation are recognized in the ballad 'Seven Hundred Elves', which tells of a farmer who destroys a wood and is punished by its indwelling spirits:

> He felled the oak, he felled the birch,
> The beech nor poplar spared,
> And much were grieved the sullen elves
> At what the stranger dared.
> He hewed him baulks and he hewed him beams
> With eager toil and haste,
> Then up and spake the woodland elves,
> 'Who's come our wood to waste?'

The spirits of the trees did not forgive those who had driven them out, for the ultimate result of ecological destruction is the Wasteland, which is as much a spiritual as a physical state.

TREE CLUMPS

In parts of Britain a clump or grove of pine trees on the crest of a hill is called a 'folly'; such trees are strongly affected by the wind. The Greeks heeded the oracular sound of the wind rustling in Zeus's prophetic oak at Dodona; the wind in the reeds creates the syrinx sound of the great god Pan. When we visit a hill-top grove, the sound of the wind may create mental images of the roaring sea, a blazing fire or supernatural voices. In *The*

Old Straight Track, Alfred Watkins noted in the Herefordshire border country frequent 'one-tree' hills and compact tree clumps, which he knew to be landmarks for travellers on ancient trackways.

Ancient apple orchards are another remnant of Celtic sacred groves. Their inviolability is enshrined in common law under the privileges of British Free Miners. Chartered associations of independent miners were permitted to prospect for and extract coal and minerals in areas where they were plentiful, including Cornwall and the Forest of Dean where they still operate. Their royal charters, which have precedents in ancient Welsh law, give them the right to dig on any land, with three exceptions: the sacred ground of the king's highway, churchyards and orchards. Even today, many people look upon the destruction of an orchard as an act of sacrilege, and not only because a valuable living resource is being wiped out. The tradition continues of 'wassailing' the orchards at midwinter, when offerings are made to fruit trees and shotguns are fired into the air to ward off evil in the coming year.

SINGLE TREES

Celtic veneration of trees came from twin sources: as a direct outgrowth of archaic animistic beliefs, and also by way of Graeco-Etruscan influences on central Europe in the Hallstatt and La Tène periods. Throughout the northern hemisphere, single trees were the foci of shamanic activities, and from them arose more formalized, sophisticated religion. To the Greeks and Celts, each ancient deity had her or his own type of holy tree. The oak was sacred to Zeus and Taranis, the myrtle to Aphrodite, the thorn to the Queen of the May. The Scholiast of Aristophanes notes that the olive tree was Athena's temple and her image before the times of temples and images. Today, certain rose and thorn trees are sacred to Our Lady.

The close similarities between the Celtic and the Greek traditions emphasize the essential unity of European polytheism. A venerated single tree known as a *bile* was part of any sacred place where Celtic kings were inaugurated. The French place-name Billom recalls the Celtic Biliomagus, 'the plain of the sacred tree'. Ancient Ireland knew five such sacred trees, which the *Rennes Dindsenchas* described as no longer in existence even then. One stood for each province; they were the trees of Ross and Mugna, Tortu and Datha, and the branching ash tree of Uisnech, which stood alongside the Stone of Divisions, the navel of the land. Mugna's tree was an evergreen oak which bore three varieties of fruit: in addition to acorns, it produced apples and nuts, perhaps from grafted branches. Offerings and the remains of ceremonies were hung upon bile trees. Also, some sacred trees were not left in their natural state, but were tended and altered somewhat in the fashion of the later trained lindens of mainland Europe.

'Druim Suithe', a medieval Irish poem about the yew tree of Ross, reveals the multivalent symbolism of the tree to Celtic sensibilities. It is full of allusions and kennings, describing the famed oracular tree of Leinster, the 'word-pure man':

> Tree of Ross:
> A king's wheel,
> A prince's right,
> A wave's noise,
> Best of creatures:
> A straight, firm tree.
> A firm, strong god,
> Door of Heaven,
> Strength of a building,
> The good of a crew,
> A wood-pure man,
> Full-great bounty,
> The Trinity's mighty one,
> A measure's hours,
> A mother's god,
> Mary's Son,
> A fruitful sea,
>
> Beauty's honour,
> A mind's lord,
> Diadem of angels,
> Shout of the world,
> Banba's renown,
> Might of Victory,
> Judgment of origin,
> Judicial doom,
> Faggot of sages,
> Noblest of trees,
> Glory of Leinster,
> Dearest of bushes,
> A bear's defence,
> Vigour of life,
> Spell of knowledge,
> Tree of Ross.

TOWN AND FAMILY TREES

Despite their longevity in comparison with human life, trees, like all living things, have a limited existence. When a notable tree dies, Celtic custom directs that a new one should be planted in its place. If possible, the new tree should be grown from a cutting of the old one, or from a seedling of its fruit. As such, continuity is possible over thousands of years. When we lose this understanding a dead tree is sometimes preserved as a spectacle, and the opportunity to plant anew rejected. A sad example of this concerns one of the most celebrated Celtic trees, Merlin's Oak at Carmarthen.

As a symbol of stability and living continuity, the Celtic battle-standard was the oak tree. The Irish poem, *The Battle of Moyragh*, tells us:

> In O'Loughlin's camp was visible a fair satin sheet
> To be at the head of each battle to defend in battle-field.
> An ancient fruit-bearing oak, defended by a chieftain justly.

The Murtenlinde at Fribourg in Switzerland, as it appeared in its last years, growing in the middle of the road opposite the city hall and St George's Fountain. It is removed now, because it was killed when a car collided with it. Happily, its offspring flourishes nearby.

The Welsh archers who fought with the English army at the Battle of Agincourt carried images of Merlin's Oak, but in the nineteenth century Carmarthen's venerable tree was killed deliberately by a Nonconformist who disapproved of the crowds of people that congregated there day and night. Nonetheless, for many years afterwards its dead bole stood in the street, propped up by concrete and iron. No attempt was made to plant a new tree. Inevitably, the dead wood was finally taken away to the museum, making a mockery of the tradition that the spirit of the town was embodied in Merlin's living tree:

> When Merlin's Oak shall tumble down,
> Then shall fall Carmarthen town.

Whatever spiritual sustenance the tree afforded the town is no more. A happier story of continuity can be told about the Midland Oak at Lillington, near Leamington Spa, one of the places reputed to be the centre of England. When it died, a new tree was planted to replace it in 1982. A similarly happy fate befell the Murtenlinde, the town linden tree of Fribourg in Switzerland. Planted in 1476, it stood in a triangular enclosure in the middle of the street near to St George's Fountain and the city hall. Traffic was its downfall, for in 1983 a car crashed into it, inflicting fatal damage. In the next year, the one or two remaining branches still bore leaves, but two years after the accident the Murtenlinde was declared dead and cut down. A new tree, propagated from a cutting of the original tree, was planted and flourishes today near to the fountain in the square fronting the city hall.

THE TREE OF INSPIRATION

The Celtic bardic tradition is intimately interwoven with trees. The Irish bardic alphabet, ogham, is linked expressly with them. Each character has a corresponding tree, for example: B, birch; D, oak; S, willow; etc. Each species of tree is thus an embodiment of the quality expressed by the ogham character. In the Welsh language, many words for awareness, knowledge and writing are related to the word for wood, *wydd*. They include *cywydd*, 'revelation'; *gwyddon*, 'a wise man'; and *derwydd*, 'druid'. Traditionally, since at least the time of Taliesin (520–70), the bards of the island of Britain have used the wood metaphor for poetry and 'carpenters of song' for themselves. Taliesin wrote:

I am the fund of song,
I am a reader,
I love the branches and the tight wattles.

Likewise, Iolo Goch (1315–1402) wrote:

I will bear for Owain
In metrical words, fresh and slow,
Continually, not the hewing of Alder wood,
By the chief carpenter of song.

The ensouled nature of trees makes them perfect media through which we can draw inspiration, and there are historic instances of specific trees associated with places of learning. In the bardic tradition, William of Waynefleet founded Magdalen College at Oxford expressly near the Great Oak, which survived until 1788. In north Wales, the Caerwys Tree is a rare survival of a bardic tree. It is a sycamore, and it was planted in the mid-twentieth century as a replacement tree of inspiration. From 1568, when Queen Elizabeth I authorized the first official eisteddfod at Caerwys, competing bards sat around the base of the tree to compose their poems, then went across the road to read them at the Eisteddfod Hall.

The poem *Afallenau* tells how Merlin, running in terror from a battle, enters the Wood of Caledon and becomes a wild man who hides in an apple tree when he is hunted. Myth and reality converged at Boscobel in 1651, when, following his defeat in battle at Worcester, King Charles II hid in the Boscobel Oak. After the Restoration, the tree was revered by royalists as 'The Royal Oak'. It died in 1704 as a result of the depredations of relic-takers, but 'The Royal Oak' remains a popular name for inns throughout England, where the King's head is portrayed amid the foliage in the manner of the Green Man. Relic-takers were also the bane of St Craebhnat's Tree at Killura. Irish seamen and emigrants took pieces of the tree in the belief that anyone who carried a piece could not drown. During the great emigrations of the mid-nineteenth century the tree was torn apart and is no more.

The practice of bardism is ancestral, the recounting of history and genealogy being among their more important functions. Occasionally, therefore, bards plant trees to commemorate famous events. At Dalilea House, Moidart, Scotland, the Jacobite bard Alasdair Macdonald planted an oak in 1745 to celebrate the return of Bonnie Prince Charlie. Sometimes people plant whole woods whose shape recalls or symbolizes a notable event. Estates all over Scotland once possessed woods whose shapes and spatial relationships reflected the disposition of the military units at the Battle of Waterloo. Notable examples exist on the promontory at the eastern entrance to the Kyles of Bute at Loch Striven, and the Glenearn Woods by the Bridge of Earn in Tayside.

The tradition has continued into modern times. At Rothesay on the Isle of Bute there is a wood in the shape of a crown, planted in 1948 to commemorate the birth of Prince Charles. In Scotland, isolated rows of thickly planted trees – 'Bell Trees' – are regarded as sacred, commemorating ancestors of families and clans. Sometimes the fortunes of families are bound up more intimately with the fate of individual trees. At Dalhousie Castle near Edinburgh was the Edgewell Tree, upon whose condition the destiny of the family of the same name was said to rest. It was also customary to plant commemorative spirit-trees on the graves of wizards and bards. One of the reputed graves of Merlin, near Paimpont in Brittany, is marked by a holly tree. A venerable yew in the ruins of Strata Florida Abbey in Dyfed grows over the grave of the fifteenth-century bard Dafydd ap Gwilym. It is contemporary with the grave. As living monuments, these bardic trees serve as trees of memory.

FAIRY THORNS AND SACRED PLACES

A notable tree is often the outward manifestation of the otherwise invisible spiritual qualities of a place. According to Irish lore, a single thorn growing in the middle of a stony field or on a hillside is protected or inhabited by the fairies. It is especially sacred when it grows close to a large boulder or over a holy well. Also, thorn trees growing on a bank, especially when three or more wax together naturally to form an L- or V-shape, indicate a special place. Specific classes of supernatural being are present in certain trees. In Cornwall, it is said that people who buried treasure always planted a hawthorn over it to guarantee its protection from the Piskies. It is probable that this tradition refers to offerings deposited at sacred bushes. In Ireland, the Lunantishees guard the blackthorn bushes. Raftery, the Irish bard, sang the praises of the Killeaden Fairy Thorn of Lis Ard.

'Gentle Bushes', sacred thorn trees, play an important part in the Celtic elder faith. Fairy thorns are held in such regard that not even dead branches lying under them should be taken away. Sometimes, a branch broken off accidentally will be tied back into its original position rather than being removed. Naturally, it is considered very unlucky to destroy a sacred tree. 'Don't tamper with the lone bush,' we are warned. In former times, deep respect for these trees was a universal *geis* (prohibition), which, if broken, was certain to bring misfortune not only to the perpetrator of the deed, but also to the locality of which the tree was a protector. Cutting down a sacred tree might result in the release of harmful spirits held in check there, causing an imbalance which would be manifested in poor crops, sickness and general misfortune. Only by planting a new tree of the same species at that place could the imbalance be rectified.

Whilst certain Christian missionaries made it their speciality to fell Pagan sacred trees, it seems that on occasion certain ones were protected and allowed to stand. In ancient Greece, sacred trees were often considered more holy than the altars associated with them, and it is likely that the same tradition was current among the Celts. A humorous story is told of St Martin of Tours, who travelled through northern Gaul in the late fourth century, destroying Pagan shrines – and trees in particular. In one place, the local people made a deal with him: he could cut down their holy tree only if he would stand beneath it as it fell. Sensibly, Martin declined their challenge and went elsewhere. It is probably not coincidental that some churches dedicated to St Martin, such as St Martin at Thorn in Norwich, still retain their tree epithets. The Irish town of Killarney is named after the 'Church of the Blackthorn', Cill Airne, whilst the Madonna and thorn tree at Ballyhaunis, County Roscommon, are the object of a pilgrimage. In most cases, it is likely that the ancient holy trees remained when the temenos was appropriated by the incoming faith, for today many venerable and venerated trees, especially ancient yews, remain in churchyards.

In more recent times, Dermot MacManus has recounted the story of the thorn tree that was felled to clear the ground for a new hospital at Kiltimagh. Although he was warned of the consequences, the workman destroyed the tree, only to suffer a stroke from which he eventually died. The place where this happened was cursed by the sacrilege and the building never became a hospital. Many years later, an Ulster fairy thorn was cut down because it was in the way of a new factory where the DeLorean car was to be made. The disastrous fate of that enterprise is well known. The theme of 'Seven Hundred Elves' is manifested in another way.

The precise meaning of the sanctity of fairy trees is not fixed. As with all sacred places, in some respects it depends upon one's religious viewpoint. Wearyall Hill at Glastonbury bears a single thorn tree that is visible from great distances. Although a classic 'fairy tree', this thorn is associated with the legend that Joseph of Arimathea planted his staff there, and it put forth leaves. The present thorn is a pleasant example of replanting. An earlier thorn tree, implausibly claimed to be the original, was destroyed by a Protestant who objected to it as an object of superstition. It is said that he suffered swift retribution. A similar thorn that still grows in the churchyard of St John's in Glastonbury High Street flowers around midwinter and cuttings are sent to the reigning monarch.

Sometimes a miraculous revelation of the feminine divine comes through trees. In Brittany, two important pardons in east Morbihan celebrate images connected with trees. The pardon of Notre-Dame-de-la-Tronchaye at Rochefort-en-Terre commemorates a black Madonna image found in the twelfth century in a hollow tree. At Josselin, the pardon of Notre-Dame-du-Roncier reveres Our Lady of the Bush. According to legend, by chance a ploughman discovered an image of Our Lady in a rose bush. He took the image home, but during the night it transported itself miraculously back to the bush. Eventually, a shrine was made there at the rose bush, which gained a reputation for curing people with epilepsy. Along with many other sacred relics, the image of Our Lady was burned by revolutionaries in 1793. However, a fragment was retrieved from the ashes, and this is enshrined in the modern chapel that marks the site.

The basilica of Le Folgoët, 'The Fool in the Wood', owes its existence to a comparable miraculous manifestation: it is the result of divine madness. In the fourteenth century, a shepherd called Salaün ar Foll lived by a spring over which a tree grew in a wood near Lesneven. Considered to be an imbecile, he shambled around the area repeating continuously the words 'O Itroun Gwerhez Mari' (O Lady Virgin Mary). Sometimes he would climb into the tree over the well to pray. In 1358 he was found dead and was buried by the well in which he was known to have sat in water up to his armpits while he prayed. When a lily grew upon his grave, people noticed that its leaves bore the miraculous words 'Ave Maria'. This was recognized as a divine sign, and in 1365 Duke John IV founded a pilgrimage church over the spring. A pardon, one of the largest in Brittany, is held there each year on the first Sunday after 8 September.

A similarly miraculous bush was the origin of the veneration of Our Lady at the pilgrimage shrine of Ave Maria at Deggingen in south Germany. In the fourteenth century, a rose-thorn bush of ancient veneration was about to be cut down when it was noticed that each leaf bore the words 'Ave Maria'. Thereafter, the bush was venerated, and later a chapel, now called Alt-Ave, was erected on the site. This was a period when the feminine aspect reasserted itself in the Christian religion with the revelation of the rosary.

TREE-BUILDINGS AND TRAINED TREES

We may occasionally encounter the results of a technique in which certain trees are altered into special shapes as they grow. This ancient northern European custom is not modern topiary, but is a continuation of its symbolic forerunner. Because of its essentially transitory nature, we have relatively few surviving examples of the tradition. There are two basic results of tree-alteration: the trained tree, where it is formed into an image of a cosmic ideal; and the tree-house, where a habitation, or at least a kind of building, is fashioned from the growing trunk and branches. The latter custom appears to go back to the ancient veneration of trees, building on them in order to gain their support. In the *Volsunga Saga*, we are told that King Volsung built a noble hall on the site of an oak tree, so that 'the limbs of the tree blossomed fair out over the roof of the hall, while below stood the trunk inside it, and the said trunk people called *Branstock*.' English folk-memory recalls that the hall of Huntingfield in Suffolk and the Old Manor House at Knaresborough in Yorkshire were built around living sacred trees, as was the timber-framed Cross Keys Inn at Saffron Walden in Essex.

In former times in the west of England, especially Devon, there was a type of 'village tree' that was altered as it grew. Mainly oaks or elms, their branches were trained horizontally to make a kind of floor. On feast days, villagers erected a wooden platform on these branches, upon which dancing and feasting then took place. Other trees were altered so that a series of circular platforms positioned one above another gave them the shape of the cosmic axis, in which different planes of existence are stacked one above the other. They are first recorded around 1200, when, in his *Parzival*, Wolfram von Eschenbach gives the account of how Sigune sits weeping in the crown of a linden with the corpse of her lover. From about 1501, we have an illuminated page by Jean Bourdichon in Queen Anne of Brittany's Book of Hours (in the Bibliothèque Nationale in Paris). It shows a Maying scene in which two youths carrying flowering 'May Branches' are coming out of the woods. Nearby grows a three-tiered tree, on which eggs and apples hang. This tree's tiers are supported by rings that reflect the circles of existence. Speed's map of the town of Flint, dated 1610, shows one with a maypole and stocks in the central square outside the church. Living examples have survived into modern times in the Netherlands and Germany, though they do not appeal to contemporary sensibilities. If they are not maintained, they soon grow out of shape. It is rare for old ones to be maintained, and there are few, if any, examples of new ones being created.

OFFERINGS TO TREES

The commonest way of honouring a special tree was to tie wool, string, ribbons or rags to it. Usually, but not always, this was done by those seeking a cure at a holy well. Frequently, it was stipulated that the offering had to be tied to the tree with raw wool, a material that was believed to absorb harmful and polluting substances. Sometimes, however, the ribbons or rags were nailed to a tree. The Oak of Maelrubha on the holy island in Loch Maree was studded with nails to which ribbons were tied. Coins, buttons, buckles and horseshoes were also nailed to trees. Near to Angers in Anjou was an oak called Lapalud: every hammerman who passed it, whether journeyman, carpenter, joiner, metalsmith or mason, would hammer a nail into it. A similar tree, Stock-im-Eisen, is preserved, still full of nails, in a glass case on the corner of a building in Vienna. While it stood, it was the last remnant of the nemeton of Vindobona which once grew at the place where St Stephen's Cathedral now stands. Every hammerman who passed through Vienna made sure to hammer a nail into it for luck.

The holy well of St Fintan at Clonemagh, County Laois, was halfway up a tree. It may appear strange that a tree could contain anything called a well, for no water can flow from it. But St Fintan's well-tree perpetuates the belief that when a holy well is profaned, it will cease to flow. The spirit of the well will migrate to a nearby tree. It must then be recognized in its new home by offerings hung there. The practice of hanging relics and remains of sacrifices in trees, originally Pagan, appears to have been continued by the Celtic Christians. Several *Lives* of Celtic saints recount incidents where objects were hung in trees used by the saints as stopping-places. While travelling, Celtic priests spent the night in or under trees, hanging their valuables in the branches. This had both a practical and symbolic purpose. The tree would protect the traveller physically, whilst its spirits would be honoured by the presence of sacred objects. St Senan actually died beneath a thorn tree at Kileochaille near Rossbay.

Sometimes valuables were accidentally left behind, and because this absentmindedness made a good story, the incidents were woven into the bardic recollections of the saints' lives. The Irish priest, St Muinis, is particularly remembered for this reason. One morning he left his crozier on a tree; when he complained about it, it was found miraculously hanging on another tree nearby. He was later sent to Rome to collect some relics but left them behind in a hollow elm tree. This time they were not recovered.

According to Flodoard, St Moderan, a Celtic bishop from the Rennes district, was crossing Monte Bardone in the Italian Apennines near Parma. Like Muinis, Moderan left his relics hanging in the branches of an oak tree. When he realized his mistake, he sent his assistant back to the tree, but the latter could not reach them. Moderan also tried but could not reach them. With typical Celtic flair, he turned this failure to recover his relics from a potential disaster into a good omen. He therefore made a vow that he would leave a portion of the relics there in a chapel dedicated to St Abundius, and built a new monastery at Berzetto nearby.

Festival Trees

Because sacred trees were such important elements in the elder faith, Christian ceremonies, especially weddings, were conducted at them. Until the last century, marriages were celebrated at an oak at Brampton in Cumbria. At special times of the year, services were and continue to be held out of doors beneath notable named trees. One is held annually at Old Polstead Gospel Oak in Suffolk, and the practice continues in many other places, particularly in south Germany where outdoor services are conducted at notable oaks on Whitsunday. Although the custom is most vigorous today in Germany, the May tree once had a strong showing in Celtic lands. Often, as in present-day Westphalia, a whole birch tree was cut on May Eve to be erected at the appropriate place in the village or town, where its presence ensured the fertility of the coming season. Celtic traditions of festival trees are best recorded from Wales and its border with England. One of the earliest references we have is a fourteenth-century poem from the bard Gruffydd ap Adda ap Dafydd. He laments the fate of a birch felled to become the May tree at Llanidloes, contrasting its proper place in the wood with its new location by the town pillory. But the principle of setting up the May tree is to re-create for a short time the forest within the town, bringing back to it the wild spirit of growth.

At the beginning of the twentieth century, before the Great War, it was still the custom in Herefordshire to fell a tall birch on May Day, to deck it with streamers and to set it against the stable door to bring good luck for that year. (This practice continues today in Germany.) Until the middle of the last century, it was customary in that part of England to make crosses of birch and rowan twigs and to place them over doors on May Morn. Like the birch, these would be left in place until the next May Day. Seedbeds and pigsties were protected likewise by these sacred woods on May Morn.

In south Wales this ceremony was called *Codi'r Fedwen*, 'raising the birch', and in the north *Y Gangen Haf*, 'the summer branch'; the tree was decorated with precious items, such as pocket watches, silver tankards and dishes, to represent the jewel-bearing tree. *Y Fedwen Haf*, 'the summer birch', was erected on the Feast of St John at Midsummer. At Caple Hendre, Carmarthenshire: 'The dance was to begin on St John's Day and to continue, if the weather were favourable, for nine days. There were one or two harpists, and the assembly, both male and female, used to dance. They used to set a birch tree in the earth and decorate its branches with wreaths of flowers.' This custom was kept up until 1725. William Robert o'r Ydwal, the eighteenth-century 'Blind Poet of Llancarfan', described the raising of the birch in his poem 'Taplas Gwainfo'. The pole was trimmed by a carpenter until it was round, and was then decorated with pictures. Young women next adorned it with ribbons and wreaths. A weathercock with ribbons streaming from its tail was set on its apex, beneath which a banner was unfurled. Sadly, under the influence of Nonconformist religion, these Welsh May and St John's customs have ceased completely.

Sacred Stones

A T THE MOST basic level, stone is the fabric of the earth, and as such is a symbol of the everlasting. The anthropomorphic view of the world sees stones and rocks as the bones of Mother Earth. They are the fundamental structure that supports all other aspects of physical existence and contains traces of earlier earthly life-forms. This is the outer reflection of our inner fabric, for the bones inside our bodies determine the human physical form. They are the components of the physical body that endure the longest after the spirit has departed. Within the human psyche, stone signifies the eternal substance of existence, at a level deeper than the ego-consciousness. When we touch a stone, we commune with this eternal substance, and we feel that the virtues present in the stone are transferred to us. Traditionally, stones are receptacles for spirit, which can be attracted if correct procedures are adopted. The ancient philosophers, among them Iamblichus, Porphyry and Proclus, stated that gods and demons, when attracted to stone images through rituals, take up residence in them, using them as media for their manifestations.

NATURAL AND MODIFIED STONES

When we look at sacred stones in the landscape, it is often difficult to determine whether their forms stem from nature or result from human activity. They span the whole range between natural simulacra and artificial structures. Natural rocks, especially those with some notable quality, were acknowledged as stopping-places of sacred or supernatural beings. Unusual stones had been thrown there by gods and giants; stones with strange depressions were the pillows of heroes and saints; others were clearly the abode of demons or monsters. Their existence was a recognized part of everyday life. Visitors and passers-by would acknowledge them through prayers and offerings. Certain classes of stone attract greater reverence than others: these are the stones which have a human dimension and about which sacred legends are told.

The Ladykirk Stone, at St Mary's Church, Barwick, Orkney, is a classic Celtic footprint stone.

At many places in the Celtic realms we can see human-size footprints carved into the living rock or upon detached slabs. Carved footprints are known from megalithic times onwards. A passage-grave on the crest of the hill of Petit-Mont Arzon in Brittany contains a stone with a pair of feet, toes pointing upwards. Similarly, the footprinted Calderstones, preserved in Liverpool, may come from a Lancashire passage-grave. The Romans were accustomed to carve pairs of footprints on a stone with the inscription *pro itu et reditu*, 'for the journey and return'. They used them for protective rites of leaving on a journey and for thanksgiving for a safe return, when the traveller would place his or her feet in the footprints to mark the beginning or end of the undertaking. In Celtic contexts, they are also associated with the rites of passage. Most footprints are accompanied by appropriate legends and lore, but in a few cases these are now lost.

In northern Europe, rock footprints are associated closely with kingship. Saxo notes: 'The ancients, when they were to choose a king, stood on stones planted in the ground to proclaim their votes, signifying from the steadfastness of the stones that the deed would be lasting.' Several reputedly royal footprint stones survive in former Pictish power-places. A pair of footprints are carved in a stone slab in a causeway at the broch (drystone tower) of Clickhimin in Shetland, whilst at Dunadd, erstwhile capital of Dalriada, there is a stone slab bearing an image of a boar facing a single human footprint. It is reputed to be that of Fergus, eighth-century king of the Picts. Close to this is a rock-cut basin for ceremonial ablutions. Another footprint used for the inauguration of kings and lords of the isles can be seen on Islay. Wherever the traditions are still spoken of, it is said that the ritual culminated when the king's foot was set in the print, the Celtic equivalent of crowning the monarch. The sacred stone, in which the goddess of the land dwelt, served as the royal foot-holder, which in other times was the ceremonial duty of certain young women.

Because most of the upper echelons of the clergy of the Celtic Church were drawn from the nobility, the associations of stone footprints seem to have been transferred to Christian abbots and bishops. Many extant footprint stones commemorate specific acts of saints. They exist in all Celtic lands. A crag near the chapel of Keil, between Dunaverty Bay and Carskey in Kintyre, has two footprints carved at the place reputed to be where

St Columba first landed in Dalriada. A single footprint, reputed to be that of St Cybi, was formerly visible on a rock at the eastern end of Holyhead church in Anglesey. Close to St Ólann's Well at Coolineagh, near Coachford, County Cork, are the footprints of St Ólann on a boulder.

In addition to footprints, other rock impressions are spoken of as the traces of notable people. They were often revered because a saint or hero was accustomed to pray there. At Portpatrick on the island of St Kilda there is the impression of a pair of knees and a right hand, said to be those of St Patrick. In Cornwall, St Newlyna knelt on a stone and left the impressions of her elbows and knees, and at Llangynnlo are Olgliniau Cynllo, the knee-prints of the praying King Cynllo. Some of these impressions are in river-beds. At Troedraur in Dyfed, the knee-marks of St Gwyndaf Hên can be seen impressed on a flat rock in the bed of the River Ceri. These 'prints' in rocky river-beds are 'potholes' created by the grinding effect of stones in the river current. They contain large pebbles that smooth and are smoothed by the rock-holes. To those who view the earth as a living being, these holes appear to nurture the growth of new pebbles from the mother rock. At times of low water they are natural 'bullauns' (see below).

Traditions of body-prints remind us that Celtic monks prayed in rivers, holy wells and beneath waterfalls. Perhaps they continued the practice from the druids' veneration of sacred waters. Folk belief ascribes healing powers to water taken from these depressions, which is used to treat sickness, wounds and sores, and to prevent cattle from falling ill. Those of St Cynwyl in the river at Caio and of St Beuno at Llanaelhaiarn were famed for this. St Gredfyw had a particularly impressive record with rock imprinting. At Llanllyfni are found his rock bed, a stone with his knee-prints, and his rock seat. On other rocks there are the prints of his horse's hoof and the mark of his thumb. This recognition of ancient traces serves to humanize the cold rocks, with the marks taking on the function of linking present-day people with the spirit of the saint. Finally, the rock hoof-prints that exist are usually associated with royal horses, which in former times were animals sacred to Epona, the horse-goddess. A classic example, near Castell Cilan in Gwynedd, is Ol Troed March Engan, a stone embedded in the ground bearing the hoof-print of King Einion's horse.

NATURAL STONE CONTAINERS

Water held in natural rock basins (other than supposed body-prints) is also reputed to possess curative powers. Water that seems to appear from a place as if by magic is especially potent. Such a place is Ffynnon y Cythraul (The Devil's Well), near Llanfihangel-y-Pennant. It is a rock basin with no obvious supply of water, which nevertheless is always full. Similar rock basins exist in many caves; the water is empowered by the virtues of the rock and the place. In Ireland, free-standing boulders with natural water-filled depressions, known as 'bullauns', contain healing waters. A famous healing bullaun exists at Boherduff in County Galway. Another can be seen by the churchyard gate at St Dogmael's Abbey in Dyfed. It is possible that at least some of these stones were once receptacles for libations to the gods and spirits. At many places in the Scottish Highlands, milk is poured into special hollowed stones called *Leac na Gruagach* or 'dobby stanes', in honour of the Gruagach, the guardian-goddess who protects the cattle. The power ascribed to these container-stones reflects the legend that the Holy Grail, which contained the power to heal and restore the Wasteland, was also a stone. Like some holy wells, basin-stones were used in rites of raising the wind. Supplicants placed offerings on the side from which the wind was required. Because the cupped surface of a dobby stane is a little artificial cave reflecting the dome of the heavens, it is a microcosm of the rising of the winds. By making an offering, one could invoke the ruling wind-spirit dwelling in that quarter.

CHAIRS

Many places possess open-air 'seats' of stone, usually associated with ancient authority figures. Known variously as druids', brehons', saints' or inauguration chairs, they are always stone. Some are naturally shaped places in the living rock, but often they show signs of having been cut deliberately and carved into throne-like shapes. Others are free-standing boulders from which a portion has been chiselled to make a seat. Such rock chairs are reputed to be places where kings or priests sat to meditate or command. They are infused with the primal strength of the rock from which they are cut, imparting their power to any who sit in them. Because of this, some are ascribed healing qualities. For instance, the seat of St Délo, a granite block at Guengat in Finistère, was resorted to as a cure for fever. Many rock chairs are associated with holy wells, and, when used in the prescribed manner, produce cures. In former times, St Canna's Chair at Llangan was resorted to for the cure of mysterious complaints. The patient would first make an offering of a pin to Ffynnon Ganna, then drink some water and finally sit in the chair to be healed.

It appears that the strength innate in rock chairs gives the sitter the power to command, both on a physical and at a psychic level. Temporal power resided in those rock chairs that served as royal thrones, and some rock seats are named after kings. Close to the holy well at Abererch near Pwllheli is Cadair Gawrdaf, the boulder chair of King Cawrdaf. This was a chair of regal command. The power to command the otherworld is reputed to dwell in a rock chair at Altadeven in County Tyrone. Above the well dedicated jointly to St Patrick and St Brigid is St Patrick's Chair, a throne-like rock from which one or other of the saints is said to have commanded demons. Commanding demons is essentially a psychic activity, and it seems that those who undertook the task needed to draw upon the power and protection afforded by the stone.

But not all chairs of psychic power were employed so dramatically. Just as some were used for healing the body, others could heal the soul. As part of the earth, rock chairs are ideal for meditation. The Hag's Chair at Lochcrew is a stone in the side of a cairn which faces north. Carved with concentric rings, arcs and zigzags, it is reported to be a place where magical strength can be drawn from the stone by sitting upon it. Those who have meditated there tell of transformative experiences. Certain seats on high points were in places that served as windows to otherworldly visions. A classic instance is the rock-hewn seat of the astronomer-prince Idris on his holy mountain, Cader Idris in Gwynedd. It was said that anyone spending the night there would, on the next morning, be either dead, insane or a poet of the highest inspiration. This story is reminiscent of the Lappish and Norse practice of *útiseta*, 'sitting out', where a person sat out under the stars to hear inner voices and commune with the cosmos.

In a few cases, the virtue of one chair was transferred later to another. St Michael's Mount had two chairs. The earlier one was a rock-cut seat in classical Celtic fashion: 'Who knows not St Michael's Mount and Chair, the Pilgrim's Holy Vaunt,' wrote Richard Carew in 1602. This Holy Vaunt was 'a bad seat and a craggy place called St Michael's Chair somewhat dangerous for access and therefore holy for the adventure.' It was sacred because it was said to be the site of an apparition of St Michael. But at some point this was superseded by the second 'St Michael's Chair': a broken medieval stone lantern on top of the church tower. Access to it has an element of danger, as does access to the Blarney Stone in Cork, for the would-be sitter has to climb out over the battlements of the church, high above the sea, to sit precariously facing the seaward side.

Sadly, only a few of the most famous Celtic chairs still remain. Disintegration of belief and the breakdown of traditional society have led to wholesale destruction. Boulder seats in particular fell prey to nineteenth-century engineers, to whom sanctity meant less than the presence of useful materials. St Mawes's Chair, a boulder at St Mawes in Cornwall, was built into the sea wall of the Fal estuary. Others were

A phallic megalith and perron stand by the church at Clackmannan, a former inauguration-place of Pictish rulers.

broken down or blown up to build roads and railways. St Canna's Chair was lost when the well-complex was destroyed in 1840.

STONES OF KINGSHIP

Two miles (3.2 km) outside Cookstown on a tree-ringed hill at Tullaghoge in County Tyrone is the crowning-place of the O'Neills. It was the headquarters of the O'Hagans, chief justices of Ireland. From the twelfth to the seventeenth century, the king sat there upon a stone throne for his inauguration. New sandals were placed on his feet, and he was crowned by the primate of Armagh. The last king crowned there was Hugh O'Neill in 1593. The throne was smashed by Lord Mountjoy in 1602, but Phelim O'Neill, leader of the rebellion of 1641, was inaugurated at Tullaghoge without the benefit of the throne.

Although megaliths predated the arrival of the Celts by a millennium or more, as places of spirit they were resorted to for various sacred ceremonies. According to William Borlase's *Antiquities of Cornwall* (1769), stone circles were used for coronations until the fourteenth century. The king stood at the centre stone, known as the *ambre*, and his nobles, peers or barons ranged themselves around him, each standing at his own representative stone. This formation is a version of the Assembly of Tara, where the high king was surrounded on the four quarters by his vassals, and also the assembly of the Irish golden god Crom Crúaich, which gathered in the middle of a circle of twelve stone images. A phallic royal megalith still stands in the churchyard at Clackmannan, regal centre of the Picts. An Irish royal place still exists in the shape of Finn MacCumhaill's Fingers on the Cootehill road at Cavan. They are a group of megaliths that once served as the crowning-place of the local kings of Breffry.

At Tara, the Lia Fáil was said to cry out when a legitimate king was crowned. Kingship could be conferred with a portable stone that was held to contain some special virtue. The most celebrated of them, because it is still in use in the coronation ritual of British monarchs, is the Stone of Scone or the Stone of Destiny, a block of old red sandstone weighing 450 lb (200 kg). Fergus, king of the Picts, is reputed to have brought the stone to the mainland in the year 736. Subsequently, thirty-four Scottish kings were enthroned upon it before it was seized by King Edward I of England. It was taken from Scone in Perthshire in 1296 to Westminster, where a special oaken chair was made to house it. In the coronation ceremony, the new monarch sits above the stone.

THE NAVEL OF THE WORLD

Gestation within the womb is the fundamental beginning of life which all humans share. There, before birth, we were connected with our mother by the umbilical cord, and, during our whole life, the navel remains as a relic of this life-giving connection. Traditions concerning certain stones transfer the concept of the navel to a place on earth. When the earth is viewed as the slain primal giant, his navel is located at the centre. Such central points exist throughout European tradition. They are known by the Greek name, *omphalos*, 'navel of the world'. Usually it is represented by a dome-shaped stone that signifies stability or eternal existence. It is the alchemical *lapis*, something that can never be lost or destroyed.

The centre of every settlement is by analogy *the* centre. Traditionally it is symbolized by a stone that stands at the axial point between the upper and lower worlds. The central place of any settlement, the omphalos is the hypostasized centre of the world. Through the omphalos runs the vertical cosmic axis, linking Gwynvyd above and Annwn below by means of Abred – this earth. If the centre is the navel of the world, the cosmic axis is its umbilical cord. Although located in specific places, the navel of the earth is within the individual: its existence in physical reality is the outward expression of an inner reality. Many medieval cities of Europe have a stone marking the city's omphalos. Most still exist, although they may no longer be acknowledged and might therefore be difficult to find. Among them is the London Stone, associated in legend with the city's Celtic origins. The continued existence of such stones was considered essential for the city to have lasting luck and prosperity. Magically, the omphalos is a place where communication between this world and others is at its most powerful.

According to Giraldus Cambrensis, the Stone of Divisions at Uisnech is the navel of Ireland. It is the place where Midhe, archdruid of the people of Nemed, lit the first fire. From that fire all other fires in Ireland were lit. The Uisnech omphalos had five ridges which indicated that it was the centre-stone of the five provinces. As already mentioned, at Tara, the royal centre of Ireland, there is the Lia Fáil, the Stone of Destiny. Local tradition called it Bod Feargius, 'Fergus's Phallus'.

Another significant Celtic omphalos-stone is the Blue Stane at St Andrews in Scotland. Although it is actually composed of reddish sandstone, the generic name 'blue stone' denotes its geomantic function as a central marker. This name is used also in the Netherlands to denote the centre of a city, as at Delft. Scottish knights swore allegiance on the stone at St Andrews, and the men of Fife raised the standard of Robert the Bruce over the stone before marching to Bannockburn. Farmers in the city on market day patted the stone for good luck, as students in Tübingen today pat a similar stone. Like many stones, the Blue Stane has been moved from its original position several times.

THE CELTIC CROSS

In the Hallstatt period, the continental Celts erected aniconic stones that seem to be the direct forerunners of later insular Celtic crosses. In their humanoid form they resemble much older aniconic representations of the Great Goddess. The head parts of these stones have an X-pattern seen on later Cornish stone crosses, but dating from almost a millennium

47

The form of the Hallstatt-period Celtic 'cross' from Kilchberg near Tübingen, Germany, is a forerunner of many insular stone crosses, such as this one from Kirkinner, Dumfries and Galloway, a millennium and a half later.

before the adoption of the cross as a Christian emblem. Much later, these shouldered, humanoid forms appear in Welsh stone crosses, such as those at Carew and Nevern in Dyfed.

Before it was adopted as an exclusively Christian sign, the cross had geomantic connotations. Cicero, in his *De Divinatione*, records that the staff with which the Roman augurs marked out the heavens was in the form of a cross. A non-Christian cross of iron was discovered in the remains of the Temple of Mithras near Caernarfon. The Celtic cross itself has a provenance in the earliest period recognized as Celtic, six hundred years before Christian worship began. A Hallstatt-period pillar-cross from Kilchberg near Tübingen in south Germany closely resembles later crosses in Cornwall and Ireland. Crosses exist in the carved diaper-work of Celtic memorials from the La Tène period. A fragment from Steinenbronn, now in the Landesmuseum in Stuttgart, has patterns that appear later in both Irish Christian manuscripts and church carvings. Another artistic strand that helped to inspire the Celtic cross was Coptic iconography. An example can be seen on the cover of the *Codex Brucianus*, a Coptic gnostic treatise from Egypt in the Bodleian Library, which has an illuminated ankh-cross which in many ways foreshadows the typical Celtic cross. It

*Menhir at St Duzec, Brittany,
altered in the sixteenth century
into a Christian Calvarium.*

amalgamates wheel and cross, decorating it with the interlace and diaper-work that became and remains today the hallmark of the art of the Celtic Church.

Another source for the Celtic cross may be found in Celto-Roman Gaul, where Jupiter Columns were erected to honour the sky-god. They are most plentiful in the areas of the Vosges, the Moselle, the Middle Rhine and Neckar. An original column stands on a road in Stuttgart. Typically, the monument is a classical pillar rising from a cubic base. Carved figures on the base represent the four seasons, and sometimes the planetary deities of the weekdays are present. Above them rises the column which is surmounted by a capital, sometimes with Celtic heads, acorns and oak leaves. Above this, Jupiter rides down a giant or demon, whose head is smashed by the horse's forehoof. The mounted sky-father appears to be a singularly Celtic interpretation of the Roman deity. A Jupiter Column still standing in its original position at Cussy, near the source of the River Arroux, has the god facing towards the east.

The Saxons also erected holy pillars. The most sacred, called Irminsul, stood at the Eresburg (now Ober-Marsberg in Westphalia). Rudolf of Fulda described Irminsul as 'a universal pillar supporting the whole'. According to the historian Widukind, this and similar pillars were connected with Mars, and their location represented the sun. In later times, similar columns were erected to the hero Roland. These various pillars were the forerunners of the Christian high cross. Later, in France, the Low Countries, England and Scotland, the column reappeared as the perron, topped by a stone ball, a symbol of the sun.

In the early days of the Church, megaliths were Christianized by being marked with crosses. A Cornish *Life* of St Samson recounts how he did this to a Pagan stone at Tregeare. A ninth-century cross is carved on an earlier ogham-inscribed standing stone at Bridell in Dyfed. Perhaps many megaliths were carved into crosses, but surviving examples in Brittany are late. There, megaliths were still being converted into crosses well into the seventeenth century. In 1674, a megalith at Penvern had Christian images carved upon it and its peak cut away to make a cross when a chapel dedicated to St Duzec was built a short distance away. The Croix des Douze Apôtres near a farm at Rungleo in Finistère is a megalithic menhir, similar to others in Brittany and Ireland, upon which Christian figures have been carved. Breton crosses are adorned with the symbols of the Passion, which include a ladder. According to Breton tradition, the cross itself is a ladder from earth to heaven, down which Christ came and up which human souls can travel to paradise. A very late conversion took place near Althorn in Alsace in 1787, when the megalith called Breitenstein was recarved as the Twelve Apostles' Stone in fulfilment of a vow.

But the vast majority of stone crosses are architectural in form and carved from dressed stone of high quality. In its fully developed form, the wheel-headed Celtic high cross is a version of the world axis. It stands on a foursquare pyramidal base representing the world-mountain whose roots are buried in the earth. From the centre of this arises the shaft, the axis proper. Close to the top is the Celtic cross itself. It is a sunwheel, reproducing a natural phenomenon observed occasionally in the skies when the sun's light, shining through ice crystals, is diffracted into a cross-and-circle pattern. At the centre of the wheel is Christ, the cosmic man. The cross is topped by a house-like form, the hall of heaven, the abode of god, resembling a Celtic reliquary.

The majority of stone crosses that existed in England and Wales were destroyed by Puritans for religious reasons or by treasure-hunters who believed that riches were deposited beneath them. An English anti-witchcraft law of 1542 refers to people who had 'digged up and pulled down an infinite number of crosses within this realm, for despite of Christ, or for love of money.' This craze continued until well into the seventeenth century. However, the practice of erecting stone crosses as memorials was not completely suppressed by Protestantism, as many nineteenth- and twentieth-century examples attest.

Everything in the world is subject to the ravages of time and must be replaced periodically if there is to be continuity. However, modern restorations sometimes violate the spirit of the place and it would be better to do without them. One such object is the concrete replica of St John's Cross on Iona, erected in 1970 in front of the Chapel of St Columba as a substitute for the original, which had been blown down several times by storms.

The wheel-headed cross at Kildalton on the island of Islay is the most striking Celtic cross remaining in Scotland, its pierced form reflecting the holes of the Kilchberg and other continental pre-Christian Celtic monuments.

ROCKING STONES

Large boulders perched on others in such a way that they rocked but did not fall were the focus of legend. Although today they are recognized as natural, in past times they were deemed to be artificial: giants, saints and heroes had erected them as monuments and places of worship. In antiquity, rocking stones were noted in his *Natural History* by Pliny the Elder, who told that once such a stone is made to move, it cannot be stopped. According to Apollonius of Rhodes's *Argonautics*, Hercules erected a stone over the grave of one of the sons of Boreas, the north wind. It would move in the slightest breeze, 'hovering' over the rock below in a supernatural way. In earlier times, there were several notable rocking stones in Great Britain that seemed to share the characteristics of Hercules's stone. The Cornish rocking stone Men Amber was so perfectly balanced that a child could put it in motion. The Roulter Rocks, an outcrop of gritstone-containing rocking stones in the southern part of Stanton Moor in Derbyshire, were kept in almost continuous motion by winds blowing across the moors in wintertime. As they moved, they ground against their base rocks, producing eerie sounds. These were stones that spoke, used by seers for oracles. It must have been an awesome experience, in the days before the noise of machines was everywhere, to encounter these primal sounds wafting across the empty moor. In Derbyshire, local legend connected the noisiest of them, the Minstrel of the Peak, with otherworldly spirits. Similarly, the Irish *Carricknabuggadda* or rocking stones at Island Magee and Highwood in Sligo were held in awe by local people as places frequented by the 'gentry'.

In his *Caractacus* (1759), the Reverend William Mason described the tradition that rocking stones were used as oracles by ancient Britons:

> Turn your astonished eyes; Behold yon huge
> And unhewn sphere of living adamant,
> Which, pois'd by magic, rests its central weight
> On yonder pointed rock: firm as it seems,
> Such is its strange and virtuous property,
> It moves, obsequious to the gentlest touch
> Of him whose breast is pure; but to a traitor,
> Tho' ev'n giants prowess nerv'd his arm,
> It stands as fast as Snowdon.

But because they were considered objects of superstition, many rocking stones were overthrown by the Puritans, especially during the English Civil

War. Men Amber was associated with a prophecy of Merlin, which said that it would remain until Britain had no king. The advent of Cromwell's Commonwealth was the occasion for the local military governor to topple it. Another, near Balvair in Scotland, was destroyed by Parliamentarians for the same reason.

The antiquary William Borlase referred to them in his *Antiquities of Cornwall* as 'rock deities', notable stones in the landscape that were the object of popular veneration in his day. Following Cornish folk tradition, he concluded that in former times Celtic priests had revered such stones as holy images. This observation was popularized by an engraving of the rocking stone near Rishworth in Yorkshire. Published in *Archaeologia* in 1773, it shows a mistletoe-carrying druid pointing at the structure. Although modern archaeologists have sometimes used this picture as an example of antiquarian fantasy, the local popular sanctity of such stones in the vernacular tradition is unquestioned.

During the eighteenth century, antiquarians' reports made the stones famous and, inevitably, tourists began to arrive to witness the astonishing spectacle of moving and noisy rocks. But they brought with them a problem many people consider to be uniquely modern – deliberate vandalism. It is sad to reflect that most rocking stones were disrupted in this manner. The most famous ones went first: in 1799, a gang of youths pushed the Minstrel of the Peaks from its pedestal. A few years later in Cornwall, the Logan Stone near Treen was unseated by naval hooligans. This stone was located at a place of giants, close to the apex of Castle Treryn, a promontory that contains a rock shelter called the Giant's Grave. Nearby were two rock chairs, the Giant Lady's Chair and the Giant's Chair. Before it became a tourist attraction, sick children were rocked upon the Logan Stone in rites that included visits to the holy well of St Levan nearby. But in 1824 a Royal Navy boat crew led by Lieutenant Goldsmith toppled the stone for a wager. When the crime became known, there was a public outcry, and the Lieutenant was compelled to re-erect the stone at his own expense. But it never rocked so well again, having suffered considerable damage. Since then, most of the famous rocking stones of Britain have suffered the same fate.

SACRED MEGALITHS

To secular people, megaliths were respected as places of the ancestors and spirits at which the deities of the elder faith were acknowledged. Until recently, many people worshipped the spirit of stones as well as going to church on Sundays. In the Channel Islands, sixteenth- and seventeenth-century manuscripts describe dolmens as 'altars of the gods of the sea'. Some were dedicated to the god Hus, who was acknowledged with ceremonies and offerings. The stone circles of the Orkneys had similar traditions: in 1703, Martin Martin wrote that the stone circles at Stenness and Brodgar were 'believed to have been Places design'd to offer Sacrifice in time of Pagan Idolatry; and for this reason the People called them the Ancient temples of the Gods.' An engraving made in 1823 of the Ring of Stenness, known then as the Temple of the Moon, shows a woman hallowing her promise of betrothal at the stones. Despite the existence of written law, until the nineteenth century the eternal quality of stones was used to empower legally binding oaths. Before 1814, when it was destroyed by a farmer, the Odin Stone, a holed stone at Croft Odin, Orkney, was used for oath-taking. In 1791, a young man was arraigned by the Elders of Orkney for 'breaking the promise to Odin', that is, breaking an oath sworn on the stone. When visiting the stone ceremonially, it was customary to leave an offering of a stone or a piece of bread, cheese or cloth.

When the Christian Church was predominant, there was an ambivalent attitude to the power of standing stones. The Catholic Church allowed many to remain, lightly Christianized, but puritanical Protestants tended to see them more as foci of traditional Pagan worship, and many were overthrown by them, especially in the seventeenth century. The name of 'Stonekiller' Robinson, who destroyed many stones at Avebury, is still vilified by megalith-lovers. But during the same period, non-Christian people continued to erect stones. In 1699, a man was arraigned before the Kirk Sessions at Elgin, charged with idolatry. He had set up a standing stone and raised his cap to it. The tradition has continued to the present day. A humanoid stone unearthed by a farmer at Granish in County Cork is revered today as the 'god stone'. It is treated as an aniconic image and dressed at certain times of the year. Also, in Scotland's remote Glen Calliche, off Glen Lyon, is Tigh nam Bodach, 'The Hag's House', a small drystone structure containing aniconic images, water-shaped stones known as 'the Cailleach and her Children'. From May (Beltane) to November (Samhain), the stones are stood outside the shrine-house by the local shepherd, who maintains the custom. In the winter half of the year, they are safely housed 'indoors'. Until the Great War, the house was rethatched on May Eve. At Samhain, the thatch was removed, the images placed inside and the gaps in the stones sealed with moss.

Furthermore, the custom of erecting megaliths to commemorate various notable people and events from Welsh history also continues to flourish. For instance, in 1736, the Alleluia Stone was set up near Mold by Nehemiah Griffith. It marks the site where a Welsh army under St Germanus defeated a Pagan alliance of Saxons and Picts in 429. A granite megalith was erected in 1953 at Cilmeri in Powys near the site where Prince Llewelyn was killed in 1282. Finally, on Sirhowy Top, overlooking Ebbw Vale, four inscribed limestone megaliths commemorate the Socialist politician Aneurin Bevan (1897–1960). They were set up in 1972.

EISTEDDFOD STONES

Although tradition tells of bardic gatherings since the earliest days of British Celtia, the assemblies of the bards of Wales are documented historically only from 1176. History is uncertain about how frequent they were before the eighteenth century, but by then a significant interest had arisen. In 1789, an eisteddfod was held at Corwen, the following year at St Asaph, in 1791 at Llanrwst, and in 1792 at Denbigh. Also in the latter year, and more significantly for later developments, Iolo Morgannwg summoned an assembly of Welsh bards in London at Primrose Hill. 'This being the day on which the autumnal equinox occurred,' reported *The Gentleman's Magazine*, 'some Welsh Bards, resident in London, assembled in congress on Primrose Hill, according to ancient usage.' A temporary circle of stones was formed, surrounding an altar stone, the Maen Gorsedd. Although this was an innovation, the custom of setting up new stones for ritual purposes had never died out, and in 1819 a stone circle was erected at Carmarthen for the traditional eisteddfod. After that, assemblies were held on a sporadic basis, but in 1860 the custom was institutionalized when the first official Welsh National Eisteddfod was held at Llangollen. Since then, it has been the central pillar of Welsh culture. Stone circles are erected in an appropriate place, usually a local park, to commemorate permanently the Eisteddfodau. By introducing the stone circle and other features, Iolo at once continued and formalized an ancient Celtic tradition which is continued to this day. He was an inspired mystic whose contribution to rescuing Welsh culture in its hour of most drastic decline cannot be underestimated. His romantic interpretations of ancient druidism revitalized the tradition, and created new ones that continue today – for where the bards sing, the land is sanctified.

Virtuous Stones for Wishing and Cursing

Probably the most celebrated of all stones in Ireland is the Blarney Stone. It is the most potent example of the ancient belief that anybody who touches a certain stone will acquire a portion of its virtue, bringing with it special powers or abilities. However uncertain its origin may be, today it is part of a wall at Blarney Castle, near Cork. The castle has a high, square keep, situated on a massive rock above two caves, one of which is in part human-made. The stone is located about 80 feet (24 m) above ground level beneath the machicolation of the parapet. To kiss it, pilgrims used to be suspended precariously by the ankles over the battlements. In more recent times, access has been gained less perilously by lying on one's back and leaning through a gap in the wall to kiss the inner side of the stone.

Beliefs about the Blarney Stone are part of a larger folk tradition of wishing and cursing stones. In 1703, Martin Martin recorded the 'blessed stone of St Columba' on Iona that had the power to grant one wish. But the Blarney Stone is different, for it is famous throughout the world. Its powers were popularized by an Irish bard of the early nineteenth century, Francis Sylvester Mahony. Writing under the *nom de plume* of Father Prout, he spread its fame through the lines:

> There is a stone there, that whoever kisses,
> Oh! He never misses to grow eloquent:
> 'Tis he may clamber to a lady's chamber,
> Or become a member of Parliament.

After this was published, pilgrims began to flock to Blarney Castle and continue to do so today.

Certain stones associated with churches, but of earlier provenance, are deemed to possess protective powers. At Tomfinlough, County Clare, the 'Plague-Stone', carved with circles and a sunwheel and built into the church wall, is reputed to ward off disease from the parish. Dust scraped from this and similar stones, then drunk mixed with holy well water, was once considered an efficacious remedy for many ills. Scrapings could be taken from holy boulders, megaliths and church stones. Certain pillars in the megalith-based St Beuno's Chapel at Clynnog Fawr were prized as the source of a famous remedy, as were the stones of Stonehenge and the church door-pillars at Warburg in Westphalia.

Directly related to the practice of leaving stones on cairns is the custom of laying small stones on tombs and the drystone altars called *leachta*.

Stones left behind at a graveyard as votive offerings to the spirits carry the prayers of those who left them. Sometimes, the stone is used to hold down a piece of paper upon which is written a petition or prayer to the spirit of the dead person. Commonly, the stones used have some special or notable quality. In Ulster and the Western Isles, pebbles – often of quartz – and crystals called 'godstones' or 'adder-stones' are left on graves or tombs. In parts of Ireland, ancient *leachta* in old Celtic monasteries bear large pebbles, occasionally carved with sacred sigils. The eleven *leachta* on the island of Inishmurray, each of which has its own name, bear collections of stones that are rotated by people making wishes. The altar called Clochabreacha is resorted to especially by those making curses.

At Killin in Perthshire, pebbles from near the church protect people and livestock from drowning in the torrent that rushes into the loch. In former times they were kept in a niche in the east gate of a mill. Every Christmas the stones were taken out and placed on a bed of rushes that had been pulled from the riverbank. Stones from sacred places are deemed to be empowered by their origin. Throughout the Celtic world, green stones are considered most lucky. They can be found on Iona, and it is said that anyone owning an 'Iona Stone' cannot be drowned. Similarly, St Cuthbert's Beads, crinoid fossils found around the holy isle of Lindisfarne, are prized for bringing good luck to their owners. Unlike the modern viewpoint, Celtic folk belief does not reduce good luck to little more that a random happening, rather it holds that it originates in the good will of the spirits that affect events. This belief leads to direct supplication for good luck and the search for lucky objects ensouled with beneficial spirits. St Colman's Well at Churchtown, on the shore of Lough Neagh in County Antrim, is visited in early summer by pilgrims who drink the waters and search for the amber-coloured stones called Cranfield Pebbles. They are prized for their powers of saving women from the pains of childbirth and, like the green stones of Iona, preventing men from drowning at sea. Kerry Stones are stones from Ireland, considered magical in England so long as they do not touch the earth there, when they are immediately disempowered.

Until the last century, certain individual small stones were renowned throughout Ireland for their magical powers. The amulets of Imokilly and Garnavilla and the Ballyvourney Murrain Stone were balls made of stone or crystal reputed to possess remarkable powers of healing. Closely related to them are the Bloodstones that were attached to the scabbards of swords or carried by scythemen, which held the power to staunch bleeding and heal wounds. In the north of Ireland, dumbbell-shaped amulets called dicket-stones were used for healing. The Relig, a brown dicket-stone kept in a hollow of a broken cross near Bruckless on the north side of Donegal Bay, was formerly resorted to for cures. It was taken from its place of power to anyone needing its virtue. On one occasion in the last century, it was sent across the Atlantic to cure a man who had emigrated from the district. After use it was returned to its keeping-place.

Stones containing special virtues are most prized as offerings or as luck-bringers. Crystals most obviously demonstrate natural geometry, the spiritual ordering principle within matter. They are stones that contain a hidden essence, something precious. In former times quartz was crushed for gold, since it occurs as veins in which metallic ores are found. This was done in Wales at Ogofau (Cynwyl Gaio). Here, quartz crystals can be viewed as containing the essence of the Philosopher's Stone, the mother of gold. In the north of Ireland, golden-yellow crystals are most prized, for they are said to encapsulate the internal light, the ultimate spiritual essence. Similarly, the Cornish legend of how St Piran discovered tin symbolizes the way in which the fire of spirit transmutes the soul, bringing forth its spiritual essence. Once, it is said, the hermit-saint was cold and so made a fire, resting the kindling on some black stones that he found near his cell. As the fire heated the stones, so silvery streams of tin flowed from them: thus, shining consciousness, symbolized by the saint's wisdom, emerges from the dark unconscious, represented by the black stones.

STONES OF MEMORY

Dressed stones that are placed deliberately, such as a cross or tombstone, have four sides orientated permanently relative to the four directions. They relate their location to space and time in two principal ways: a stone can be a memorial of the time it is set up; or it can be a means of telling the time, as astronomical megaliths and sundials are. Sometimes both are combined. Memorial stones record dates and events, their setting being related to time, encapsulating information that can only be read by those educated to read the signs. Medieval Irish and Welsh metaphysical traditions preserve the knowledge of esoteric sytems of correspondences that can be projected back into the earliest Celtic period. As elements of the Western Mystery Tradition, these systems were a means of preserving and transmitting knowledge. *The Triads of Britain* tell of the stones of Gwydden-Ganhebon from which initiates 'could read the arts and sciences of the world'. Such records were both literal, in terms of

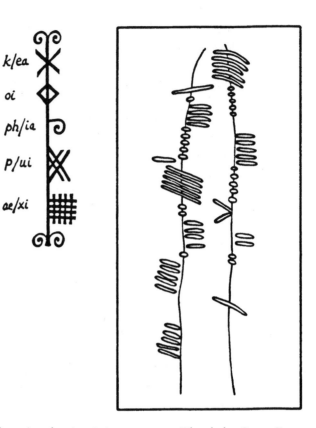

58

Above: An ogham inscription on a stone at Kilmachedor, County Kerry, Ireland.
Left: The characters of the ogham alphabet, used mainly in Ireland and western Britain. Customarily, they are cut along the druim at the edge of a dressed stone or wooden stave.

inscriptions (whether in the ogham script, Latin characters or pictograms), and also involved more esoteric symbolism, such as location, geometry, proportion, measure and colour.

Ogham is a peculiarly Celtic form of inscription, being a cipher that uses a variety of the ancient Greek method of signalling at a distance with torches. There, the alphabet was divided into five columns, four with five characters and one with four. Flaming torches were hidden behind two temporary walls or shields with a space between them. Torches were then exposed to view, those on the right representing the group, and those on the left the number of the letter within that group. The principle of ogham is very similar, indicating each letter by a number of strokes that signifies its place in a group. It is possible that ogham also reproduces a form of bodily sign language, being written across the edge of a stone with strokes that could signify fingers. As with many Celtic mysteries, ogham was far more than merely a system of writing. Each ogham character was assigned correspondences within the animal and plant kingdoms, with colours, and even with tones in harp tablature. Certain famous Irish fortresses were known by its letters, and ogham still has a place today as a divination technique.

A stone of memorial is not merely the record of the name and exploits of a person buried at that place. Just as the life of a worthy person reflects the cosmic order, so should their memorial. Traditionally, places of sepulture are also records of other things celestial. At Caernarfon in former times there was 'a stone of enigmas', the tomb-slab of the ancient Welsh astronomer Gwydon ap Don, carved with symbols intelligible only to the cognoscenti. There is also the hint in the *The Triads of Britain* about the stones of Gwydden-Ganhebon. But, despite these legends and suggestions, we can only speculate on the meaning their makers intended to convey.

LABYRINTH STONES

The labyrinth is the path that leads from the outer to the inner world. At the centre is the omphalos, which, although it can be seen, can be reached only by travelling the whole pathway. It is a very rich symbol, containing within itself the mysteries of human consciousness, birth, transformation and death. For more than a millennium it has been a symbol of pilgrimage in the Christian tradition, and in recent years it has re-emerged in the women's movement as a symbol of the Great Goddess. In the British Isles there are a number of ancient labyrinths carved on stone. All of them come from Celtic contexts. The largest of these is a boulder called the Hollywood Stone. Now in the Museum of Antiquities in Dublin, it bears a clearly incised and carefully executed classical labyrinth. This inscribed stone was found at Upper Lockstown in County Wicklow close to the ancient pilgrims' track, known as St Kevin's Road, that links Hollywood with the monastic settlement of Glendalough. Most probably, the Hollywood Stone marked a stopping-place on the way to this exceptional sanctuary. St Kevin founded the monastery in around 550, and the labyrinth carving may date from a similar period.

Two classical labyrinths are carved on a rock wall next to a ruined watermill in Rocky Valley in Cornwall. One suggestion is that they may

The Inchbrayock Stone. A characteristic of the multivalency of the Celtic vision appears repeatedly in surviving artworks, where, as in the natural world, forms fade into one another, nevertheless remaining expressions of the underlying geometrical scheme.

date from the early sixth century, when a Celtic monk who was known as St Nectan is said to have lived in a hermitage further up the valley by the waterfall now known as St Nectan's Kieve. If this is the case, then they, like the Hollywood Stone, may have marked a pilgrims' path. But the Tintagel mazes are probably later, perhaps dating from the eighteenth century, and are connected with the mill itself, whose owner at that time, although illiterate, had the reputation of being a brilliant natural mathematician. A later carving of a labyrinth can be seen at the Church of St Laurence at Rathmore in County Meath. It is of a later design that is sometimes called the 'Christian Labyrinth', similar to those laid in the pavements of cathedrals in France.

Celtic folk tradition perpetuates a practice where labyrinths are carved on small, portable stones, usually of slate. A rare example is preserved in the Witchcraft Museum at Boscastle, not far from Rocky Valley. It is a classical labyrinth carved on an irregular piece of slate small enough to be easily carried. It came from a farm at Michaelstow nearby, having been donated by a daughter of the famous wise woman, Kate 'The Gull'

*Celtic labyrinths. Top: Carvings on a rock face in Rocky Valley, Tintagel, Cornwall.
Middle: Angel corbel with labyrinth from the Watts Mortuary Chapel, Compton, Surrey
(left); The Hollywood Stone, a stopping-place from St Kevin's Road, near Glendalough,
Ireland (right).
Bottom: Medieval stone-carving of a Christian labyrinth from Rathmore, Ireland (left); Wise
woman's Troy Stone from the Isle of Man (right).*

Turner. It was a magical object that, in typical Celtic tradition, had been handed down from woman to woman. We are fortunate here in having some documentation of how such a rare and usually secret artifact is preserved through generations of use, unseen and unknown. Its final user had inherited the stone from Nan Wade, a Manx 'sea-witch', who in turn had had it from Sarah Quiller of Ballaveare, Port Soderick. The latter had inherited it from an earlier wise woman, and it appears to have been handed down through many generations.

These Troy Stones, as they were known, were used by wise women to commune with the otherworld through states of altered consciousness. The wise woman would trace her finger through the labyrinth, back and forth, whilst humming a particular tune, until she reached an altered state. This surviving Troy Stone is unusual, for most are either still in use, or were destroyed at the death of the last owner. A Cornish Troy Stone was destroyed in 1958 after the death of a wise woman, who had stipulated in her will that it should be smashed and the pieces disposed of.

Springs, Wells and Places of Healing

WATER IS the primary symbol of life: it is the source of vitality, for without it life cannot exist. Because of this, water, and most especially water sources, have been revered since the earliest times. In Celtic belief, natural waters – springs, streams, rivers, ponds and lakes – are ensouled with indwelling spirits which must be acknowledged and nurtured. This is in total contrast to the modern experience. Today, most of us take our water from the domestic main supply. To us, water comes out of a tap at the end of pipes of whose origin we have little, if any, idea. Perhaps the water has been piped to us from distant sparkling lakes in the mountains; equally, it may have been recycled at the local sewage works. Wherever it happens to originate, our water is heavily processed: sterilized, filtered, perhaps demineralized, then chlorinated and fluoridated. However high its quality, and however pure in a scientific sense, it is no longer natural water.

Water from holy wells has a quite different character. It comes directly from the waters that exist unseen beneath the earth, the mysterious chthonic realms of Annwn. When we take water from a holy well, we are participants, not consumers. We have a personal relationship with the origin, literally drawing our water from the source. Each holy well is unique. It bears a name that expresses a personality born of the subtle interaction between geology, topography and human activities since time immemorial. In myth and custom, Celtic sacred waters are associated with the three archetypes of light: the sun, the eye and consciousness. When we use sacred waters, we commune with these archetypes, which manifest themselves to us as deities, legends, traditions and folk practices.

RIVER AND LAKE SPIRITS

Celtic rivers have their own indwelling deities which express their character. Rivers in all of the former Celtic realms bear the names of ancient deities: for example, the Aisne in France (Axona) and the Boyne in Ireland (Bóinn). Surviving origin-legends of Irish rivers strongly suggest that every Celtic river formerly had its personal mythos, expressed through the attributes and legends of its presiding deity. Although entire rivers were deemed sacred, notable features have special virtues. Certain waterfalls, for example, were reputed to possess healing properties, especially for sprains and muscle pains. Typical is Pistyll Brido near Old Colwyn, where sufferers allowed water to run over their afflicted parts. Sometimes a natural feature assists the power of the waterfall. One at Scorrybeck on the Isle of Skye has a natural rock hollow beneath it in which sick people would bathe. In a similar vein, early Celtic churchmen sat in meditation beneath waterfalls, in rivers and in holy wells, as perhaps the druids did before them.

Lakes, too, are inhabited by water spirits. Many still bear names that recall their spirit guardians. Some, such as Lake Dee in Dumfries and Galloway, are named after a Pagan deity (in this case, Deva), or a Celtic saint, such as Loch Ciaran. Like special places in rivers and holy wells, many lakes are reputed to be endowed by their guardian spirits with healing powers, often to cure skin diseases or wasting illnesses. They show a close affinity with holy wells and, indeed, some healing lakes in Wales have the word *ffynnon* (fountain, holy well) in their name.

Making offerings to the gods and spirits of rivers and lakes is a venerable Celtic tradition. Rich parade armour and weapons of the Iron Age have been found in England in the Thames at Battersea, in the River Witham in Lincolnshire and in Lake Geneva. Numerous Celtic artifacts have been found in Switzerland at Lake Neuchâtel and again at Lake Geneva. The artifacts from Lake Neuchâtel come from a place called La Tène, which has given its name to a phase of Celtic culture. There is literary evidence, too: Strabo tells of the treasures thrown by the Gauls into the sacred lake near Toulouse. Sacrifices to the lake were considered necessary for the well-being of the surrounding land; when the treasures were stolen, disaster ensued. The necessity of observing a lake-offering is recorded in medieval Arthurian legend. The magic sword Excalibur was taken by King Arthur from a holy lake (said to be Dozmary Pool) with the permission of its spirit, the Lady of the Lake. But once its destiny in this world was fulfilled, it was essential that Excalibur should be returned to the waters.

Veneration of lakes has been continuous from antiquity into modern times. In the early nineteenth century, people observing Garland Sunday at Loughharrow made sacrifices to the lake. Around 1820, a Mr O'Connor wrote in an *Ordnance Survey Letter*: 'The people ... swim their horses in the lake on that day to defend them against incidental ills during the year and throw spancels and halters into it which they leave there ... they are also accustomed to throw butter into it that their cows may be sufficiently productive.' In 1845, the *New Statistical Account of Scotland* tells of a lake called Dowloch, into which food and sick people's clothing were thrown in thanksgiving for cures that took place there.

CELTO-ROMAN WATER SHRINES

Large and complex shrines of water-deities came into being shortly before the Roman expansion into Celtic territories. Some enshrined the sources of major rivers, whilst others were centred around holy wells. Their function involved veneration of the *anima loci*, involving ceremonial purification, with spiritual and physical restoration of pilgrims. An important example of such an enshrined river-source is that of the Seine near Les Vergerots, north-west of Dijon. Many votive offerings to the goddess Sequana have been found there in a shrine that endured for several centuries. Where Celtic lands came under Roman rule, the major Celtic water-shrines were incorporated into fully fledged temple complexes. Religious practices became increasingly sophisticated as certain aspects of Roman civilization were introduced. Later, when polytheism gave way to monotheism, many such shrines were occupied by churches.

One of the most important holy places in Germany, the Imperial Cathedral at Aachen, stands over the Celtic curative sacred wells of Aquae Granni. To the Celts, it was a sacred place of the solar deity Grannos. To the Romans, he was Grannus, equated with the sun-god Apollo. Another magnificent temple of Apollo Grannos stood at a holy well inside the Celtic *Viereckschanze* at Faimingen, and shrines dedicated to Apollo Grannos are also known in France and Scotland. A temple of Apollo Grannos stood at Trier. Clearly, Grannos is a male solar deity, not a water-god. His name is cognate with the modern Gaelic word *grian* meaning 'sun'. But symbolically, waters are feminine, and generally the preserve of goddesses. Grannos's shrines are thus subtly different from places where water-goddesses alone were venerated. They are places where his presence in waters

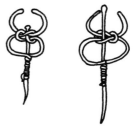

Wire caducei. Pagan votive offerings discovered in a Celtic holy well at Finthen, Rhineland, Germany.

sacred to a local or general water-goddess was acknowledged in a mystic marriage of opposite principles. The Celts believed that at night the sun sank beneath the waters, emerging from them again at sunrise. During the night, the illuminating and healing power of the sun was absorbed by the waters. The tradition of incubation at holy wells, where the patient slept all night near the waters, invoked the nurturing powers of the underground sun.

Hot springs were considered supremely the subterranean stopping-places of the night-time sun. Mont Dol, near St Malo, was such a stopping-place, where four holy springs were sanctified by solar ceremonies at sunrise. Morning ceremonies at these and other sources celebrated the sun's emergence from the underworld, its brilliant light reflecting on and empowering the holy waters. A significant solar-water shrine existed beside the River Cure at Les Fontaines Salées in Burgundy. Excavations have revealed a sanctuary in the shape of a sun-wheel. Dating originally from the Hallstatt period, it was equipped with wooden catchment vessels fashioned from single oak trees, from which the healing water was channelled to well-heads through oaken pipe-work. In later Celtic times, the shrine was expanded, and, under Roman rule, circular baths and ancillary buildings for pilgrims were constructed.

Sirona, often dismissed as the consort of Grannos, was the indwelling deity of the waters into which Grannos descended at night. She was venerated widely. At Pforzheim, a wooden image of the goddess was discovered in a Roman well. An inscription of the year 223, found by the holy source at Alzay, dedicates an altar to Venus, Grannos and Sirona. Water-shrines acknowledged a number of goddesses in addition to Sirona. At Badenweiler, the Roman baths that extended the Celtic holy well-place were dedicated to Diana Abnoba, the goddess of the Black Forest. The hot springs at Buxton, known to the Romans as Aquae Arnemetiae, were sacred to the goddess of the grove, and those at Bath, Aquae Sulis, to Sul, whose name means 'sun', but who, as a goddess, was assimilated with the Roman Minerva. Red wells, whose water is coloured by iron deposits, were seen as symbolizing the menstrual blood of the goddess. Later, under Christian influence, the 'blood' was transferred to Christ or his martyrs.

Burmanus, or Borvo, was a deity who presided over seething, turbulent waters, especially hot springs. A ceramic image from Vichy shows him attended by a horned serpent and a dolphin. His indwelling well-goddess was Damona (or Burmana). As in the case of Diana Abnoba, Burmanus was identified with a larger sacred forest area, the *Lucus Burmani*, around

Cervo in Liguria. Nodens, the Roman version of the British god Nudd, in some aspects related to the sea-deity Neptune, was revered in the forest spring-sanctuary at Lydney. In the late fourth century, when Pagan shrines were being suppressed in other parts of the Empire, Lydney was expanded to become a place of pilgrimage, a Celto-Roman sanctuary of healing, equipped with rich temples, baths and accommodation for visitors.

During the first century, the Celtic holy wells at Heckenmünster in the Rhineland were surrounded by a large Celto-Roman sacred complex with baths, a temple, theatre and accommodation for pilgrims. Today, the healing waters still spring up there from the Victoria-Quelle and the Wallenborn, both of which have a healing reputation. Most places of healing waters never attained the complexity of Aachen, Bath, Heckenmünster or Lydney. Most remained small holy wells serving local deities and local needs. Just as the Roman deities absorbed their Celtic counterparts, Celtic or Catholic saints assimilated the earlier polytheistic deities. This is true for all sacred places, but is most notable at holy wells.

67

Built against a rock outcrop is the holy well of St Seiriol at Penmon in Anglesey. The present well-house dates from the eighteenth century, but the well has been revered since at least the sixth century.

The little shore chapel of St Trillo at Llandrillo-yn-Rhos in north Wales is built over the saint's holy well, beneath the altar upon which devotees place their prayers and offerings of thanksgiving.

HOLY WELLS

Although the great water-shrines are no more, holy wells remain in all Celtic lands. Many are venerated still, continuing to acknowledge their Niskai or sprites. Almost every saint in Irish, British and Breton tradition has a holy well named after him or her. It is clear that many holy wells existed before the introduction of Christianity, and that this renaming was a monotheistic reinterpretation of the spirit that dwells within and guards the often healing waters. These sources are not wells in the sense of deep, stone-lined shafts, but rather are natural springs enhanced and protected by constructions or buildings. Many are like small versions of the Celto-Roman sanctuaries, often with provision for drinking, bathing, contemplation and worship.

A classic instance of a present-day holy well-shrine exists in north Wales at Llandrillo-yn-Rhos. The little chapel of St Trillo nestles almost hidden at the base of a low cliff on the foreshore. Its reason for being is to enshrine a holy well, whose waters rise beneath the stone altar table. Like many important sacred loci, St Trillo's well-chapel is a paradoxical place. Here, through some seemingly miraculous agency, curative fresh water flows at a location where the salty waters of the Irish Sea should dominate. St Trillo's is still very much a sacred place: believers write votive prayers on scraps of paper which they leave on the altar. They ask for healing and peace, and give thanks to God for prayers answered. Almost identical practices can be seen at the Liebfrauenbrunnen Chapel at Werbach in Germany. Like St Trillo's, it is built over a Celtic holy well which rises on the bank of a stream bridged by the chapel. The Liebfrauenbrunnen Chapel contains modern ex-votos thanking the Madonna for the curing waters. St Trillo's is administered by the Anglican Church in Wales, and the Father God is thanked; the Catholics at Werbach thank the Blessed Virgin Mary, but it is to the healing waters that they all come.

Throughout the Celtic world, well-visitors particularly value well-water taken on special days. Most auspicious are New Year's Day, Palm Sunday and Ascension Day. New Year's Day is a transference from the winter solstice, the time of the longest night when the sun spends the most time beneath the earth, and the waters are especially empowered. It is customary to make a pilgrimage on the holy day of the well's saint. When we draw water on the well's holy day, we perpetuate tradition in the conscious knowledge of the empowerment that taking water on that day will bring. On these days, the most prized water is the 'cream of the well', the first water drawn after sunrise. Naturally, this can only be taken by one person, and in the past in some places there was fierce competition to get it. Sometimes there would be a contest in which competing women ran at sunrise from a customary stopping-place to the well. The winner then 'took the cream'. But in other places, as in south Germany, well-water was taken in a dish which was held up to catch the rising sunlight before being distributed to every woman at the well. In Scotland, where 'creaming' continued until recently, the 'cream' was given to cows to increase their milk yield. Any water left over was used to wash the utensils of the dairy.

In Cornwall, there used to be notable official pilgrimages to the holy wells at Gulval, Roche and Nantswell. Pilgrims went to the wells on the eve of the saint's day and spent the night 'waking' there in a vigil, and perhaps undergoing the ceremony of *bowsenning*, that is, being immersed in the healing waters. Unlike in Catholic Ireland and Brittany, where patterns and pardons continue to flourish, Celtic pilgrimages on the British mainland have dwindled. Those that continue, such as the annual holy communion held at St Deiniol's Well at Penally, are rarely publicized. In Ireland and Brittany, however, well-devotions are more public. The first Sunday in September is the pattern day for St Ciarán's Well at Clonmacnois, when pilgrims follow the pilgrimage pathways called the Short Station or the Long Station, and hang offerings on a thornless hawthorn or throw them into the well. Another of St Ciarán's wells is at Castlekieran, County Meath. Pilgrims go there with torches at midnight on the first Sunday in August, on or near Lughnasa, the old Celtic festival of the solar god Lugh. They try to glimpse a mysterious trout, which appears only at this time.

A notable pilgrimage place in Wales is St Winefride's Well, sacred to St Gwenfrewi. Situated on the west side of the Dee estuary, 4 miles (6.4 km) north-west of Flint, the well is in fact much more impressive than any other. It is a two-storeyed late Gothic building. Above, a small chapel protrudes from the hillside, whilst a polygonal well-chamber with five recesses guards the sacred waters below. It is surrounded by a processional passage. The spring is the most copious in the principality, being reckoned among the 'Seven Wonders of Wales'.

Holywell is unusual in Great Britain because of its continuity as a traditional sacred place. It has been in unbroken use probably since pre-Christian times, and certainly throughout the upheavals of Christian sectarianism into the present day. In the medieval period, it was under the control of monastic orders. Unusually, it was spared destruction at the Reformation, and although the sacred images were removed, somehow a resident well-guardian priest remained. Priestly guardianship continued until 1688, when Protestants ransacked the chapel and drove out the resident priest. But people continued to visit the well, and in 1851 and 1887 the Pope granted indulgences to pilgrims visiting the well. Today it remains the primary holy well of Britain.

WELLS, SKULLS AND CURES

According to the principle of correspondences, where topographical features are equated with parts of the human body, springs correspond to the tear ducts. Thus, spring waters may be likened to tears emerging from the eye socket, beneath which, invisibly, lies the skull. Celtic lore venerates the head as the place of the soul and consciousness, and undoubtedly there is a strong connection between wells and the human head, both symbolically and in physical remains. It is said in Scotland that holy well-water drunk from the skull of one's ancestor is an effective remedy against epilepsy, and human skulls were often kept at holy wells for the use of pilgrims. Usually those of holy men or heroes, they were preserved by well-guardians, who continued into recent times the ancient cult of the severed head, as recalled by the myth of Bendigaidvrân. A related north European myth is that of Mimir, whose head was cut off by the gods. Odin took the head, which he preserved with herbs in the Celtic manner, and placed it in a well called Mimirs Brunnr. He then magically empowered the head with prophetic speech. But in order to understand this intuitive otherworldly speech, Odin plucked out one of his eyes and gave it to the well.

As a place of the sun at night, the well symbolizes the inner light of life as contrasted with the outer light of the visible world. The abyss from which the waters issue represents the hidden source of wisdom in the unconscious, which we can tap if we relinquish our egoism. The well itself is the channel from the unconscious to the conscious. By giving an eye to the well, Odin was able to gain inner enlightenment at the expense of outer vision. Related to this myth is the power of holy springs to cure eye diseases. Just as the sun's light emerges from the well at daybreak, dispelling darkness, so dim eyes can be illuminated once more by the sacred waters. There are many 'eye-wells' whose use today attests to a continuing perception of their effectiveness. I have personal experience of the power of the holy well at Mont-Sainte-Odile in the Vosges mountains.

In addition to the eyes, head-wells are reputed to cure other diseases located in the head and neck, such as whooping cough, epilepsy and toothache. Well-water was drunk from a skull at Drumcondra in Dublin to cure toothache. Sometimes the skull was kept by a dewar family, perhaps descendants of the deceased. Until the nineteenth century, hereditary skull-guardians administered water to epileptics at Tobar a' Chinn (The Well of the Head) in Wester Ross. Similarly, in Wales people with whooping cough resorted to St Teilo's Well at Llandeilo Llwydarth to drink the waters from Penglog Teilo, a skull reputed to be St Teilo's. It was kept by a dewar family, the Melchiors, one of whom had to administer the water if it were to effect the cure. The custom ended when the last surviving Melchior sold the skull to a curio-collector. Presumably the waters are no longer effective. Another notable skull was kept at Ffynnon Llandyfaen, also in Dyfed, for treating whooping cough. This was not the cranium of a holy man, but of an ancestral hero-knight, Gruffydd ap Adda ap Dafydd; it seems, nonetheless, to have been as effective as the others.

Also part of the Celtic well-head mythos are the legends that relate how many a healing or prophetic source sprang up spontaneously when someone was beheaded. This is recalled in *The Life of St David*, where a spring wells up in a hazel grove at the place where a damsel is decapitated. The Celtic sacred springs of Alesia in Burgundy, in use long before the Christian religion, are said to have been the result of the beheading of St Reine. The identical legend is claimed by St Jutwara, St Lludd, St Noyala and St Tegiwg. Naturally, the most famous Welsh holy well of them all, that at Holywell, is said to have sprung forth when St Gwenfrewi (Winefride) was beheaded. When her head touched the ground, the waters burst forth.

CUSTOMARY CURES OF MIND AND BODY

In former times, healers recognized that curing bodily ills also involves treating the roots of the affliction in the psyche. Because of this, the curative virtues of holy wells depend as much on the spiritual as the physical dimension. The total experience of healing is important, and the emphasis on the head underlines the role of both the conscious and unconscious mind in this process – undertaking the pilgrimage, its rituals, contemplation, prayer and purifications as a prelude to bathing in or drinking the mineral waters.

Visitors to some Welsh holy wells practised incubation, an ancient technique of psychological transformation and healing through sleep. Just as the sun was believed to be regenerated through his nightly marriage with the waters of the underworld, so a sick person could be renewed by sleeping at a holy well. In the morning, as the sun rose, the patient would likewise experience a new awakening to a disease-free life. Until the eighteenth century, children were immersed in Ffynnon Gelynin at Llangelynin, then wrapped in a blanket to sleep in the farmhouse near the well while the cure took effect. Sometimes the patient had to sleep at a special place associated with the well's presiding spirit. At Ffynnon Redifael at Penmynydd, people subject to fits would take the waters and then lie for a night on Bedd Gredifael, the saint's stone, and similarly at Ffynnon Gybi, by Llangybi Church, near Lampeter. In 1699 Edward Lhuyd recorded Welsh incubation practices then current: 'On Ascension Eve, they resort to Ffynnon Wen; after they have washed themselves, they go to Llech Gybi, that is an arrow's flight from the well. There they put the sick under the Llech, where, if the sick sleeps, it is an infallible sign of recovery; if not, of death.' In the early part of the eighteenth century, crutches and wheelbarrows used by the sick were to be seen around the well. But this sight was not acceptable to the sensibilities of later generations and they were removed. Nonetheless, the chest for offerings remained in the church.

In the Welsh language, epilepsy is called *Clwyf Tegla* (Tegla's Disease), after the saint whose curative holy well at Llandegla was the resort of people with epilepsy. Writing around 1740, Bishop Maddox of St Asaph's described the Ffynnon Degla customs: 'In this well the people that are troubled with convulsion fits or falling sickness called St Teccla's Evil do use to wash their hands and feet, going about the well three times, saying the Lord's prayer thrice, carrying in a handbasket a cock, if a man, and a hen if a woman offering 4 pence in the said well. All this is done after sunset.' After further prayer and sunwise circumambulation of the church, the patient went into the church to 'sleep under the communion table ... till break of day'. Thus purified and empowered, the patient could then expel the evil spirits that had caused the illness. The sufferer took the cock or hen and put its beak into his or her mouth. By breathing into it, the sufferer transferred the illness to the unfortunate bird, which was then left in the church. Then the patient returned to the well for more prayers, hopefully of thanksgiving for a cure. The last time this was done seems to have been in 1813, when Evan Evans, son of the parish sexton, was so treated.

On the island of Maelrubha in Loch Maree there was a healing well dedicated to St Maree, to which people seeking a cure for insanity were brought from miles around. The presbytery records at Dingwall tell of the derilans who officiated as (non-Christian) priests on the island. It is possible that their title comes from the Gaelic *deireoil*, 'afflicted'. Seemingly, the well-guardians were people enthused by 'divine madness' in the manner of shamans the world over. In 1774 Thomas Pennant visited the island and witnessed the rites. A person suffering from insanity would be brought to the 'sacred island' and 'made to kneel before the altar, where his attendants leave an offering of money. He is then brought to the well, and sips some of the holy water. A second offering is made; that done, he is thrice dipped in the lake.' The shrine was profaned in 1830 by a man who attempted to cure a mad dog. As a result its healing virtue was lost for about a decade, after which visits resumed for a while. The well is now dry.

There are now few well-guardians, and none like the derilans of Maelrubha. An example of how the practice came to an end is furnished by Ffynnon Eilian, near Abergele, which 'stood in the corner of a field, embosomed in a grove'. In the early nineteenth century, the well was guarded by a 'priestess' named Mrs Hughes. A struggle arose, however, between her successor, Jac Ffynnon Elian (John Evans), and the local vicar, who wanted to destroy the well. On two occasions Jac Ffynnon Elian was sent to prison. He was punished for reopening the well after it had been filled in. It was blocked permanently in January 1829. 'Here there is, I think, very little doubt that the owner or guardian of this well was, so to say, the representative of an ancient priesthood of the well,' commented Professor John Rhys in 1893. 'His function as a pagan ... was analogous to that of a parson or preacher who lets for rent the sittings in his church. We have, however, no sufficient data in this case to show how the right to the priesthood of a sacred well was acquired; but we know that a woman might have charge of St Eilian's Well.' Tragically, when the ancient well-customs were suppressed, so was a vast quantity of ancient Celtic skills and wisdom.

SALT AND SALT WELLS

Until recently, in the English North Midlands people swore oaths on salt instead of the Bible, and in the Outer Hebrides cattle were *sained* (blessed) with salt before being moved between pastures. Symbolically, salt is the incorruptible essence of life, because, like water, it is an essential human requirement. The sea is the greatest source of salt. Like rivers and lakes, the sea has its divinities: around Britain it is sacred to the Irish and Manx god Manannan MacLir and the Hebridean god Shony. In Wales, salt was won from the sea on the sacred Salt Island off Holy Island, Anglesey. In the Celtic heartlands of central Europe, many days' travel from the sea, salt was mined or won from natural saline springs. The proto-Celtic Hallstatt culture is named after one of the most important of these sites in Upper Austria. Several significant early Celtic sites owed their opulence and wealth to the salt trade. In Celtic times, Schwäbisch Hall in Germany was important because of its wells where salt water issued from the earth. The octagonal well-head of the main salt well still exists, but sadly it is no longer respected. Passers-by throw in empty drink cans and cigarette packets. In Britain, too, salt wells were formerly used and honoured; but today, as in Germany, their importance is no longer recognized. For example, only the name of the Salt Wells Inn at Dudley in the English West Midlands recalls an important saline holy well. Until quite recent times, the salt springs and brine pits of Nantwich and Northwich in Cheshire were garlanded and blessed by local priests. The custom was kept longest at St Richard's Well in Droitwich, Worcestershire.

SYMBOLIC FISH

Certain Celtic holy waters contained fish that were *geis* (forbidden) and never molested or caught. All of the fish in Loch Siant on Skye and in Loughadrine in County Cork were sacred, but the fish that lived in holy wells had greater symbolic significance. They were often elusive, being glimpsed fleetingly as a scaly reflection of light in the dark depths. Symbolically, the fish that lives in the well swims in the channel between the unseen and seen, the unconscious and the conscious. It denotes the usually unrecognized reality that our unconscious mind is not empty or

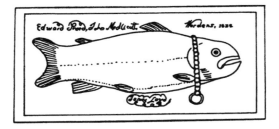

A painting by James Lloyd, dated 1828, shows the chain-wearing sacred fish that lived in the holy well at Peterchurch, Hereford and Worcester, England.

dead but contains living qualities of which we are scarcely aware. When we are sick and need to enter the healing process, or in a critical situation mentally, we must establish a relationship with our unconscious to restore our inner balance. So if we go to the sacred waters in the right frame of mind, then we glimpse the fish – the unconscious opens itself up to us. In this altered, meditative state, the mysterious depths freely reveal those elements that were previously hidden from us. Suddenly we see where before we could not. All that seemed dark and dangerous is illuminated, and we are opened to creative living possibilities that enable us to realize our human potential fully. The archetype of the fully realized human being is Christ, who is symbolized by the fish.

According to Celtic belief, a fish may be a manifestation of a spirit or a metamorphosed human being. An instance of the latter is found in *The Book of the Dun Cow* in the legend of the inundation of Lough Neagh. Overtaken by the flood, a woman survives transformed into a salmon. She lives in the lake for three hundred years until she is recognized by Congall, who restores her to human form as Muirgen 'the Sea-born'. Perhaps many wells with fish had legends of transformations. Also, sacred well-fish recall another Irish legend, that of the Well of Connla, over which the hazel tree of inspiration and wisdom grew. Its magic nuts fell into the water and were eaten by the salmon that lived there. The hero Finn MacCumhaill gained illumination by taking in the essence of this magic salmon. A related myth is told about St Neot's Well in Cornwall, which always contained two fish. In a vision, an angel told the guardian priest that if he took only one a day there would always be sufficient to eat. But when he was sick, a servant took and cooked both fish. At this outrage, the priest ordered them to be thrown back. Miraculously, they were restored to life. The story symbolizes the abundance and regenerative powers of divine waters. Perhaps it is a monkish version of an old myth about the water-deity Nechtan. A similar tale is told about St Corentine's Well at Plou-Vodiern in Brittany.

Where their species is recorded, most well-fish seem to have been trout. In the 1690s Martin Martin noted sacred trout in a well at Kilbride on the island of Skye. At Glenelg, Inverness, there were formerly two holy wells, each with trout. St Bean's Well, at Kilmore in Argyll, Scotland, contained the Easg Siant, two 'mystical or sanctified fishes', black in colour, which were probably not trout, and a well at Llandeloy, Pembroke, had resident eels, fish that resemble snakes. In many places, they were looked after by a well-guardian. At Ffynnon Wenog in Cardiganshire, the trout in the holy well wore golden chains, sacred to the sun. A painting of such a fish is exhibited in the church at Peterchurch, west of Hereford, representing the fish of the local Golden Well.

Sadly, the custom of maintaining fish in holy wells lapsed in most places during the nineteenth century. When new fish were put into Ffynnon Beris at Llanberis in 1896, it was so unusual that it was reported in the *Liverpool Mercury*: 'There have always been two "sacred fishes" in this well; and there is a tradition in the village to the effect that if one of the Tyn Y Ffynnon fishes came out of its hiding-place when an invalid took some of the water for drinking or bathing purposes, cure was certain; but if the fishes remained in their den, the water would do those who took it no good.' Such omens seem to have been a significant part of fish-lore. If the eel that lived in Ffynnon Gybi at Llangybi coiled around the legs of anyone who stood in the water, it was taken as a sign that the sought cure would be effective. In other places, different information was sought. The Anglesey holy well of King Elaeth contained an eel, whose movements were interpreted by a resident ichthyomant, and the fish of Ffynnon Fair on the same island were consulted concerning the course of love affairs.

GIFTS, VOTIVE OFFERINGS AND WELL-DRESSING

Custom requires that after using a holy well the pilgrim should leave a gift. The water-spirits are tolerant, for almost anything will do. Human artifacts, including coins, buttons, beads, corks, keys, buckles, ribbons, rags and humanoid 'dolly' figures are favoured. Natural objects are also permissible: flowers and fruit, cones from trees, thorns, stones and crystals, as well as offerings of food and drink, milk, bread and cheese. Whenever a miracle cure takes place, the grateful patient should leave his or her crutch or other sign of infirmity in thanksgiving and to give hope to others.

In his work on Irish religion, *Traces of the Elder Faiths of Ireland*, W.G. Wood-Martin quotes a visitor to St Bartholomew's Well at Pilstown,

County Waterford, in 1855: 'The venerable thorns which overshadow it bore a motley appearance, being covered with red, blue, and green ribbons, and rags, as if torn from the dresses of pilgrims, and tied up as a finale to their "rounds" and prayers. An old crone engaged in going her "rounds" said, they were tied up by each, to leave all sickness of the year behind them.' So long as the offering exists, there is a tangible link with the healing powers of the well, and the benefit continues. But under no circumstances should any object deposited at a holy well be removed (as at any sacred place), not least because it was believed that the giver's illness would be transferred to the taker. The exception to this rule was made with money. In the Middle Ages, when the Church had developed an efficient organization, the non-Christian custom of leaving a gift for the spirit of the well was exploited as a source of revenue. Collecting-boxes were set up at holy wells, and sometimes a priest was employed as money-collector and guardian. A most lucrative example of this practice was Our Lady's Well at Whitekirk in East Lothian, which was administered by the monks of Melrose Abbey. The flow of pilgrims seeking a miracle cure was so great and so profitable that they erected a large shrine to cope with them.

Traditionally, people honour holy wells on the saint's day by 'dressing' them with garlands, flowers, branches and moss. Also, the local priest may take a portable altar to the well and hold services there rather than in church. The most highly developed customs of well-dressing are practised in the English Midlands and southern Germany, where complex shrines made of flowers are erected over the wells at Easter or around their patronal day. At one time the English custom seems to have been restricted to Tissington, Derbyshire, where the five wells – Holy Well, Coffin Well, Hand's Well, the Town Well and Yew Tree Well – were decked, it is said, in thanksgiving for the end of the plague in 1350. Maundy Thursday is the traditional day for these dressing ceremonies. In recent years, the practice has spread, or rather returned, to other parts of England.

MAGIC WELLS

People visit wishing wells today, but seldom do they attempt to use them magically. However, in the past certain wells were reputed to be effective for the performance of magic. A few holy wells were reputed to affect the weather. Fishermen and farmers would make supplication to the spirit of the well to alter the weather in some way. Manx fishermen used to use water from the *chibbyr* (holy well) at Lezayn in wind-magic. They threw handfuls of the water towards the airt or eighth of the horizon from which they wanted a good wind. Further north, on the holy island of Iona, were two wind-wells: the Well of the North Wind, which still exists, and the Well of the South Wind, which is lost. In former times, both were visited by seamen, who brought offerings to them for wind in the required direction.

It is clear that, like everything on earth, sacred waters are subject to transformation through human or other agency. They can be empowered or disempowered – like the Maelrubha well. Just as in Pagan times sacred waters were empowered by Grannos's nightly visits, so in later times people believed that sacred waters could be charged with a healing force by contact with various relics and power-objects. At Ludlow in Shropshire, a pilgrim on his way to St Winefride's at Holywell blessed the Boiling Well, and it acquired the power to heal sore eyes. The virtues of the healing Loch Manaar at Strathnaver were reputed to have come from a magic white stone thrown there by an old woman. Until well after the Second World War, during the Vigil and Feast of St Clothilde holy relics were dipped in her fountain at Le Grand Andely in Normandy. Then sick people plunged into the waters in hope of a cure, for the water was said to be effective only at this time. From the evidence of ex-votos, the last cure seems to have been around 1963. It is now acknowledged only as a wishing well, which tourists throw coins into.

Common to all holy wells is a belief in the power of transformation, usually of a beneficial nature. In former times, aged pilgrims to the holy island of Iona would bathe at dawn in the Well of Age to recover their youthful powers. But sometimes transformation is not to human advantage. In Kerfeunteun parish in Finistère, Brittany, is the Church of St Mélar, which contains his holy well in the middle of the crypt. Legend tells that, on some future Trinity Sunday, the well will overflow and a flood will destroy the church. Because of this dire warning, the priest never celebrates Mass there on Trinity Sunday, but at the nearby chapel of Kernitron instead. An archetypal Celtic flood legend is localized at this place, having a predicted local effect, destroying the church. This legend recalls the Irish myth of the origins of two major rivers, the Boyne and the Shannon. Both came into being when a goddess profaned a holy well: Boann, the Well of Segais, and Sinann, the Well of Coelrind. Both overflowed, forming mighty rivers along the courses where they pursued the goddesses to their deaths. Manifesting the law of the unity of opposites, as well as giving life, water can also bring death.

Holy Mountains

*The steeple-house, and the ground wherein it
stands, is no more holy than this mountain.*

George Fox at Firbankfell, 1652

SINCE THE earliest times, high places have served as the altars of the
gods, and every religion preserves traditions of mountains as the
places from which the gods hand down wisdom or commandments
to their earthly followers. Mountains are sites of divine power: in antiquity
the Greeks revered Olympus, and in central Europe the Hörselberg, the
Brocken, Mont Blanc and Mont Pilatus were places of holy dread. In
Pagan times none could look upon Iceland's Helgafell without first washing his or her face. Wales has five holy mountains, the most important of
which is Pumlumon, near to which rise the rivers Severn and Wye. These
holy mountains are manifestations of the archetypal cosmic mountain at
the centre of the world, an access-point to the upperworld of the gods.

The physical nature of mountains gives them a special character quite
different from other landscapes. They are paradoxical places where the
weather and the seasons differ from those in the valleys below. Winter lasts
longer here: it may be spring at the top when it is high summer lower
down. The highest mountains have eternal winter, in the shape of permanent snow-fields or glaciers: they are the upperworldly 'White Land' of the
gods. Others are eternal places of the winds, where the irresistible elemental powers are at their strongest. Mountains are places of vision, both in
physical terms because one can see a long way from their summits, and
also because the power of inner vision is enhanced there. They are also
places of the exultation of the soul: it is from mountain tops that spirits
ascend to the empyrean, and upon them that inspired teachings may be
received. Carn Ingli, the Mount of Angels, near Nevern, is one such place,
where St Brynach experienced angelic visitations. Visions or apparitions
have been experienced on most Celtic holy mountains, among them
Glastonbury Tor, Ben Nevis, Menez-Bré and Ben Bulben.

Climbing in itself is hazardous, and in the past few people who had no business there would have dared to venture upon a mountain, especially one with eternal snows. But because they are places of vision, mountain-tops are attractive to mystics and magicians. Anyone who reaches a place of vision on a mountain will have done so through undertaking a life-threatening pilgrimage whose effect will have been transformative. The initiatory nature of climbing can be given no better example than the ritual climb performed on the holy island of Scelig Mhichil. There, after offering and praying at holy wells at the foot of the mount, the votary climbs a steep pathway which leads to a narrow chasm called the Needle's Eye. After squeezing through this gateway, he or she then continues high above the sea across a perilous ledge called the Stone of Pain. Beyond this, the next stopping-place is the Eagle's Nest, where there is a stone cross. Lastly, the climber must sit upon a ledge overhanging the sea, 460 feet (140 m) up, to kiss a cross carved on the rock. Those who succeed in completing this pilgrimage are respected as brave and pious individuals who will be rewarded in the next life for their devotion.

Before 1930, when the last inhabitants were evacuated at gunpoint by the Royal Navy, the young men of St Kilda had to pass a challenging test before they were allowed to marry. This was to climb the perilous Stac Biorach (236 ft, 72 m) in Soay Sound at the south-west end of the island. At the summit, the climber would balance on one heel on the Mistress Stone, perched high above the sea, grasping the other foot in his hands. To do this was to achieve the blessing of Mother Earth by setting foot on her special sacred stone. Only when this feat was accomplished could the young man take a wife. He had proved his ability to collect eggs from the most dangerous cliffs and thus his ability to support a family.

GODDESS AND GOD HILLS

Mountains have a dual nature. Whilst they function as sacred places of higher, heavenly beings, they remain rooted in the earth. Upon certain mountains are shrines dedicated to the sun, sky-gods and wind elementals, usually male in aspect. All European religions revere a divinity of the sky, who is seen as the all-father of gods and humans alike. He is known variously as Zeus, Jupiter, Tîwaz, Ziu and other names. His manifestations are frequently through the medium of mountain-tops, and it is easy to think that the mountains themselves are aspects of the

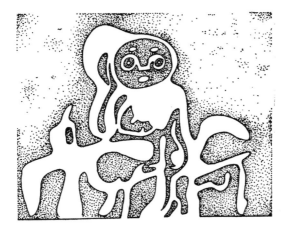

*The Celtic hill-figure of Gogmagog that existed on a hillside at Wandlebury, south of
Cambridge, according to T.C. Lethbridge. Such hill-figures were the largest images
of the 'anima loci' and were visible from great distances.*

deity. However, like the holy well, where the male sun was seen to enter
the female waters, the manifestation of sky-gods is upon the feminine
ground of Mother Earth, the mountains themselves. Physically part of the
earth, they are the linking-point of the earthly and heavenly powers at
which the heavenly light becomes present upon the earth.

The Celtic god who manifests himself on mountains is Poeninus, from
whom the Italian Apennines and British Pennine mountains are named.
His status as sky-god was acknowledged by the Roman priests who assimilated him to Jupiter Poeninus. His temples were erected at high points
where he appeared and at places where his aid was necessary, such as the
summits of mountain passes. The Little St Bernard Pass in the Alps was
perhaps his most important shrine. In Cisalpine Gaul, the deity of the
mountain passes themselves was the goddess Brigida, consort of Poeninus.
The Brigantes, who appear to have claimed descent from the goddess,
dwelt in the Pennine region of Britain. Later, the Church assimilated
Brigida as St Brigida or Brigid.

As high points of the earth, mountains are dedicated to goddesses. In
medieval times, the Hörselberg in Thuringia was famous throughout
Europe as the Venusberg, where the Lady Venus held court. Famous bards
including Thomas of Ercildoune and Tannhäuser are reputed to have
visited her there, and it was the scene of an apparition of the goddess in
1398. Certain hills in the British Isles are holy to Brigid, whilst others commemorate Ana, the Celtic mother of the gods. Cormac wrote of the mountains called the Two Paps of Ana, west of Luchair in County Kerry, where

her breasts are manifested as twin holy mountains. Through them the body of the goddess is manifest in the landscape.

Traditions exist that hold that holy mountains often remained Pagan long after the creation of Christian sacred places on lower ground. They were remote and subject to infrequent visits, so the expense and trouble of building churches upon them meant that they were of less immediate interest than other places. Also, powerful and vengeful deities resided there. Until the nineteenth century the fairy goddesses, Aine and Fennel, were honoured at two hills near Lough Gur in County Limerick, 'upon whose summits sacrifices and sacred rites used to be celebrated according to living tradition.' Mont-Beuvray, the sacred mountain of the nature-goddess Bibracte located west of Autun, was Christianized in 1876 when a church dedicated to St Martin was built upon the site of her Celto-Roman temple. Unique in Britain is the Roman Catholic island of South Uist in the Hebrides, where the roadside shrines and stopping-places are still maintained and revered. In 1957, Rueval, 'The Hill of the Miracles', was acknowledged as a mountain of the feminine principle when a gigantic Madonna-and-Child image called 'Our Lady of the Isles' was erected there.

MOUNTAINS OF LIGHT

Mountains are places of light and illumination because the sun is visible there in the morning before it becomes visible below. Likewise, in the evening it can still be seen when it has already set at lower altitudes. This made mountains ideal places for sun-worship, which included what would now be called astronomy, the observation of the azimuths and altitudes of solar phenomena through the yearly cycle. Because of this, traditions survive of solar mountains in the Celtic realms. Although Christian influence has renamed many of them, Beinn-na-Gréine, near Trotternish on Skye, still bears its ancient Gaelic appellation of 'The Mountain of the Sun'.

In the Vosges of Alsace is the impressive Mont-Sainte-Odile. Surmounted by the monastery of Hohenbourg, it is associated with a legend that shows it to be a mountain of illumination. Around 660, we are told, the wife of Etichon, duke of Alsace, gave birth to a blind daughter. The baby was taken away and eventually put into a convent where she became a Christian at the age of twelve. At her baptism, her sight was miraculously restored. She was given a new name, Odile, meaning 'daughter of light'. Subsequently, Odile became the abbess of a convent built on

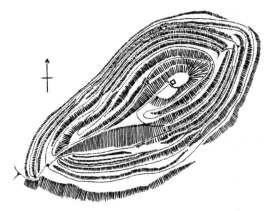

*Plan of the terraced holy mountain of Gwynn ap Nudd, Glastonbury Tor. The dotted line
is the labyrinthine pathway first noted in 1968 and used subsequently for ceremonial purposes.*

the summit of the holy mountain which had previously been a Celtic
sacred place. At the foot of the rock upon which the monastery stands,
Odile made a spring appear. Its water is a sovereign remedy for sick eyes.

The dedication of holy mountains to sight and the sun reflects the classical tradition that certain mountains express the qualities of one or other
of the seven planets of the mundane system. Among other things, the planetary ruler depends on the shape of the mountain. The attributes of planetary mountains are recorded in medieval geomancy and alchemy (for
example, in C.A. Balduinus's *Aurum Hermeticum* of 1675). Traditionally,
mounts with the shape of the Tor have a solar attribution.

In the Christian tradition, certain mountains of light are dedicated to St
Michael. Usually, like Mont-Sainte-Odile, they are isolated hills, notable
landmarks visible for miles around. There are several in southern England,
among them St Michael's Mount, St Michael de Rupe on Brentor, St
Michael's at Burrow Mump and Glastonbury Tor. According to Christian
cosmology, Michael's physical body is the sun, and his place in the
company of archangels is like the sun in the congress of planets. As solar
angel of the East, representative of the region of light and fire, St Michael
forces the demonic elements back into the dark underworld. But he does
not transform them, and, though bound, they remain dangerous.
Repression rather than acceptance and transformation of the unconscious
means that the conflict is unresolved, and will emerge again later in some
form or other.

Unusually, the local legend of St Collen's Christianization of Glastonbury Tor contains some elements of transformation. To the Pagan Celts,

The central pillar of the Chapel of the Cross at Mont-Sainte-Odile, Alsace, France. The bound hands at the foot of the pillar recall the legend of the slain giant, Gargantua, who is the foundation of the earth.

the Tor was the sacred mountain of the god Gwynn ap Nudd, 'The White One, Son of Darkness', who was the lord of the fairy kingdom. Collen lived as a hermit in a cave in the side of the rocky hill. One day he overheard two men talking in reverent tones about Gwynn ap Nudd, so immediately he berated them for worshipping the *genius loci*. Shortly afterwards a fairy messenger appeared, summoning Collen to Gwynn's court atop the holy hill. At first Collen refused, but finally he agreed to go and, reaching the summit, he beheld a magnificent castle. Collen entered, and was received graciously by Gwynn ap Nudd, whom he repaid by throwing consecrated water everywhere. At this, the castle disappeared into thin air, leaving the monk sitting alone on the grassy hill-top. After this, a church dedicated to St Michael was erected there. But because Gwynn ap Nudd was a powerful deity who prevented the demons of the underworld from swarming upwards into this world, the Christian God gave him special dispensation to remain at his post, guarding the portals of Annwn. The Tor's status as *lapis manalis* or 'pot-lid of Hell' was thereby reconfirmed by the newer faith.

There are few more striking holy places than the two holy mountains that are neither totally in the sea nor on the land, being connected to the mainland by causeways that are passable only at low tide. These are St Michael's Mount and Mont-Saint-Michel. There are traditions at both places that for the Pagans the mounts were sacred to the sun. Legend tells that in the year 495 fishermen beheld an apparition on the western side of the Cornish mount. Christians identified it as St Michael, and the mountain was thus renamed in his honour. The place of the saint's epiphany was made into a shrine, monks founded a monastery and pilgrimages began.

A remarkable parallel exists on the other side of the English Channel in Normandy at Mont-Saint-Michel. It is a conical granite island which bears a close resemblance to its Cornish counterpart. During Celto-

Roman times this island-mountain was a solar sanctuary called Dinsul or Belen. Around the year 708, the local bishop, Aubert, made a pilgrimage to Apulia to visit the shrine of St Michael at Monte Gargano. Like the northern St Michael's mounts, Monte Gargano was also a solar shrine, latterly associated with Mithras. The name of Monte Gargano appears to refer to Gargantua, a primal giant whose body was dismembered to make the world. When Aubert returned to the Channel coast in 710, he rededicated Dinsul to St Michael and built an oratory near the summit. Then he dispatched a deputation of monks to Gargano to bring relics for the new monastery church. Other notable Celtic St Michael's mountains include Burrow Mump in Somerset and Montagne Saint-Michel near Brasparts in Brittany. Near Carnac is a tumulus of the megalithic era, dedicated to St Michel, with a chapel built on top.

85

The fortified monastery-town of Mont-Saint-Michel in Normandy stands on a holy mountain dedicated by the Celts to solar worship.

A steep rocky island is a mountain whose base is upon the seabed, so the dedication of such places to St Michael is natural. There are a number of notable St Michael's islands in the Celtic realms. Steep Holm, in the Bristol Channel, held a priory of St Michael from the Norman Conquest until around 1270. Looe Island in Cornwall is also recorded by Camden as being dedicated to St Michael, and Drake's Island, in the middle of Plymouth Sound, once bore a chapel to St Michael. But the most impressive of all St Michael's mountains is the Great Skellig rock, 7 miles (11 km) into the Atlantic off Bolus Head, County Kerry. On it was the monastery of Scelig Mhichil, founded by St Filian. In this harsh and isolated environment, the monks built an oratory, surrounded by drystone beehive huts. As at other rocky monasteries, soil was brought from the mainland to make a graveyard. Scelig Mhichil flourished until the thirteenth century, when it was abandoned and the monks resettled at Ballinskelligs on the mainland. Today, there is a round of pilgrims' stations on the rock.

The Upper and Lower Classes

The noble dynasties of Europe once claimed descent from divine ancestry. Each family had an ancestral guardian spirit, and the holy hill was the locus where its power was most accessible. For this reason, land-owning families were identified with specific holy hills or mountains. Being high is a symbol of power that is based on a physical necessity. In addition to possessing divine qualities, high points are always of strategic importance. In former times, each lord had his own hill-fort, constructed on a high place from which he could see everything and thereby control the surrounding countryside. From the earliest times, high points in the landscape were thus places of government. The hill was the place of the ancestors where the chief nobleman received divine inspiration to make favourable decisions for the well-being of his kinspeople. The high king of Ireland sat at the Hill of Tara. The German noble families from whom kings and emperors came have the element 'high' in their name, recalling their mountain castles of Hohenstaufen and Hohenzollern. With the advent of more urban ways of living, the mountainous high point was transmuted into a high seat or bench of state within the royal hall. This, however, was a model of the godly Throne of Majesty, the seven-stepped holy hill of heaven, raised above the surrounding floor-level. Sometimes the seat was actually made of stone, or contained one, linking it to an earlier time when the throne itself was a physical part of the mountain of the king. Such a

A Celto-Roman image of the goddess Brigantia, tutelary deity of high places, now in Edinburgh.

throne is the British Coronation Chair in Westminster Abbey, beneath which the Stone of Destiny serves as the monarch's inauguration stone.

In his assembly hall, the king sat on high, raised on steps above his nobles and clergy, who themselves were at a higher level physically than the lower orders. Literally, society was divided into upper and lower classes, and the assembly hall reflected this, being divided by a screen rather like that found in churches. In Wales, this was called a *corf*, a name applied to a boundary-wood planted on the steep bank of a stream. These woods marked the point of division between the upper and lower parts of a land-holding. Thus, the structure of a building that served as a microcosm of the country reflected the ideal layout of the land itself. The corf, as a sort of natural terrace across the land, resembles the artificial terracing of holy hills such as Glastonbury Tor. The form of these hills reflects the Throne of Majesty, and may have been used for class-stratified assemblies like that of the Manx Parliament on the artificial hill of Tynwald.

87

UNDER THE HILL

When we die, our physical bodies return to Mother Earth. What might happen to any other components is a matter of religious faith. In northern Europe it was believed that the souls of the dead go into the hills and spirit-mountains, where they live among otherworldly beings. There are local traditions throughout the Celtic lands that certain hills are fairy strongholds, and in Scandinavia they are inhabited by the Hill-Folk, a race of halflings somewhere between elves and humans. Formerly, every district had its own fairy hill. In general, there is an indistinct boundary between departed souls, fairies and other supernatural beings.

The custom of interring the dead in earth mounds was widespread among the Pagan Celts. The remains of upper-class people were buried within a chamber, surrounded by possessions and ritual artifacts. A mound of earth, sometimes surmounted by wooden posts, stones or a statue, was raised over the chamber, which was a representation of the underworld itself, for artificial burial mounds were made in imitation of spirit-mountains. Constructing special hills for the dead was thus the creation of a model of the otherworld. The otherworld is a symbolic realm in which everything must be done correctly, according to canonical principles that reflect the underlying structure of existence. Those who go inside the mound leave the world of the living and re-enter the womb of Mother Earth. At death, part of the human spirit goes into the otherworld to be regenerated and reborn; the goods are taken into the fairy kingdom; and the mound serves as a memorial to the life and deeds of the departed, a landmark for travellers and a stopping-place for the devout.

We are fortunate that through the skill and expertise of archaeologists we can look into the Celtic world of the dead. The grave of a sixth-century BCE Celtic lord at Hochdorf, near Stuttgart, excavated in the late 1970s, contained all of the symbolic elements of belief that were recorded a thousand years later in medieval Celtic literature. Among the grave-goods is an enormous cauldron. The relationship between the cauldron and the mound is significant, demonstrating the principle of correspondence between the inner and the outer. The shape of the earthen mound in which the cauldron was buried reflects the dome of the heavens, which is the container of the earth on which we exist. The shape of that which is above is created below on earth.

The inside of the cauldron also reflects this shape, but it is inverted. Within this enormous bronze cauldron, large enough to hold a man, was a golden bowl a few inches across. The golden vessel appears to represent the container of the essential spirit, which emerged a millennium after Hochdorf as the Grail legend. Celtic lore recorded later holds that the cauldron was sacred to the goddess Cerridwen, symbolizing rebirth and plenty. But to be reborn, we must first die and enter the cauldron of the underworld, the uterus of spiritual rebirth. With the cauldron was a finely constructed four-wheeled wagon, the sacred vehicle of the dead, carefully built according to numerological principles. Other grave-goods include vessels and aurochs drinking-horns whose numbers correspond with the holy numbers of Greek and Celtic spirituality. Nothing at Hochdorf is without its symbolic function. Even the clothing of the buried man is significant: his hat is the birch hat of the dead, made from the tree of the regenerative goddess of springtime, signifying the expectation of rebirth.

HILLS AS STOPPING-PLACES

Conical piles of stone by the trackside or on hill-tops are a common sight in Celtic hill-country. They are spiritual way-stations that commemorate those who have passed before, both travellers in this world and the dead. Throughout the Celtic realms it is customary for the traveller to leave a stone at any cairn he or she passes. Because the stone is a symbol of the self, each passer-by thus leaves something of her- or himself on the stone-pile. Cairns occupy liminal areas, places of transition in history (decisive battles), travelling (mountain passes), and territory (borders between counties and countries), and sometimes cover burials. Irish tradition asserts that five stones constitute a cairn, being a microcosm of the whole island of Ireland.

It is as places of the dead that they are most numinous. Memorial cairns were erected wherever someone died out of doors. In many places, cairns at the summits of steep hills or beside water are customary stopping-places of the dead. Funeral cortèges would halt there for prayers and rest. On leaving the stopping-place, every mourner would add a stone to the cairn, perpetuating and reinforcing its presence. Another reason why people add stones to a cairn is in commemoration of completing a personal sacred act. Cairns at shrines have this function. The Priest's Grave, a cairn near St Buonia's Well at Killabuonia in County Kerry, is honoured by pilgrims who make nine sunwise turns around the well and then place a stone on the cairn. In former times, there was frequently a more direct relation between cairns and the dead. In commemoration of a British victory over Irish invaders, King Caswallon is said to have erected cairns of Irishmen's bones at Holyhead, the nearest point to Ireland. Such macabre trophies of war, not uncommon in the ancient world, have long since been removed. But cairns of stones have proved more durable. In Cumbria, a cairn at Dunmail Raise, the pass between Steel Fell and Seat Sandal, commemorates a battle in 945 between the Scots under King Duvenald and the Northumbrians under Edwin. Before the battle, each Scot put a stone on the pile; afterwards, all survivors took one away. The remainder served as a receptacle for the spirits of the dead, numbering the fallen, creating a place to be honoured in hero- and ancestor-worship. In later times the cairn acquired another function, marking first the boundary of England and Scotland, then that of Cumberland and Westmorland.

Cairns are best known as stopping-places on trackways. In rough country they are intervisible, so that the traveller is always in sight of one and cannot stray far from the right route. In ancient times, cairns and small mounds that served as way-markers were dedicated to Jupiter and called by the name of 'Mons Jovis', later corrupted to Montjoie and Mountjoy. Topographically, a Mountjoy is any hill that marks the way for travellers and pilgrims, artificial or natural. A good natural example is at the hill of La Montjoie at Mortain in Normandy, which bears a chapel of St Michael on its highest point. It was from there that pilgrims travelling to Mont-Saint-Michel could first see the holy mountain that was their destination.

CALVARIES

For the first twelve centuries of Christian belief, the name Calvary meant the place in Jerusalem where Christ's Crucifixion was enacted. Pilgrims to Jerusalem were accustomed to walk the path known as the Way of the Cross, halting at the stopping-places where the dramatic events of Christ's Passion had happened. Later, the Islamic conquest made it impossible for Christians to make pilgrimages to Jerusalem. But devotion to the Way of the Cross did not cease. In the thirteenth century, *Meditations on the Life of Christ*, a Franciscan text attributed to St Bonaventure, popularized the re-enactment of Christ's Passion as a means of religious devotion. To this were added the ideas of St John of the Cross, who, in *The Ascent of Mount Carmel*, visualized the ascent to the divine being as accomplished by ten upward steps. In the thirteenth century, the Dominican mystic Heinrich Suso also developed a 'path-working' meditation involving visualization in stages of each locus and event of the Passion, ending with the Crucifixion. In these and other mystical writings on the Passion, the upward ascent by means of distinct steps or stages was emphasized.

Once the Way of the Cross had been removed from the physical reality of Jerusalem into the landscape of the mind, it was possible to project it outwards onto any appropriate place. This is an important principle of correspondences in geomancy facilitating the recognition and creation of new sacred places. When someone recognizes a place that resembles or reproduces the essence and virtues of another, then the new place reflects both the particular essence of the original and its deeper archetypal qualities. In this case, natural hills whose topography suggested the traditional Hill of Calvary were modified with a pathway that re-created the ritual landscape of the Way of the Cross. The stopping-places – the Stations of the Cross – were marked with images or chapels. The path itself reflected the course of the Passion, its varying roughness, steepness and narrowness emphasizing the events commemorated in the stations.

Pilgrims climbing a Calvary hill have their senses assailed by physical hardship and mental devotion, undergoing a transformational experience not possible in the more intellectual realms. It is a symbolic journey on several levels, interpreted through the specific imagery of Christian myth. A nineteenth-century manual for pilgrims states of the Stations of the Cross that the pilgrim 'must reach [them] by difficult roads, as he must arrive by steep paths at the several Stations of Virtue.' Thus, the outer pilgrimage reflects and reinforces the inner archetype within those who 'have sought the source of virtue at the summit of the Calvary, which they have climbed, inspired by the thought of him who first ascended there.'

The earliest Calvaries had seven stages, reflecting the Mountain of God, derived from the seven-planet cosmology of the mundane system, the number ascribed by medieval numerologists to St Michael. The number was later increased to reflect more fully the scriptural account. In 1734, at the behest of the Franciscans, Pope Clement XII fixed the number at fourteen, and so it remains now. One of the earliest examples was the Sacro Monte at Varallo in northern Italy, founded by Bernardo Caimi in 1481 to house an olive-wood cross brought from Palestine. It served as a model for others, first in Italy, then in France and elsewhere. In Celtic lands, the Way of the Cross fitted in perfectly with the numerous pilgrimage ways that led to the summits of holy mountains. Stopping-places, hitherto general places of prayer, were made into the specific Stations of the Cross. Thus, to the old Pagan and Christian attributes of specific holy mountains was added another layer of meaning. Brandon Mountain in County Kerry is a good example. At the summit is the oratory and monastery of St Brendan where he received a vision of the mystic island of Hy-Brasil, far out in the Western Ocean. The summit is reached by the Old Saint's Road, a holy trackway whose stopping-places are marked by the Stations of the Cross.

TEMPORARY HOLY HILLS AND PERRONS

In Celtic lands there was a widespread custom of erecting temporary hills to celebrate the harvest festival of Lammas on 1 August. Writing in 1792 about customs in the Lothians, James Anderson recalls: 'The celebration of the Lammas Festival was most remarkable. Each community agreed to build a tower in some conspicuous place, near the centre of their district. This tower was usually built of sods. … In building it, a hole was left in the centre for a flag staff, on which was displayed the colours on the great day of the festival.' On Lammas Day, the participants danced and sang, took part in sports and banqueting, 'drinking pure water from a well, which they always took care should be near the scene of their banquet'. Research conducted in 1942 by the Irish Folklore Commission identified 195 assembly sites in use then. Most were on hill-tops, and only 17 of the 195 had any connection with the Church. In Ireland, the Pagan celebration of Lammas continues to the present day. Sometimes the festivities are held on Garland Sunday, the nearest Sunday to Lammas Day. The ceremonies centre around a girl, seated in a chair on the hill-top. Garlanded with flowers, she personates the goddess of the hill. In some places, people set up a female effigy decorated with ribbons and flowers. Round the image circle dancing girls, who pick flowers or ribbons off the figure as they dance.

Some ancient Celtic crosses are raised above ground level on stone steps which seem to recall the Lammas hill tradition. Notable stone crosses such as those at St David's, Llantwit Major and Trelleck surmount formidable multi-stepped 'pyramids' or perrons that follow the pattern of the Throne of Majesty or terraced holy mountain. Often, the stepped base of the perron supports an image in stone of a wooden post, the world tree, topped by a sphere representing the sun or the upper world. It represents the world-mountain that supports the cosmic axial tree. These stepped bases sometimes reached enormous proportions. At Winsford in Cheshire the stepped base contains a room formerly in use as a lock-up, for it was customary to punish wrongdoers at the base of crosses, as surviving stocks and pillories attest. In the perron we can recognize the ascent of levels expressed in different ways in the stratification of society or the Way of the Cross. The stepped mountain is a symbol of cosmic order and stability, each level representing a stage of attainment in the cosmic hierarchy. Naturally, then, perrons were symbols of law and order, often connected with the reading of proclamations. The prime example is the terraced law-mound on which the Manx Parliament assembles to promulgate laws. The ball-topped perron at Clackman- nan stands close to the much earlier phallic megalith that symbolized the power-centre of the Pictish kings.

Like the step-pyramid and ziggurat, the perron is an image of the cosmic holy mountain, whose steps lead to the summit where the image of divinity is found. This one is at Winsford in Cheshire.

Sacred Caves and Subterranea

Then Aeneas climbed the rocky hill
Where, on the crest, the temple of Apollo stands,
And there the fearsome cavern of the awesome Sybil lies,
Whence came her prophecies.

Virgil, *The Aeneid*

THE BREATH OF THE EARTH

FOLK TRADITION associates caves with the breath. In anthropomorphic symbolism, caves parallel the throat. Caves where wind emerges from the ground are places where the earth is felt to be breathing. In former times, a cave called Breuant, 'The Windpipe', existed in Gwent. Nennius describes it as 'having wind blowing out of it constantly'. Breuant was reckoned as the Eighth Wonder of Britain. Clement of Alexandria says of it in his *Stromata*: 'in the island of Britain there is a cave situated under a mountain, and a chasm on its summit … accordingly, when the wind falls into the cave and rushes into the bosom of the cleft, a sound is heard like cymbals clashing musically. And after, when the wind is in the woods, when the leaves are moved by a sudden gust of wind, a sound is emitted like the song of birds.'

Sometimes other caves emanate mysterious noises. They may be grinding or cracking sounds created by strain along faults in the rocks, the throbbing and gurgling sounds of underground streams, or the booming waves of the sea. Giraldus Cambrensis describes the wonderful noise he heard at a cave on Barry Island, where the clash of the waves rolling in sounds like smiths labouring in the bowels of the earth. In the sounds of caves other people have heard the echoing notes of a bowed instrument, rumbling drums, droning bagpipes, howling dogs, wailing spirits and 'the good people's music', the sounds of otherworldly life. Because of this, Fingal's Cave on the island of Staffa is called in Gaelic *an Uaimh Binn*, the

'Melodious Cave'. The mysterious singing of birds sometimes heard in caves is associated in Celtic belief with the otherworld. The bird is often rather menacing. St Patrick's Purgatory is reputed to be the home of the monstrous demonic black bird called Cornu. Goose images in caves go back as far as the Magdalenian era, and there are cave carvings of geese from Celtic contexts, especially in Fife. Folk tales about caves also tell of geese. Here, the goose appears to be an image of the Earth Mother-goddess as guardian of the dead. She appears in goose form as one of the archaic goddess images of old Europe, and in modern times as the doyenne of fairy tales, Mother Goose.

The Irish bards had a group of stories called 'Caves', but few have survived in anything but fragmentary form. However, in Ireland many legends surround two particular caves: the Cave of Cruachan at Rathcroghan in Roscommon and St Patrick's Purgatory in Donegal. The former, otherwise known as Ireland's Gate of Hell, was viewed as a way between this world and the otherworld. It was greatly feared, for people considered it to be the abode of demonic beings. Legend tells of Cruachan as the source of plagues: it is 'the fit abode' of the horrid Morrigan. Periodically, on Samhain, *in t-Ellén trechend* – 'the three-headed Ellén' – and other demonic beings would come forth. They included a destructive swarm of red-ochre coloured birds – birds of the dead – whose breath withered fields and orchards, and a teeming multitude of abominable supernatural swine. Demonic denizens were found elsewhere, too: on the Isle of Man, cave-noises are said to be the breathing of a sea-monster called the Cughtage. In the Danes Hills near Leicester was Black Annis's Bower, a fearsome cave reputed to be the lair of the eponymous demoness who hunted and devoured little children, hanging up their skins to dry.

ENTERING THE UNDERWORLD

Frequently, caves are portrayed as entrances to the underworld or the fairy kingdom, or perhaps, in a Christian interpretation, hell. In legend, this underworld may contain treasure and ghostly guardians, cave fairies or sleeping armies awaiting their recall to this world. Like holy wells, caves are passages that lead from the daylight world of the visible into the dark underworld of permanent night, whose contents cannot be seen. The physical cave reflects the cave within, the dark unconscious that lies behind the conscious mind. To enter the underworld of the unconscious is to take a step towards transformation. In entering the cave, we breathe the breath of the earth, making contact with the unconscious. The decision to enter is the prelude to an encounter that may bring a drastic change in personality.

Legend tells us that, despite the daunting residents, people have braved the dangers of the underworld in order to acquire charmed artifacts and gain visions of the future. The Welsh epic, *The Spoils of Annwn*, recounts how Arthur and his knights mounted an unsuccessful expedition to capture the otherworldly cauldron, female symbol of bountifulness, and bring it up to this world. In the Irish saga *The Adventures of Nera*, Nera enters the Cave of Cruachan and has a vision of evil events to come. But to enter the dangerous uncharted territory of the subterranean kingdom takes great courage or folly. This is implicit in the common Celtic tales of the musician – a fiddler, piper or drummer – who enters the perilous passage accompanied by a dog. He never returns, but the animal emerges again, burnt by the underworldly fires. This tale is told of a number of locations, including Smoo Cave at Cape Wrath, the Piper's Cave O' Gowend in Galloway, and certain caves on Colonsay, Islay and Mull.

Men who visited the otherworld through caves sometimes learned new skills which they brought back into the world of mortals. Flannery, the celebrated piper of Oranmore in Galway, learned his musical skills underground from an otherworldly tutor. In addition to new skills, fairy gifts were bestowed upon the fortunate. The pipe known as the Black Chanter of Clan Chattan was given to a MacPherson piper by a fairy woman who loved him. A Macrimmon piper who visited the Piper's Cave at Harlosh Point on Skye was given the gift of music by the Fairy Queen herself in the shape of the Silver Chanter of the Fairy Woman. With this, he founded the hereditary bagpipe school of Borreraig, whose members served as pipers to the MacLeod of MacLeod. Years later he was summoned to return to faery. Leaving the magic chanter to his son, he entered the cave sounding his pipes, accompanied only by his dog. His companions, too fearful to enter, followed above ground, guided by the sound of the pipes. When they reached Fairy Bridge, the piping stopped. The dog suddenly appeared from a hole in the ground, its hair singed off. But the piper was never seen again, having been taken back into the kingdom of faery.

Often pipe music is ascribed to a departed spirit playing a lament. According to A. MacCulloch, writing in 1841, bagpipes were heard frequently in the Piper's Cave O' Gowend in Galloway: 'Some think the piper a devil, others fancy the musician to be some kind of carline, who reveres the memory of departed highlanders, who were anciently smothered in the cave.' Sadly, such tales were sometimes based on real events which impress upon us the callous barbarism of life in former days: for instance, in 1006, Bishop Muiredhach was smothered in a cave in County Sligo by King Ua Ruairc. In 1135, King Echri Ua Taidhg of Feara-Lí and his wife and brother were suffocated in a cave by the members of the Uí Thuirtre clan; and on Eigg in 1578 the MacLeod clan killed 393 MacDonalds by driving them into a cave and setting a fire that asphyxiated them.

CAVES OF INSPIRATION

Caves are very much places of the breath, and suffocation, loss of breath, is a fitting way to die in a cave. Caves can be lethal or inspiring. There is a very fine dividing line. Those containing noxious gases smother victims who inadvertently stray into them, for when we are inside a cave we breathe the breath of the earth for good or ill. The breath is an aspect of the subtle cosmic breath that dwells within caves. Those listening to the natural breath of the earth within caves sometimes hear voices that may be intelligible. Sound becomes our link with the otherworld. Our own breath is at one with the chthonic breath. The earth's breath is intermittent, so it is most accessible to those, such as sybils and hermits, who inhabit caves and are present when it appears. Caves are thus places of oracular pronouncements, where the voice of the earth speaks through inspired people. In the primal darkness of an oracular cave, the conscious mind is suppressed and contact with elements of the unconscious can be achieved. The Cave of the Bard on the Orkney island of Bressay is such a place.

Although most surviving folk tales are about men in caves, they were primarily places of women's mysteries. Names such as White Woman's Hole (in the Mendips, near Leighton, Somerset) are redolent of sybilline occupants. Sometimes it is the horrid Morrigan, sometimes the Fairy Queen and sometimes a wise woman who inhabits the cave. But whatever female being was there, men entered them to gain instruction, like the individual who was taught to play the pipes in the cave at Harlosh Point. Bagpipers must employ the breath; likewise, the seeress uses her breath to pronounce oracles. The inspiration for musicianship as much as for seership lies in the unconscious. Sacred caves were places of mediums such as Mother Shipton, whose cavern at Knaresborough can still be visited. In the side of the Teck, an ancient Celtic holy mountain in southern Germany, is the Sybillenloch. This cavern was the seat of a benevolent being who gave counsel to local people and made fields and flocks fertile by passing around them in her chariot. Finally, legend tells us, the Sybil of the Teck decided to leave in despair at the behaviour of her renegade sons, who robbed and oppressed the people she had formerly helped.

This story may represent the arrival of patriarchal religion, in which the priesthood of wise women had no place. Misogyny was one of the less admirable aspects of the Celtic Church. Women were often excluded from churches and sacred fanes, areas over which formerly they may have presided. Another instance of expulsion took place at the Cave of St Beatus, which is situated in a hillside overlooking Lake Thun near Interlaken. According to legend, this Irish priest drove out a dragon so that he could meditate in the cave, perhaps symbolizing the expulsion of Pagan female qualities.

The dragon's attribute is her fiery breath, the visible aspect of the Nwyvre, which has traditionally feminine qualities. In a sixteenth-century engraving, Beatus lashes out at it with his staff. His cave is a place of intense inspiration, located on a major fault line. A powerful waterfall emerges from it. When he visited the cave, Goethe conceived his ideas of metamorphosis from contemplating the dragon-like ivy vine that grew at its mouth.

A Dominican legend asserts that the Christian tradition acquired an important otherworldly treasure from the feminine underworld. According to the Breton Black Friar Alain de la Roche, who flourished around 1470, the rosary beads were received from the spirit-world in 1214 by Dominico de Guzmán. Having failed to convert the Cathars to Roman Catholicism, Guzmán went into retreat. He resorted to an ancient Celtic holy place, a cave in a wood near Toulouse. After three days' penitential fasting, he experienced the apparition of the Madonna, three queens and fifty maidens. From them he received the rosary, which rapidly became an essential element of Catholic devotions.

St Patrick's Purgatory

Station Island in Lough Derg is the site of one of the most curious pilgrimages in Ireland. It began in the twelfth century when a knight named Owen spent a fortnight in prayer and fasting there. He spent the final night of his vigil in a cave, where he received visions of the afterlife, both heavenly and hellish. Owen recounted his experiences to a Lincolnshire monk, Gilbert of Louth, who spread the story among the Cistercians. They recognized that Owen's visions were similar to those of St Patrick, who, unable to convince his congregation of the existence of heaven or hell, prayed to be shown a place where people could experience them. Patrick then discovered a cave where these visions were accessible. Owen was declared to have rediscovered it, and it was henceforth called St Patrick's Purgatory. It became an important place of pilgrimage, though only pilgrims who were considered worthy, and who had purchased the appropriate permits, could enter the cave. Once there, they were shut in to experience demonic visions of torment. They were warned not to sleep, for, as in all otherworldly myths, once one sleeps in the otherworld, one can never re-enter the world of the living.

The Augustinian Order was put in charge of the cave, but in the late medieval period there were allegations that the cave was no longer effective in giving visions. So in 1497 the Pope ordered the cave-shrine to be closed on the grounds that it was inauthentic. But this was not done, for in 1503 the Bishop of Armagh petitioned the Pope to grant indulgences for those who entered the cave. Nearly five hundred years later the pilgrimage still exists, though the cave is sealed. It lasts three days and begins with a fast. Barefooted pilgrims visit a number of sacred stopping-places, including St Brigid's Cross, St Patrick's Cross and six beehive-cells, named the 'beds' of various Celtic saints. Until quite recently, it also involved plunging into the cold waters of the lough, but this has been discontinued.

There is a remarkable continuity in the use of caves for worship. In some ways, they are the oldest sacred places: according to Porphyry, before there were temples, religious ceremonies were conducted in caves. Remains of early monasticism still exist in certain caves that bear the names of the anchorites who once lived and worshipped there. By Loch Kilkerran is St Kieran's Cave; on Holy Island in the Clyde is the Cave of St Moloe; and St Adrian and his followers lived underground at Caplawchy in Fife. One of the most striking is Physgyll, St Ninian's Cave, near Whithorn, described in an eighth-century poem as an *horrendum atreum*, an awesome cavern. It has crosses carved on walls and several stone grave-markers. The fifth-century Latinus Stone was found there in 1891. The cave of St Rule at St Andrews is mentioned by Sir Walter Scott in *Marmion* as a place resorted to by wayfaring pilgrims:

> To fair St Andrews bound
> Within the Ocean cave to pray,
> Where good St Rule his holy lay
> From midnight to the dawn of day
> Sung to the billows' sound.

At Galmisdale on the island of Eigg is the Cathedral Cave. In the seventh century it was the retreat of St Donnan, but its fame lies in its later use. In the Reformation it served as a church for Roman Catholics whose observances had been proscribed. Another cave used for clandestine worship can be found on Rona in the Inner Hebrides. This is the Warriors' Cave, which contains sitting-stones for fifty people arranged around a stone altar. During the seventeenth and eighteenth centuries, the island was the home of the Broken Men, people who did not belong to clans and were therefore outcasts from Scottish society, living by brigandage. Denied the church, they worshipped in caves. Even in the nineteenth century, caves could still be used religiously. In the 1880s, Archibald MacKinnon, the art teacher at Campbeltown Grammar School, had a vision of the Crucifixion of Christ. Around the Cross were emblems of the ills of the world. He vowed to paint it in a cave on the island of Davaar, at the entrance to Campbeltown Loch. The project took some time, for MacKinnon worked in secret. When, finally, someone discovered him to be the artist, he left Campbeltown, only to return shortly before his death in 1935 to continue and restore the work. Because a sea cave is not the best place for a mural, it deteriorated rapidly. It was restored in the 1950s and again in the 1970s.

Occasionally, although more associated with secret love affairs, official marriages were celebrated in caves. Joining together in the womb of the earth was held to be a sure recipe for a fruitful relationship. It is probable that they were used for baptism, itself a transformation. The Cave of Dwynwen, the patroness of secret lovers, on the Tresillian Dingle contains the Bow of Destiny, about 8 feet (2.4 m) below the roof of the cave. At high water a boat can pass over the bow. The rite is to enter the cave at low tide and throw a pebble over the arch. Formerly, non-Christian marriages were celebrated in the cave.

ROCK BASINS AND FONTS

Caves are places of transformation from which one may emerge a changed person. Folk tradition ascribes healing powers to certain caves, especially those connected in some way with water. Some contain actual springs of water that are considered curative holy wells: for example, St Medan's Cave on the shore at Kirkmaiden near the tip of the Mull of Galloway. More common are the natural or artificial receptacles that catch and hold water dripping from above. Symbolically, these rock basins are reflections of the otherworldly cauldrons of Celtic myth. Like holy wells, they are ascribed various beneficial properties. A cave near Sanna at Ardmaurchan in the Highlands has a rock basin whose water is said to make people happy and strong. Where they occur in a Christian context, it is probable that they were used for baptism. A cave near Campbeltown, reputed to have been the residence of St Kieran, contains a rock basin actually called St Kieran's Font. But, despite its name, water from this is believed to have curative qualities.

Rock basins are kept full of water by constant dripping through the cave roof, and this is the key to some cures. To the remarkable clarity of sound made by water when it drops into a rock basin in a cave was ascribed the power to restore the capability of a human being to make or receive sound. Thus the Dripping Cave at Craigiehowie was reputed to cure deafness. The patient lay on the floor of the cave and allowed water from the roof to drip into one ear, then the other. The 'dropping cave' in Kirkmaiden parish called Peter's Paps was used to treat whooping cough, a breathing ailment. Patients stood in the cave, face upwards, to catch drops from the ceiling in their mouths.

CAVES OF THE DEAD AND SLEEPING HEROES

Celtic folklore of caves often tells that they contain beings from bygone times. For instance, the Irish cave fairies are said to be descended from the second race that settled in Ireland, the Tuatha da Danaan. After their defeat by the Milesians, the Tuatha da Danaan went underground into the caves, especially those by the coast. This reflects the legend of heroes who did not die, but disappeared into the earth to lead a subterranean existence with their ancestors.

Caves contain secrets, and secrets must be guarded. Their guardians may be physical or supernatural, or on the borderline between. In the eighteenth century the cave of Tangrogo at Denbigh was kept by three fairy sisters, whose footprints were often seen nearby. They were the guardians of 'hidden treasures'. In some places, legend particularizes the spirit guardian into an immortalized hero-figure. Of these, King Arthur is the most widespread, having once descended into Annwn to steal the mystic cauldron. According to Welsh tradition, the tomb of Arthur was a mysterious, hidden place, something about which it was considered unwise or irreligious to enquire. Its location, on the otherworldly Isle of Avalon, was indeterminate. This is borne out by a passage in 'The Stanzas of the Graves' in the twelfth-century *Black Book of Carmarthen*, which states:

A grave for March, a grave for Gwythur,
A grave for Gwrgan Red-Sword,
A hidden thing is the grave of Arthur.

This is because Arthur, unlike the other heroes, was believed not to be dead but sleeping in immortality. Similar tales are told in Germany of Frederick Barbarossa, who sleeps in the Kyffhäuserberg, and elsewhere of the equivalent national heroes of other countries. The myth of Arthur is related to a tale about a former god who, at the end of a golden age, was exiled to an island in the Western Ocean. He sleeps there still in a cave, awaiting his recall. Seen in terms of the universal symbolic values in the land, every cave is Arthur's resting-place, where, reunited with his slain comrades, he awaits his second coming. A number of caves in different parts of Britain have legends of him sleeping there with his knights and his treasure. Only two British caves are actually named after the King: Ogof Arthur in Anglesey and Arthur's Cave in Herefordshire.

A legend about Craig y Ddinas near Glynedd tells how a wayfaring wizard once came upon a Welsh drover carrying a hazelwood staff, and asked to be shown the tree from which it came. Reaching the tree, the wizard uprooted it, revealing a cave. They entered, and came to a subterranean chamber containing King Arthur and his knights amidst a pile of treasure. At the chamber's entrance was a bell. The wizard told the drover that he could take as much treasure as he wanted, so long as he did not ring the bell. But of course the drover did accidentally ring it. The knights woke and asked: 'Is it day?' The drover replied with the stock answer in such situations: 'No, sleep on.' The bell ringing a second time, the knights woke again, but were quelled by the same reply. The third time, however, he forgot to answer and was beaten so badly that he was permanently disabled.

Another Arthurian character, Merlin, is connected with caves. At Tintagel in Cornwall, Merlin's Cave penetrates the neck of the peninsula where the castle ruins remain, 250 feet (76 m) above the sea. The cave runs right through from one side to the other. At low tide one may enter it and walk through to the beach on the other side, but at high tide the sea enters and it becomes impenetrable. Merlin's Cave is an example of a paradoxical place, where it is dark during daytime and where the sea is beneath the earth. Another cave connected with Merlin is in the woodland near Old Dynevor Castle, up the Tywi from Merlin's town, Carmarthen. There, according to Edmund Spenser, Merlin communed with the spirits. Like Arthur, Merlin is said to lie in sleep in a cave on Bardsey Island.

ARTIFICAL UNDERGROUND STRUCTURES

The curious artificial underground structures known as souterrains occur in all Celtic countries. Although they have different names in different places, their structures are similar. They are not tunnels carved into the rock, but trenches and chambers dug in the earth and roofed with flag-stones. Usually, there is a long, sometimes winding passage, with abrupt changes of level or other features that may disorientate the visitor. The passage leads to a larger chamber or chambers roofed with stone. There may be side passages, known as 'creeps', through which one may only pass on hands and knees. But beyond this generalization, no two souterrains are alike. Their plans vary considerably, and from the surface they are impossible to predict. A typical souterrain exists at Grainbank, near Kirkwall. It has a pillared, flag-roofed chamber dug out of the earth. It is lined with drystone walling, and roofed with flat lintels supported with orthostatic pillars. Archaeologists have found that some Irish souterrains were roofed with wood, and of course there is the possibility that some may have been composed entirely of wood. But such structures would not have lasted long, except in exceptional circumstances.

In western Britain there are a number of massive drystone field-bound-aries known as great walls that are as thick as 12 feet (3.7 m). The purpose of these archaic structures remains a mystery, although there is no short-age of theory to account for them. One thing is certain: their size makes them inefficient field-boundaries. Sometimes they contain hidden struc-tures; the Cornish fogou or souterrain of Pendeen Vau is located partly in such a great wall. In Ireland, souterrains are found in the earthen ramparts of 'raths' (earthwork ring-forts). Some were made when the rampart was built, but others were constructed later. No souterrain in Ireland has been shown to be older than the sixth century.

Documentary evidence for souterrains is sparse. It is known that in 866 the Dublin Scandinavians plundered the 'caves' of north Kerry. It is proba-ble that this refers to souterrains, but also other accounts refer to much more ancient passage graves. Several *Lives* of saints and sagas, dating from the tenth century and later, refer to a type of subterranean structure called *uaim*, which is translated as 'cave'. The descriptions make it clear that most of them were souterrains. The *Historia Norvegicae*, dating from around 1200, describes the Picts of Orkney as working in the mornings and evenings, but losing strength at midday and hiding through fear in underground houses. These accounts tell of multiple uses for artificial caves: worship, refuge and storage of treasure and supplies.

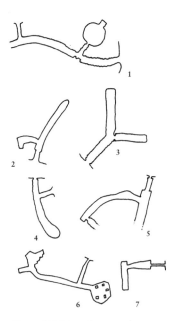

Plans of Celtic underground
structures. The first four are Cornish
fogous. *1. Carn Euny; 2. Boleigh;
3. Pendeen Vau; 4. Halligey,
Trelowarren; 5. Scottish earth
house at Chrichton; 6. Saverock,
Kirkwall, Orkney; 7. Souterrain
at Ballyanly, County Cork.*

At least one remaining Cornish souterrain has a literary pedigree. Various thirteenth-century versions of the Tristan and
Isolde story – Gottfried von Strassburg's
Tristan, the Norse *Tristramssaga* and the
English *Sir Tristram* – refer to a Cornish
cave in which the lovers took refuge.
Gottfried described it as a secret place in a
hillside beside a certain spring, vaulted
and dug deep in the earth and protected by
a holy tree. In a Tristan romance by the
Anglo-Norman poet Thomas, the author
identifies the place as a *locus amoenus* or
earthly paradise, built by giants. The location, form and dimensions of this feature
are identical with the fogou at Carn Euny
in Sancreed parish. Close to it was a holy
well, known as the Giant's Well until the
Ordnance Survey mapmakers renamed it
after St Euny. At some time in the medieval
period the fogou was filled in, seemingly to
prevent its use for purposes of which the
authorities disapproved. Medieval legend
tells of Minne, the goddess of love, who possessed grottoes hewn by giants
in the wild mountains. Gottfried von Strassburg described such a lovers'
cavern: entered by a bronze door, it had a green marble pavement and
contained a bed of crystal, engraved with characters that proclaimed its
dedication to the goddess of love.

In the classical world as well as northern Europe, caves were often
places of sacred sexuality, such as the *dictyria* of ancient Greece, the cave-
temples of Rhea Dictynna. Children conceived in such places are inspired
with the spirits of the cave. In the north, the myth of Odin drinking
Kvasir's mead of wisdom whilst making love to a giantess in a cave appears
to allude to sexual ceremonies of enlightenment. The parallel here
between the womb and the cave is explicit, for in the Odin legend Bragi,
god of eloquence, is born there as a result. When a man enters a cave to
engage in sexual activity, he enters first the womb of Mother Earth and
then that of woman. The female counterpart of this symbolic doubling is
when a woman gives birth in a cave. It is a double birth, from woman and

earth. The baby first comes forth from the human womb into the earth-womb, then has a second birth into the outer world from the cave mouth. Mythology tells of certain male gods coming into the world through cave-births. They include Mithras, Bragi and Jesus, born of divine females who are themselves daughters of the Earth Mother. Anyone born in a cave is thereby literally a son or daughter of the earth.

When, in periodic outbursts of zeal, the authorities attempted to suppress traditional rites, they did not succeed in extirpating them, but rather drove them underground. In parts of France, souterrains were used for Pagan ceremonies. At the time of the Tristan romances, they were so widespread that in 1266 a Church Council at Toulouse ordered all souterrains in France to be filled in at once. As usual, this command was ineffective, and people continued to make new souterrains until the twentieth century. When old ones are explored, they are frequently found to contain votive offerings which are known in many Celtic sacred contexts, including skulls and bones of animals, broken ceramics, eggs, stone balls, bone rings, whetstones and thimbles. All were placed with great care.

A most notable souterrain at Dénezé-sous-Doué, near Saumur, whose entrance collapsed in the eighteenth century, was rediscovered in 1975. It contains carvings dating from the sixteenth and seventeenth centuries. There are hundreds of human figures, some wearing animal masks and others naked, holding their sexual organs. Women breast-feed their infants whilst musicians play. The whole cave appears as a temple of Minne, recalling the festivals in which masked and costumed people revelled, as witnessed by Rabelais at Doué-la-Fontaine nearby.

In the nineteenth century a souterrain at Châtres-sur-Cher belonged to a villager who was reputed to practise sorcery. When it was opened in the 1970s, its explorers discovered votive offerings of human figures in clay, pins and broken pottery. The innermost part of this souterrain was a 'secret chapel', dated 1870, which contained ten human images carved in limestone and the broken collar of an oil lamp. According to popular belief, comparable German underground structures, called *Erdställe*, are abodes of spirits. Whatever the original purpose of individual structures, their archetypal nature as caves makes them places where those who enter may contact the unconscious. Because of this, at the present day souterrains are used as sacred places by mystics and devotees of the elder faith.

Holy Islands

ACCORDING TO traditional thinking, islands are inherently sacred, being places cut off by water from unwanted physical and psychic influences. From small offshore islets or eyots in rivers to large islands such as Erin and Britain, many Celtic islands have been considered holy. In Pagan northern Europe there were a number of smaller islands dedicated to sacred usage. Before their sanctuaries were destroyed by the Romans, the druids venerated Anglesey. Islands in general were deemed to be under the protection of specific deities, whose shrines existed on and maintained the sacred integrity of the isle. Each island was thus the *locus terribilis* of a specific deity. Many are still recognized today. The Isle of Man, for instance, commemorates the Celtic sea-god Manannan MacLir. Rügen in the Baltic and Heligoland and Walcheren in the North Sea are comparable. The deities Rugevit, Forseti and Nehalennia ruled these isles, attended by special priesthoods that conducted their worship. Certain smaller islands were also deemed sacred to specific deities, and it was on them that priesthoods continued well into the nineteenth century. Like the land, islands are ensouled with legendary, symbolic and historical names. So long as they live in local memory, they retain the character of a ceremonial sacred landscape. Groups of islands may display a rich complexity of legendary and sacred themes.

Islands enable people to adopt modes of living that are separate from the everyday world of the mainland. Spiritually, they are the undying lands, the otherworldly abodes of the dead. For the living, they have supported hermitages, monasteries and communes. Their isolation makes them separate realms politically as well as spiritually, so in Celtic tradition they often stood alone as independent territories. In Scotland, the Isle of Handa was effectively self-governing until the late nineteenth century. The 1845 *Statistical Account* records that the island was occupied by twelve families who were ruled by their own queen and parliament. The queen was the oldest widow on the island, a status recognized on the mainland nearby. Presided over by the queen, Handa's menfolk met every morning to

Left: The geomantic division of Ireland into four main provinces, with a smaller fifth, Meath, containing the omphalos of Uisnech at the centre.
Right: The four provinces of the Christian Church, with the bishops' seats, reflecting the more ancient fourfold division of the island of Ireland. The province of the Primate of All Ireland, Ardnamachana, centred on Armagh, includes both the Pagan centres of Tara and Uisnech.

decide on the activities for the coming day. Similar conditions prevailed on St Kilda. Bardsey Island, off the Lleyn Peninsula, had a 'king', appointed by the owner, Baron Newborough. The last one, Love Pritchard, ruled in the early nineteenth century. In Ireland, the peninsula of Inishowen, between Loughs Swilly and Foyle, was regarded as an island – hence its name, Inis Eoghain – and was also a separate kingdom in its own right.

FORBIDDEN ISLANDS

Certain classical writers described a holy Isle of Women somewhere in the Celtic realms. Although some have considered these accounts to be entirely mythical, yet it is not improbable that such places once existed. In later times, single-sex islands of nuns or monks were not unknown. One still exists off south Wales. Pliny recalls a report by Poseidonius of an island located in the ocean near Gaul, on which the women of the Samnitae lived without men. They were members of a sisterhood devoted to the ecstatic worship of Dionysus, to whom they dedicated mystical initiations as well as other rites. The island was forbidden to men: 'No man sets foot on the island, although the women themselves, sailing from it, have intercourse with men and then return again,' Pomponius Mela wrote of the island of Sena, inhabited by the priestesses of an oracular shrine who worked weather-magic and cured the sick. It is possible that these reports refer to the Île de Sein, in the Atlantic off Cap-Sizun, which was once reputed to support a retinue of nine priestesses. In Welsh tradition, this was Caer Wydyr, the water-girdled fortress of crystal where nine maidens dwelt in an otherworldly place of seership. Pliny also mentions Artemidorus's report that on an island near Britain women performed sacrifices like those in Samothrace, devoted to the women's mysteries of Demeter and Kore. Whatever the truth of these accounts, the people of Sein remained wholly Pagan until the seventeenth century.

When patriarchal monotheism was introduced, men-only islands came into being. On his arrival at Iona, St Columba banished cows and women from the island, which he justified by the misogynistic adage, 'Where there is a cow, there is a woman, and where there is a woman, there is mischief.' The women were deported to the island called afterwards Eilean nam Ban, 'The Island of Women'. But the prohibition was relaxed after the death of Columba, and women returned. Today, no women live on the monastic island of Caldey, off Tenby in Carmarthen Bay, but they can visit. Known in Welsh as Ynys Pyr, Caldey has a Christian history dating back to a settlement founded in the sixth century by St Pyr. Originally Celtic, Caldey was owned subsequently by Catholic Benedictines, and in this century by Anglican Benedictines. In 1929 Trappists from Chimay in Belgium took over the island, whose 350 acres of farmland support lavender and gorse from which the monks distil perfume. But the most terrible of all forbidden islands is in Scotland, near the mouth of Little Loch Broom. Gruinard Island is a real *locus terribilis* that one may not enter. This is for a profane and not a religious reason. During the Second World War biological warfare experiments by the British Army contaminated the island with the anthrax bacillus: half a century later, it is still considered too hazardous for humans to go there.

PRIESTS' ISLANDS

There are numerous 'priests' islands' around the British Isles. Some are actually called that. Priestholm lies off the north-east coast of Anglesey, whilst the most westerly of the Summer Isles, north of Loch Broom, is Priest Island. Also, islands called 'Papa' recall their use by Celtic priests. Among the Shetlands are islands named Papa Little and Papa Stour, the small and large priests' islands. In the Orkneys are Papa Stronsay and Papa

Westray, where the last great auk was shot in 1813. In the Hebrides, close to Barra, is Pabbay. There are also many islands that bear the names of the saints who lived there for some part of their lives, or whose shrines were venerated there. Barry Island near Cardiff is named after St Barruc, who was buried there. St Patrick's Island is close to Peel on the Isle of Man, whilst St Tudwal's two islands lie 2 miles (3.2 km) south of Abersoch in Gwynedd. In central Europe, too, the Celtic monks who revisited their ancestral homeland made island settlements. The island of Reichenau at the western end of Lake Constance has a favoured climate and is noted for its apple orchards and luxuriant vegetable gardens. The Celtic Christian missionaries saw in it an earthly reflection of the Isle of Avalon.

Celtic monasticism had strong links with southern Europe and the Near East, and it shared the quest for solitude with its Mediterranean counterparts. The desert asceticism of Syria and Egypt was not appropriate for northern Europe, but the island asceticism of the monks of the Tyrrhenian Sea was eminently suitable for the island-studded seas around the British Isles. Celtic priests sought isolation from the world, secure in the knowledge that evil spirits or hostile magic cannot cross water. In their search for spiritual solitude, they visited uninhabited, often almost uninhabitable islands. But dissatisfaction with some or other aspect of their new home condemned some to a life of 'island-hopping', ceaselessly moving from isle to isle.

St Senan was the archetypal restless priest. First he lived on Inis Carra, off Cork, then moved to the island of Luirghe in the Shannon. When this proved unsuitable, he sailed to Inishmore in the mouth of the Fergus, then to one of the Ennis Kerry islands. Next he lived on Inis Cunla and finally chose Inis Cathy (Scattery Island) in the mouth of the Shannon. This unending quest for solitude took the priests yet further away from inhabited land and deeper into unexplored territory. Shortly after the year 700, Irish priests reached the Faeroe Islands. They lived there until around 800, when the islands were annexed by the Norse. In the 790s, Irish monks discovered Iceland, but it, too, was colonized by Norse settlers, most of whom were Pagan, but a few of whom professed Christianity or atheism.

Some islands contain within their small compass almost every element of the sacred landscape. Iona is the classic case, with its cathedral, oratories, high crosses, holy hill, wells, bullauns, sacred road and cemetery. Similarly, the island of Inishcealtra, in Lough Derg, County Clare, the holy island of the seventh-century monk St Caimin, contains five ancient churches, the saint's graveyard, a hermit's cell and a holy well. A pattern held here in former times was famed for its bacchanalian revelry, and was suppressed finally because of the sexual licence it encouraged. Devenish Island, in Lower Lough Erne, 2 miles (3.2 km) south of Enniskillen, contains a comparable array of sacred places, founded in the sixth century by St Molaise, one of the 'Twelve Apostles of Ireland'. Island monasteries founded at that period by Celtic Christian monks have particularly intense atmospheres, engendered by the numerous sacred loci contained within a small area.

At special times of the year it was customary for people to travel to these places to participate in sacred ceremonies, and pilgrimages continue to some sacred islands. Our Lady's Island, south of Rosslare in County Wexford, has a pattern celebrated on the festival of the Assumption of the Blessed Virgin Mary. Formerly accomplished by boat, pilgrims traverse a causeway to visit the shrine of Our Lady and the ruins of the Augustinian abbey of St Mary. For shipborne travellers or pilgrims, islands can serve as sacred stopping-places. There is a chain of holy islands in Lough Erne on which stood monastic settlements that served as stopping-places on the pilgrimage to St Patrick's Purgatory in Lough Derg.

OTHERWORLDLY ISLANDS

Irish lore recalls a number of legendary or phantom islands located to the west in the Atlantic. The most famed of these is the island of Breasail or Hy-Brasil, the homeland of the Fomorians and Firbolgs. It is visited in the mythical or garbled historical stories of epic voyages undertaken by St Brendan, Maelduin and others. Occasionally, there are evanescent visions of the phantom Western Land. From north Wales it can be seen over the Irish Sea in certain weather conditions, especially at sunset when it appears in the form of a dark silhouette on a second horizon above the sea. Recorded sightings from the west coast of Ireland are too numerous to recount. 'At its own sweet will it comes,' wrote D.R. McAnally in his *Irish Wonders*, 'and, having shown itself long enough to convince everybody who is not an "innocent entirely" of its reality, it goes without leave-taking or ceremony, and always before boats can approach near enough to make a careful inspection. This is the invariable history of its appearance.' The changing locations in which it appears, and its varied appearance, sometimes with woodland, sometimes bearing a shining city, attest to the skill of the enchanter who controls it.

A similar phantom land was known to the Welsh. In his *Itinerarium Cambriae,* Giraldus Cambrensis tells of the marvels of Llangorse Lake, especially the abundance of fish and the mysterious red and green oracular currents that flowed there. Iridescent patterns created by myriad water-beetles can still be seen in summertime. On occasion, he tells us, local people saw the lake covered with buildings, or adorned with gardens and orchards. Although these accounts have a mythical base, Giraldus was not writing about the otherworld, for the lake contains a remarkable crannog, a reed- and tree-covered artificial island which once bore a settlement. Constructed of oaken planks, the Llangorse Crannog has been dated by dendrochronology to the late ninth or early tenth century. Like the royal crannog at Lagore in Ireland, the Llangorse Crannog was a rich settlement, linked to the shore by a causeway. It is thought on occasion to have housed the court of the King of Brycheiniog. Sadly, this enchanted lake is now frequently covered with motorboats and waterskiers, when it is difficult to appreciate its magical qualities through a barrage of noise and exhaust fumes.

Islands in holy lakes have a special quality, for it is through lakes that the otherwordly land of Tir nan Og may be visited. This is the 'Country of Youth', where people and non-human beings live immune to the passage of time. It is said to exist in the depths of lakes, and the legend is localized in several places such as Lough Corrib, Lough Gur and Lough Neagh. On occasion, these lands have been visited by human beings. Both the bard Oisin and the warrior O'Donoghue entered the otherworldly realm through the Lake of Killarney. To reach Tir nan Og, one must pass through the reflective crystal waters of the lake, undertaking a journey from the outer world into the inner, just as the sun enters the waters of the underworld at sunset. It is a perilous shamanic descent into the unconscious depths where timeless archetypes reside. The lake is a dangerous crystal castle where all is reflected inwards. There, the visitor may be trapped in an inner world that bears no relation to the outer one. Once entered, it is a region from which it is difficult to escape. But those who do manage to return to the everyday world are transformed by the experience. Certain material islands were reputed to possess the qualities of this timeless land. Giraldus Cambrensis wrote of the *Insula Viventum*, an island whose inhabitants knew no death. This was reputed to be Inish na mBeo, the 'Isle of the Living', in Lough Cre, east of Roscrea, County Tipperary. Unfortunately for the inhabitants, the lough dried up and so the island is no more.

ISLANDS OF THE DEAD

Celtic legend refers repeatedly to the places to which human souls go after bodily death. Belief in heaven and hell – Gwynvyd and Annwn – seems secondary to the belief in going west to the Isles of the Blest. In some ways it is an alternative to a dualistic cosmology, paralleling Thomas of Ercildoune's 'third road' that is neither the road to hell nor to heaven but to 'Fair Elfland'. This timeless island paradise lies somewhere to the west in the ocean. At death, one 'goes west'. Celtic burial islands predominantly lie to the west of the land of the living. Only by means of the ship of the dead can the deceased person be brought there. Important people were buried by the shore in the ship that carried them there across the sea, enabling them to travel onwards in the world of the dead. West is the direction in which the sun sets beneath the earth, symbolizing the end of the life-cycle, and the place to which souls must go before being reborn into another life. When King Arthur was taken away after his final battle at Camlann, he was brought westwards to the Isle of Avalon, an otherworldly realm of healing and rebirth. Avalon is associated in the popular mind with Glastonbury, whose Celtic name, *Ynyswitrin*, means 'The Isle of Glass', alluding to the crystalline otherworld. In Arthurian times, it was a real island surrounded by watery fenland. Arthur's Avalon was the island of apples, where the fruit of regeneration and rebirth grew. It is probable that the Arthurian legend is a poetic account of the transference of Arthur's body by ship to a cemetery-island. Perhaps it was the part of the former island of En Noer now detached as the small island called Great Arthur in the Scillies, where the hill-tops are reputed to contain entombed sleeping giants.

When possible, it was customary for Celtic Christians to bury their dead on islands, thereby perpetuating the Pagan tradition of sending the departed to the Isles of the Blest. In the larger lakes, and all round the coasts of Great Britain, Ireland and Brittany, there are small islands of the dead. The smallest burial islands are distinctly different in character from those formerly inhabited by monks, for they lack the complex of shrines, wells, stones and crosses that characterize monastic islands. Typical of them is Eilean Fhionnan in Lough Shiel. As the burial-isle of St Finnan, it is one of the few places where a Celtic saint's relic, his bronze bell, is still preserved. Eilean Fhionnan was the cemetery-island for the surrounding areas of Moidart, Sunart and Ardnamurchan. Similarly, Inis Chonain (St Conan's Isle) in Lough Awe served to bury local people, and in Lough Awe lies Inishail, 'The Island of Rest', with the chapel of St Findoc on a small hill at its centre. Local lore recalls that the reason for burying people here was because wolves were plentiful in the district. To exterminate them, the locals deliberately burned down the forests. But before they were extirpated, scavenging wolves would dig up and eat any human bodies buried on the mainland, so, in addition to the symbolic value, burial on this island also had a practical use.

Just as kings occasionally inhabited crannogs, certain especially holy islands were utilized as royal burial-places. The Isle of Lismore, off the Benderloch coast, is the burial-place of the Pictish kings. It contains the remains of Kilmoluaig Cathedral, founded in the sixth century by St Moluaig. In Gaelic, Lismore means 'great garden', a poetic kenning for the otherworldly garden-island of Avalon. Perhaps pre-eminent among Celtic burial islands is Iona, where forty-eight kings of Scotland, from Fergus II to Macbeth, are buried in Reilig Odhran, Iona's cemetery. There are also a few kings from Norway and France, totalling sixty royal burials on the island. In 1994, the tradition of burying Celtic leaders on Iona was continued when John Smith, leader of the British Labour Party, was buried there.

Two miles (3.2 km) off the tip of the Lleyn Peninsula is Bardsey Island, otherwise called Bangor Gadfan or Ynys Enlli, 'The Island of the Currents'. According to local legend it was the home of the wizard Merlin, who is reputed to sleep there in a cave, awaiting revitalization. The island was colonized in 516 by St Cadfan as part of the mass emigration of British who had settled in Armorica. These were known as the Gwelygordd (the Saintly Clan of Emyr Llydaw) and their leader was Cadfan. Like many other Celtic holy islands, Bardsey was a favoured place to be buried. St Lleuddad ab Dingad, Cadfan's successor, was visited by an angel who granted him requests. One of them was that the soul of anyone buried in Bardsey should not go to hell, a Christian reworking of the Pagan theme of the Isles of the Blest. Because of the island's favoured status, there are said to be twenty thousand saints buried there in the four-acre graveyard of the Augustinian abbey. Two medieval poems in the *cywydd* metre, by Hywel ab Dafydd ab Ieuan ab Rhys and Hywel ab Rheinallt, celebrate them. In his 'Death-bed of the Bard', the twelfth-century poet Meilir prayed that he might be buried on Bardsey, whose kennings are *Insula Sanctorum*, the 'Holy Island (of the Saints)', or 'The Iona of Wales'. Befitting a truly sacred island, many famous saints visited it or lived there for a while. St Dyfrig died there in 612, and the monks of Bangor Is-Coed fled there after the destruction of their monastery by the Saxons in 615. Among the saints whose dust mingles with Bardsey's soil are St Cadfan himself and St Lleuddad ab Dingad, both of whom are considered patrons of Bardsey; also buried there are St Greit and St Elgar. In 1890, Lord Newborough erected a cross at the centre of the cemetery as a sign of respect for the twenty thousand.

In medieval times, travellers made their way to Bardsey by a recognized pilgrimage route that went by way of prescribed stopping-places that supplied the physical and spiritual needs of the pilgrims. The island was thus only the final objective of a route that included travel by land and sea. Pilgrims started their journey at the dual-faith temenos of St Beuno at Clynnog Fawr, whose church and shrine are built upon and contain megaliths. From Clynnog Fawr, the route visits the church at Pistyll, where an old stone cross marks the pilgrims' track. At Pistyll was a farm that gave free water, bread and cheese on demand to any pilgrim. After Pistyll, the route visits the churches at Nefyn, Edern, Tudweilog, Penllech, Llangwnnadl and Aberdaeron, where free lodging was provided at Cwrt Farm. Beyond Aberdaeron, at Porth Meudwy pilgrims took the ferry to Bardsey. The final sea-crossing rendered it a dangerous journey, so three pilgrimages to Bardsey were considered equal in spiritual merit to a pilgrimage to Rome. This made Bardsey second only to St David's in Wales as a place of sanctity.

PLACES OF DECISION

Islands were considered neutral territory under the rulership of the island goddess or god rather than human jurisdiction. Human partisanship was suspended there in the presence of higher powers. The participants were isolated from human interference, and the will of the gods was paramount. Often linked to the shore by causeways, sometimes invisible below the water surface, these islands were used as places where contests or legal disputes were settled. Loch Finlaggan on the Isle of Islay contains two islands. The larger, Eilean Mor, was a burial island, and the smaller, as its name Eilean na Comhairle suggests, was a meeting-place – 'Council Island'. The latter island was linked to the shore and the larger one could be reached by causeways. An island-within-an-island fits particularly well the Celtic concept of repetition, parallel with the cauldron-within-a-cauldron of the Hochdorf burial, or the womb-within-a-womb of cave-births. The result of anything done in such a place is effective over the whole area that symbolically corresponds with it. A similar meeting-island, Law Ting

Holm, existed formerly in the loch of Tingwall on Shetland. It is no longer an island now, as the loch's level has been lowered.

The Norse word for formalized single combat, *Holmganga*, means literally 'going on an island', referring especially to certain small islands reserved for judicial duels. There, trial by combat was conducted on a small island in the view of appointed judges. In addition to the sacred sanction, there is no escape from a small island of combat. There can be no compromise: the conflict must be resolved, there and then, and the decision is final. Sometimes the stakes were high; the future of a whole kingdom might have depended on the outcome. There is a tradition that in 1016, on the island of Alney, near Gloucester, Canute and Edmund Ironside fought a duel to decide who would be king of England. One of the last such trials by combat in Britain took place in 1157 on an island in the River Thames near Reading. Baron Henry of Essex, the hereditary standard-bearer of England, was accused by Robert de Montfort of cowardice in battle. In the duel, Henry was defeated and left for dead on the island. But the monks from Reading Abbey nearby found him and nursed him back to health. However, he was considered legally dead, having 'died' on the isle of combat, and had thereby passed from this world. So he became a monk at the abbey, where he spent the rest of his days.

Earthworks, Enclosures and Cities

A N ARTIFICIAL enclosure separates things inside it from those that are
not. In its most basic form, the boundary constitutes a physical
defence against attack. Because a sacred place is recognized as special, separate from its profane surroundings, it must be set within a divine
framework. The boundary ensures that no one can enter the sacred space
without being aware that they have left the world of the ordinary and have
entered the realm of the numinous. This, of course, is a step away from the
viewpoint that the whole earth is sacred. The sacred enclosure is a formal
setting, protected both on the physical plane and also magically by exclud-
ing harmful psychic influences that are abroad in the profane outer world.

Celtic sacred enclosures are relatively simple in form. Located on flat-
tish ground, a ditch with its accompanying bank was considered appropriate to mark the boundary. Sometimes it was reinforced by a thorn hedge, a
fence fashioned from appropriate wood, or larger marker posts, visible
from afar. Inside this enclosure was the sanctuary, 'a place set apart'. Neo-
Platonic philosophers used the word 'sanctuary' to describe the innermost
place of the soul, illuminated by the spirit, marking its innate inner wisdom. The sanctuary contains the *anima loci*, expressing the inaccessible
elements of existence, those things that are wholly imperceptible to
humans except through the medium of symbols. The sanctuary serves as a
reminder that the gods, we human beings and the whole of nature are born
of the same origin.

TEMENOI

To the continental Celts, the temenos was the prime place of worship. It
was an enclosure, delineated by ditches, where ceremonial gatherings
could take place. In shape, the temenos was usually square or rectangular;
if irregular, it would normally have straight sides, though some circular
enclosures are also recognized. In central Europe, many examples still
exist of the square form known by the German name of *Viereckschanze*

(literally, 'four-cornered fort'). Such sacred precincts contained a number of distinct sacred things, each with a different spiritual function. A temenos might include aniconic or iconic images, sacred stones, ceremonial fireplaces, wells and ritual shafts. Sometimes the enclosure also contained a sacred tree or post, perhaps carved or adorned like modern maypoles. At Goloring, near Koblenz, a circular ditched enclosure of the sixth century BCE had a post hole at the centre. Both folk tradition and archaeology record the perambulation of temenoi in circle dancing. Inside a wide ditch at the late La Tène site at Normée, Marne, is a square floor, compressed hard by the feet of people who had walked or danced in large numbers around a central point.

Although temenoi were sometimes located close to settlements, they were not inhabited, nor were they places of burial. Any temple within the temenos appears to have been a secondary consideration and early Celtic temenoi had none. Sacred buildings were introduced to them as a result of the influence of Roman religion. Continuity was maintained when temple-sites were appropriated by the Christian religion for churches. Thus, the descendant of the ancient Celtic temenos is the churchyard, 'God's Acre', where a wall, hedge or earth bank delineates the division between the consecrated ground of the garth and the external profane world. In many places, these church garths are the sacred fanes of earlier holy structures. The 'henge' at Knowlton in Dorset is a celebrated instance, as are the circular churchyards known as *llan* in Wales and found in other Celtic lands.

TRADITIONAL MEASURE

The formal, legalistic nature of Celtic society stipulated precise symbolic distinctions within society which functioned on the practical level. Exact measure is required by any society that needs to apportion land, determine ownership and calculate amounts of seed required for areas to be sown. From correct measure comes justice. Although little research has been done on ancient Celtic metrology and there is scant literary documentation, it is known that the measure now called the natural foot was used in historical times in Wales and Scotland. In former times, this measure, which is marked on ancient Egyptian cubit rods, was used in places as widespread as Persia, Greece, North Africa, Italy, Sardinia and the south of France. The pan of Marseilles, used until the metric system superseded it, was the same as the Welsh (or natural) foot defined in the tenth-century *Venedotian Code* of land-measure.

Of course, natural measure is based on the natural world. The grain of barley is the basic unit, and twenty-seven barleycorns make a natural or Welsh foot. This is subdivided by threes. Three barleycorns make a thumb, three thumbs make a palm, and three palms a foot. Naturally, the measure of capacity, too, was based upon the barleycorn. In modern units, the Welsh foot measures 25.1 cm. Until the year 1305, when King Edward I of England reorganized weights and measures, the Welsh foot was used by the Celts to measure the land. English people used the Saxon foot. Builders and masons, whose trades were derived ultimately from classical sources, used either the Greek or Roman foot. The Welsh foot was the shortest: the Roman foot measured 29.6 cm, the Greek common foot 31.7 cm, and the Saxon foot 33.5 cm. A coherent relationship existed between Celtic and Saxon measure: the Welsh foot was related to the Saxon by a ratio of 3:4. Traditional land-measurement was carried out by means of measuring-ropes. The device known as the Druids' Cord has come down to us from former times. It is a rope composed of thirteen equal sections marked with twelve knots. Among other things, it enables the user to lay out a right angle and the seventh part of a circle by basic geometry.

THE HOLY CITY

Without a knowledge of number, geometry and measure, civilization cannot exist. The Celtic system was that of the ancient Mediterranean philosophers who understood the symbolic laws of harmony and proportion. The principle of the holy city as a mirror of the cosmos is rooted in the formalized geomancy known as the Etruscan Discipline. It was a symbolic cosmic model by means of which European nations designed their places of worship and administration, denoting the absolute oneness of land and people in an unbroken continuum of time and space.

A number of modern European cities owe their foundation to the Celts. Among the more important ancient ones are the present-day capitals of London, Paris, Vienna and Bratislava. In addition, Aachen, Lyons, Belfast, Bregenz, Bologna and Milan are flourishing modern cities on Celtic foundations. The latter city was formerly called Mediolanum, indicating its location as an omphalos, a centre of sacred order, for the ideal city should reflect the cosmos, standing at the centre of the land that it rules. It should possess four roads running towards the cardinal directions, quartering the enclosure, making the form of the Celtic cross upon the land. It is an image of completion, of wholeness. When it is modelled upon this ideal as

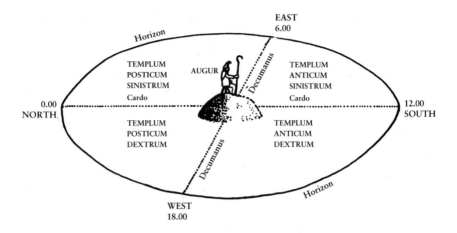

In laying out their monastic settlements, Celtic priests followed to a greater or lesser extent the core European geomantic tradition of the Etruscan Discipline, which involved a conceptual quartering of the world around the central omphalos, and other geomantic prescriptions. The Celtic Church tract 'Precincts' stated: 'One thousand paces in extent is the precinct of a saint, or a bishop, or a hermit, or a pilgrim, if it be in the plain, and two thousand paces from the precinct of every noble cathedral.'

closely as possible, a real city should reflect more or less in its physical attributes the structure of the divine. In actuality, some approach the ideal more closely than others, but in every period there have been notable instances. However, it was not until the Renaissance that the European ideal was realized fully in physical form at Palmanova, Mariembourg and Henrichemont, and later by equally skilled Baroque planners at Neustrelitz and Karlsruhe.

Wherever it exists, the holy city symbolizes cosmic order and wholeness. But, unlike the Middle Eastern concept of the city surrounded by desert, and thereby threatened with desolation, the Celtic city had to keep out the prolific wild nature that threatened to engulf it. Beyond the Celtic city was not the desert wasteland, but rather the wild wood. Outside the boundaries of the central order lay not the lifeless void, but living chaos in the shape of dark forests, uncultivated land, trackless wastes, wild animals, lawless people, evil spirits and monsters. Throughout ancient Europe, the form of the nation, its capital city, the temples of the gods and the palace of the king were representations of cosmic order. Symbolically, this was expressed as the grid, a powerful image of the structure of the world, and of divine and human dominion over it. Law, justice, rulership and order are represented by the rectilinear grid, which can be seen adorning regal and divine figures in Celtic artwork of both Pagan and Christian inspiration. The grid in the form of four squares within a square is carved on the back of a sculpture of Cernunnos from Roqueperteuse, whilst an evangelist in the *Book of Durrow* wears a gridded mantle. The image of the holy city itself is a grid laid upon the earth, with the omphalos and the cosmic axis at its centre. Law and order were symbolized by a rectilinear grid, stylized as a gameboard. In the Celtic lands, the game called *Tawlbwrdd* in Wales and *Brannumh* or *Fidcheall* in Ireland was symbolic of that order. The latter name means literally 'wood-wisdom', a poetic metaphor meaning the 'Game of the Wise'. Fittingly, one of the emblems of the office of judge in ancient Wales was a Tawlbwrdd board.

As sacral-administrative centre of Ireland, Tara was laid out according to symbolic geomancy. Although geographically it is in the east, conceptually it was the centre. It possessed a metaphysical structure that reflected the ideal order of the land in terms of number, measure and geometry. From Tara, five great roads radiated across the land, linking the centre with the periphery. One of the bardic poems of Tadhg Dall O hUiginn describes Tara as the central point on the Brannumh board of Erin: 'The centre of the Plain of Fál is Tara's castle, a delightful hill, out in the very middle of the plain, like a mark on a multi-coloured Brannumh board. Go forward there, it will be a profitable step. Leap on to that square, proper for the Branán [king], the board is fittingly yours. O white-toothed one, go to the noble squares appropriate for the Branán, let them be occupied by you. You are a golden Branán with his army with your four provincials, though, O king of Bregia, on that square and a man on each square around thee.'

The 'noble squares' of the Irish Branán are Tara, Cashel, Croghan, Naas and Oileach. When, at Samhain, the high king held the great feast or Assembly of Tara, his vassals occupied their own symbolic places in the temporary city that was convened there. As at other traditional fairs, the quarters were laid out precisely according to the principle of the holy city. Tara was at these times a symbol of wholeness, encompassing the four provinces, the four classes of society, the four directions, the four seasons and the four elements. The king was at the centre. The Munstermen were to the south, those of Connacht to the west, in the north were the Ulstermen, and to the east the Leinster entourage. In the middle of the hall, in appropriate directions with regard to the high king, sat the four provincial rulers. Traditionally, European kings had four officials – treasurer, cup-bearer, chamberlain and marshal: the high king was guarded by four men who surrounded him in the form of a cross. Symbolically, the high king sat at the centre of his country, surrounded in all four quarters by his army, which in turn faced enemies coming correspondingly from all four quarters. The ritual order of the state was especially necessary at Samhain, the chaotic time when the land was prone to attack by other-worldly, demonic forces.

The Assembly of Tara was thus a reflection of Erin, and whatever was done there affected the whole island of Ireland. Because the king at the centre was an embodiment of the land, he was compelled to observe a complex system of *geassa* (prohibitions) lest some error he might make be reflected throughout the land. For instance, whilst at Tara the high king always had to be out of bed before sunrise to ascend the walls to view the land. Because his conduct reflected correct principles, all things done at Tara according to proper form were in conformity with the divine order. Thus the land was governed in accordance with correct principles.

The Settling of the Manor of Tara tells that the Green of Tara had 'seven views on every side'. In its fully developed form, the sacred enclosure takes the form of a hierarchy of concentric enclosures with the king at the centre, representing the divine in earthly form. According to the geocentric system, the sevenfold enclosure symbolizes the seven planetary spheres of classical astronomy – Mercury, the Moon, Venus, the Sun, Mars, Jupiter and Saturn. Likewise, the Throne of Majesty upon which medieval kings sat was raised on seven steps.

The Settling of the Manor of Tara likens the 'holy city' to a foursquare Brannumh board with forty-nine squares. Significantly, a gameboard answering to this description was found in the remains of a crannog or artificial island in a bog at Ballinderry, County Westmeath, in 1934. Made of wood, it has a human head as a handle, the board thereby symbolizing the human body. Here, the microcosm of the human body reflects the mesocosmos of the landscape, which in turn is an image of the macrocosmos. Like the description above, it has seven places on every side (seven by seven, forty-nine pegholes in all). The central point where the Branán commences the game is the navel of

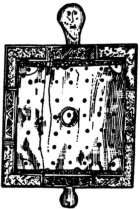

Found in a crannog at Ballinderry, close to the centre of Ireland, the Ballinderry game-board recalls the slain giant whose body is the earth.

the boardman. Sometimes the link between man, board and country was more literal. *The Annals of Clonmacnois* record that in the tenth century Muirchertach 'Of the Leathern Cloak' carried off the body of Cerbhall, king of Leinster, and made such a gameboard of his bones.

Ballinderry is not far from Uisnech, the druidic centre of the island known as 'The Navel of Ireland'. This point was defined in the second century by King Tuatha the Acceptable, who formed the fifth province of Midhe (Meath) from a small portion of each of the existing four. The former meeting-point of the four provinces was the Hill of Uisnech, which he marked by erecting an omphalos called the Stone of Divisions. Just as the Gaulish druids viewed their meeting-place at Chartres as the centre of their country, so the Irish cosmographers envisaged Meath as the middle of the island, encircled by the four provinces of Ulster, Leinster, Connaught and Munster. This was true of other northern European islands, too: like Ireland, Bornholm and Iceland were divided into four quarters. But the centre of Great Britain seems to have lost its religious significance quite early, perhaps as a result of the Roman conquest, although the medieval Welsh story *Llys and Llefelys* tells of the search for it. Significantly, there are no traces of four former provinces of Britain. Perhaps the large and irregular shape of Great Britain, as well as significant geographical and political divisions, made it impossible to quarter the island in the manner of Ireland.

In the year 554, as a result of a personal dispute, Tara was cursed formally by the Christian monk Ruadhán of Lothra. By the law of correspondences, this pronouncement was viewed as a curse on the whole island of Ireland, leading to the disintegration of the centralized power that Tara represented. Nevertheless, Christian sacred geography in Ireland followed the Pagan model. The island of Ireland was divided into four bishoprics ruled from Dublin, Cashel, Tuam and Armagh. These remain today, Armagh being the seat of the primate with both a Catholic and a Protestant cathedral. Clearly, Ireland was seen as a canonical land by both Pagan and Christian alike.

The city of St Andrews is an example of a later Celtic city-plan. It was founded by King David I (1124–53) as part of his plan for the creation of new burghs and churches throughout Scotland. The King appointed the *locator* (the title given to medieval city-founders), Mainard, to lay out the city according to geomantic principles. Two straight main streets with a central third radiate from the foundation point, a high place above the harbour where the high altar of the cathedral was located on a former Celtic church-place. The city thus looked towards the sacred place where the bishop would celebrate the holy sacraments.

Traditional geomancy recognizes that, when we acknowledge the sovereign deities of any place, we can realize divine ideals physically in the land there. When the land is in order spiritually, right orderliness will reign in human society, there will be peace and plenty, and the fields and herds will flourish. An alternative possibility is to create an 'on-lay', where a more abstract spiritual or secular tradition, originating elsewhere, is imposed upon the landscape whether or not it is appropriate there. In the case of an on-lay, the human will is the guiding principle. Unfortunately, such traditions rarely harmonize with the *anima loci*. The on-lay is at its most extreme when the will to build, the techniques used and even the inhabitants of a settlement are brought in from elsewhere. A prime example is the Ulster Plantation of 1607, which saw the foundation of several new towns by the merchant companies of London as part of an overall strategy of breaking the power of the northern Irish clans permanently. The largest of these 'plantations' was Londonderry, constructed in 1609 on the site of the devastated old city of Derry, which was renamed after the home city of the London livery companies that now owned it.

The nature of this on-lay can be discerned from Lord Macaulay's account of the foundation of Londonderry, derived from the contemporary records of the London companies:

> During the troubles caused by the last struggles of the house of O'Neil and O'Donnel against the authority of James I, the ancient city of Derry had been surprised by one of the native chiefs, the inhabitants had been slaughtered, and the houses reduced to ashes. The insurgents were speedily put down and punished: the government resolved to restore the ruined town: the Lord Mayor, Alderman and Common Council of London were invited to assist in the work; and King James I made over to them in their corporate capacity the ground covered by the ruins of the old Derry. ... The city was in form nearly an ellipse; and the principal streets formed a cross, the arms of which met in a square called The Diamond.

Thus Derry was refounded as Londonderry according to the 'holy city' plan and was the last walled city ever built in the British Isles.

While the traditional Celtic sacred landscape was undergoing drastic change, during the eighteenth century the growing awareness of Britain's druidic heritage led architects to study the archaic geomantic traditions of

Britain. According to the architect John Wood the Elder (1704–54), his native town of Bath had been the 'Metropolitan Seat of the Druids' where Apollo was worshipped. Wood made a close study of druidic and megalithic sites, and in his *Choir Gaure*, published in 1747, he wrote that Stonehenge was 'a temple erected by the British Druids'. Wood made a significant contribution to the plan and architecture of Georgian Bath, in which he sought to reproduce the mysteries of Celtic antiquity according to the canons of Georgian architecture. Most notable is the Circus, constructed according to the plan and proportional system he discerned at Stonehenge.

THE CITY OF THE DEAD

The geomantic knowledge used commonly in one context is equally valid in another. Its symbolic content allows it to function perfectly in the other context. Thus, the plan of the city of the dead reflects the city of the living. The *Life* of St Cadoc tells how in about 518, in founding the monastery of Llancarfan, the priest 'undertook to throw up a large mound of earth, and to make therein a very beautiful cemetery, to be dedicated to the honour of God; in which the bodies of the faithful might be buried around the temple. The mound being completed, and the cemetery finished in it, he made four large paths over the rising ground about his cell.' Over fourteen hundred years later, a divination ceremony enacted in the English West Midlands was a remarkable example of the survival of Celtic traditional knowledge in the community of travelling fair people. In December 1943, Patrick Collins, 'The King of the Showmen', was buried. The funeral was a major event, reported in the *Sunday Express* in a piece entitled 'Sixty-Year Ritual Fixed Grave for Showman "King"': 'There was a strange incident at the cemetery when the old man's son visited it accompanied by Father Hanrahan, of St Peter's Catholic Church, Bloxwich, to select a site for the grave,' reported the newspaper:

> When he came to seek a site for his father's last resting place it was found that the Catholic portion of the cemetery was full. The adjoining land which belongs to the cemetery was specially consecrated. When Mr Collins went to select a place for its first grave, he brought his foot forward, raised it and brought his heel down sharply on the turf, making a deep dent in it, exclaiming as he did so 'This is the spot. I want the exact centre of my father's grave to be over that mark'. He explained to the priest: 'My father used those

words and that gesture for 60 years every time that he inspected a fairground site to indicate where the principal attraction, usually the biggest of the merry-go-rounds, was to be erected. He never measured the ground, but the chosen spot was always in the exact centre of the showground. It was a ritual with him.'

The geomantic centre of the cemetery was a fitting place for the burial of a king or founder. All subsequent burials would be around him, a fitting entourage to accompany him. When St Columba founded his monastery at Iona in 563, St Odhran volunteered to be buried alive in the new cemetery as a foundation offering. His spirit became the guardian of the graveyard, known today as Reilig Odhran. In 1943 Patrick Collins fulfilled the same function. The use of the foot to mark off place and time gives us an indication of the rites that may have been enacted with the ceremonial stone footprints of Celtic rulers. The techniques Patrick Collins used to determine the centre of his fairgrounds reflected those used to lay out ancient temporary assemblies, such as the Assembly of Tara or Tynwald. Specialized traditional professions maintain customs and rites that are often incomprehensible to or just unrecognized by outsiders. They represent continuity with the ways of a former age.

DANCING PLACES

When performed ceremonially at the right time and place, a dance is a sacred act. In former times, almost every village in the Welsh borders possessed its own *twmpath chwarae*, or 'green', where the inhabitants assembled on the old festivals to celebrate with sports and dancing. The green was located on top of a hill, or upon ground higher than the surroundings. It consisted of a levelled area, usually with a small mound at its centre (the *twmpath* itself) where musicians sat and played on festive occasions. Sometimes there was a stone instead of the mound. Whatever it was, this central point was decked with oak branches before the people danced around it in a circle. As ceremonial paths marked permanently upon the ground, unicursal labyrinths are a form of 'dance-place' in which people progress along the gyrating pathway, finally to reach the centre. The important aspect of the unicursal labyrinth is that the dancers must cover the whole pathway from the outside to the centre without making a mistake. It is a symbolic journey from the outer to the inner, a pilgrimage one can undertake in the smallest of areas. The typical design of the Celtic

The private ancient Troytown labyrinth at Troy Farm in Oxfordshire is a perfectly maintained example of the traditional Welsh 'Caerdroia' cut in the turf by shepherds.

labyrinth is the 'classical' form, made in sizes ranging from the wise women's Troy Stones to those large enough to accommodate dancers.

It was customary in former days to cut labyrinths in the turf in Celtic countries. *Drych y Prif Oesodd*, published in 1740, describes the practice among Welsh shepherds of cutting labyrinths called *Caerdroia*, a name that has the bivalent meaning of 'The City of Turnings' and 'The City of Troy'. The latter interpretation reflects the traditional claim that the Welsh are descended from Brutus the Trojan. Until its destruction in 1796, during festival times the shoemakers of Shrewsbury danced on a similar turf labyrinth at Kingsland. At its centre was a representation of a human face. After threading the labyrinth, the shoemaker had to jump so that his heels landed exactly in the two holes cut to represent eyes, a reflection of the ancient rites of Celtic kingship. In the early part of the nineteenth century the custom of making labyrinths was still current among the herdsmen of Rockcliffe and Burgh marshes in Cumbria. In County Londonderry there were formerly two labyrinths called the Walls of Troy, and another with the same name near Aberdeen. There were many others in the British Isles, a few of which are maintained today. In Wales, the practice of making new labyrinths and maintaining old ones lapsed at the same time that Welsh village dancing was suppressed. But the custom did not die: it returned in the 1970s when a new labyrinth was made at Pennard on the Gower Peninsula. Subsequently, others were constructed in Wales and other parts of Britain, and the tradition now flourishes again.

SACRED EARTH

Primally, the soil is sacred to Bona Dea, 'The Good Goddess', otherwise known as St Anne, who presides over the earth and all of its blessings. Earth or dust taken from sacred stones, ancient tumuli, graveyards and the tombs of saints has a magic virtue which carries the essence of the sacred place. Collecting sacred earth was a practice understood well by the Mediterranean Pagans. The *terra sigillata*, the red earth from Lemnos, was dug ceremonially under the supervision of a priestess and distributed to the faithful as blocks bearing the seal of the head of Artemis. This was not dead dust, but rather a portion of the living, ensouled earth, in which the spirit is revealed in the material. This belief was not restricted to the Mediterranean region. There are many megalithic passage-graves in northern Europe that have been robbed completely of their covering of earth. It seems that this happened because people believed the soil to be a useful remedy for many ills. Certain soils can be used to remedy specific ailments. Breton folklore asserts that earth from the Île St Maudez in the archipelago of Bréhat has vermifuginous properties. Banagher Sand, from the tomb of St Muirdeach O'Heney at Banagher, brings great luck to believers, whilst throughout the Celtic lands churchyard soil in general is ascribed both healing and magical qualities. In Ireland, clay taken from the threshold of a house, a sacred place doubly sanctified by the continued blessings of all who enter, is a remedy for influenza.

It is an ancient belief that the earth of particular localities transfers its virtue to those buried there. Local traditions tell that no one who is buried in the churchyards at Tuam or on Bardsey Island will be condemned to hell. When a new holy place was established, virtuous soil was sometimes transferred in large quantities from an older one. When he emigrated to Iceland, Örlygr Hrappson, a Celtic-Christian Norseman, took consecrated soil from the Hebrides to put beneath the first church there. The same thing was done by the Pagan priest Thorólf Mostrarskegg, who transported his timber-framed temple, complete with the soil beneath it, from Norway to a new location in Iceland. This is the principle of transference of sanctity which underlies the practice of transferring sacred objects from one place to another, or reproducing replicas of sacred places.

On the island of Bute near Garroch Head in a green hill-top hollow surrounded by trees is the twelfth-century chapel of St Blane. Close by are the ruins of St Blane's Cell, guarding a hollow enclosed by a cashel wall. This is the notorious segregated graveyard, where men lie in the upper ward and women in the lower. According to legend, St Blane created the upper graveyard from sacred earth brought by ship from Rome. Whilst one of his monks was transporting the soil from ship to temenos on his back in a creel, the headband that supported it snapped. Blane asked a woman bystander for her belt to replace the headband. When she refused, he cursed all women and swore that they would not lie in the holy Roman soil. Two separate graveyards were made. Symbolically, however, the native women, the mothers of the island, lie in their native mother earth, whilst the men, who originated elsewhere, do not. Similarly, consecrated earth was removed from the Irish mainland to Scelig Mhichil to create the monks' cemetery, and the tradition has never died. The Carrière des Fusillés, a war memorial for Breton hostages shot by the Nazis, was erected at Châteaubriant in the 1940s. Its concrete base continues the Celtic tradition of revering sacred soil. It contains an array of small reliquary tubes, each of which contains earth from an execution-place, sanctified by the blood of the slain.

In addition to the magical or symbolic function, in former times there was a practical reason for transporting soil. The Celtic 'lazybed' system of horticulture enables crops to be grown on rocky land, bringing fertility where before there was barrenness. Fertile strips of between 3 and 9 feet (1–3 m) wide are built up within enclosures made of rocks using local peat, crushed seashells and soil brought from elsewhere. By this means the fecundity of Mother Earth was extended, in itself a sacred act. These gardens, created out of the barren wilderness, are images of paradise, where the sustaining fruits of the earth and healing herbs are grown. The miraculous mood of serenity of such gardens renders them perfect places of contemplation, separated from the harshness of the surrounding environment. Lazybeds were used widely by Celtic monks and, in later years, by crofters' families deported to barren islands during the Highland Clearances. The Inner Hebridean islands of Eriskay and Scalpay are best known for this technique today, though it is also practised in the west of Ireland.

In Brittany, the typical temenos is the 'close'. This is defined by an outer wall that encloses a graveyard and three buildings: church, ossuary and Calvary. To maintain the integrity of the sacred place, graves are not permanent. After five years of burial, the bones are exhumed from the soil and removed to the ossuary. Thus the essence of the flesh is returned to the earth, its corresponding 'material'. Every twenty to twenty-five years, all the remains are removed from the bone-house and buried together in a ceremony known as 'the great funeral'. Thus the human essence of stone – bone – is returned to the earth. The process then begins anew. In many places, an image seen over the ossuary as its protector is Ankou, the skeletal king of the dead. A fine example exists at the hill-top sanctuary of La Roche-Maurice. In the form of the last man to die in the parish during the year, he haunts the local spirit-paths by night. Those whom he encounters on his travels are destined soon to join him in the graveyard.

Trackways and Spirit-Paths

INNER BODY KNOWLEDGE

IN CONTRAST with the random scenes glimpsed fleetingly by the motorist, those who walk experience authentic contact with the places through which they pass. Through walking we can come into communion with the spirit of the land; we become one with the landscape. Its existence is part of our own inner body knowledge; it is present in our memory and our emotions. The outward reflection of this inner knowledge permeates the traditional landscape. In former times, tracks and pathways were regarded as sacred in themselves, protected by general deities of the roads and specific deities of the places they passed through.

In the era before mechanical vehicles transformed everything, any path, track or road needed to possess certain features if it were to be a viable route. For example, for reasons of comfort, when crossing ridges it was better to keep to the warmer south-facing slopes, sheltered from the cold north wind. Necessary for all travellers were landmarks for orientation, drinking water, especially from springs that did not freeze in wintertime, stopping-places for rest and refreshment, and shelter. These were sanctified by the gods of place and the general deities to which the corresponding features were dedicated. On the old tracks and roads, sacred loci propitiating the local spirits existed at every place where an awkward or dangerous course had to be followed. Each traveller who passed by could say a prayer or make an offering. This had a twofold function. It propitiated the local spirit, summoning its aid to the traveller. It also gave the wayfarer the confidence to concentrate mindfully on the walk ahead – entering a perilous bog, ascending a precarious slope or wading a hazardous ford. After successfully negotiating the difficult stretch, the walker would rest and give thanks at the next stopping-place. As Thomas Pennant wrote in 1774, describing the area of Gairloch: 'if a traveller passes any of his resting-places, they never neglect to leave an offering [to Maelrubha] … a stone, a stick, a bit of rag.'

Because each place is possessed of its own *anima loci*, human culture expresses this spirit through the place's history, legends and lore. The traditional response to the land is to give everything a name. The whole body of the land is infused thereby with names of deities, people, sprites, events, qualities and with a numinous character. For the wayfarer, the country is ensouled. Thus, an entire journey can be described geomythically in the manner of the bards. For example, in the Irish *Dindsenchas*, Cú Chulainn is asked his route. He replies: 'From the Cover of the Sea, over the Great Secret of the Tuatha de Danaan, and the Foam of the two steeds of Emain Macha; over the Morrigu's Garden, and the Great Sow's Back; over the Glen of the Great Dam, between God and His Prophet; over the marrow of the woman Fedelm, between the boar and his dam; over the Washing-Places of the Horses of Dea ...,' and so on. In this text, the geomythic names have been translated from the original Irish as an example. But, unlike names in certain languages, it is not customary to translate Celtic descriptive names. For instance, my surname is the Cornish-derived Pennick which, though it means 'hill-top', has never been given its English 'translation'.

As participants, we have a personal and collective cultural relationship with the landscape. We are not separate; we are part of the landscape. The reality is what we walk, see, touch, smell and experience. But today most people use maps when walking. While they are very useful, they are based on an intellectual concept that detaches us from a direct experience of the landscape. Maps replace body knowledge with an intellectual concept. They separate us from the living body reality of the land. People who are part of their own country do not need maps. They know the names of places without recourse to written or printed records. Often, the names on maps are the result of accidental or wilful misinterpretation by cartographers from elsewhere. As soon as this happens, there is a dislocation between the genuine local name and the official name on the map. Paradoxically, to officialdom the 'real' name is that on the map, not that used since time immemorial by the people of the land. By de-naming the land, officialdom brings psychic and then physical destruction, driving out the earth-spirit and rendering the land spiritually dead.

TRACKWAYS IN THE CELTIC LANDSCAPE

Ancient Celtic trackways survive best in hill country and mountainous territory, where modern road-building and farming methods have had minimal impact upon the countryside. Wherever they still exist, Celtic tracks show that the people who first waymarked them had a remarkably intimate knowledge of the landscape. According to legend, many of them were made first by the feet of angels, and this religious element is borne out by the number of trackways that take the form of priests' and pilgrims' paths between places of ancient sanctity. In the Welsh borderlands, for example, the walker who uses them is taken up the side of a ridge, over the top and down the other side into the next valley. The crossing-point at the top of the ridge is often marked by an artificial notch, a stopping-place visible from below only from a very narrow angle. To cross to the next valley, the wayfarer must climb straight up towards the notch that marks the easiest crossing-point. Whilst some notches may be the result of erosion by countless travellers, others have been cut deliberately. For example, two notches at Clodock, Herefordshire, cut through a ridge of rock. The trackways that traverse the ridges at Llanthony Abbey in the Black Mountains are notable for a number of them. One of the notches there marks the Rhiw Cwrw – the 'Beer Path'. A section of old hollow track aligns upon the abbey ruins, then along a curious array of three parallel paths up the opposite valley side, a striking feature visible only under certain conditions of light, or with a powdering of snow. The purpose of these three tracks has never been explained satisfactorily.

Although most are now called by a generic name such as 'the notch' or 'the crack', we may be assured that in former times each bore an individual name and was acknowledged by travellers' offerings. A few retain proper names, such as Bwlch Effengyl. Known in English as the Gospel Pass, it is a deep notch visible from near Llanthony 6 miles (10 km) away, and from Llowes 5 miles (8 km) on the other side; it is a sacred stopping-place said to be named in commemoration of Bishop Baldwin's recruiting campaign of 1188. Another notable ecclesiastical track was Llwybr Wddyn, a path over the mountain at Llanwddyn, said to have been made by St Gwyddyn to enable him to visit St Melangell at Pennant, 5 miles (8 km) away. Sadly, we can no longer take this trail, for it is submerged beneath the waters of Lake Vyrnwy.

The monastic trackways in the Wicklow Mountains and across Dartmoor are prime examples of the Celtic skill of pathfinding in difficult terrain. The Dartmoor tracks, which are still walkable today, crossed the moorland, linking several important monastic settlements. The most important are Tavistock Abbey to Plympton Priory (14½ miles, 23 km); Tavistock Abbey to Buckfast Abbey (20 miles, 32 km); Buckfast Abbey to

Buckland Abbey (18 miles, 29 km); Plympton Priory to Buckland Abbey (10¼ miles, 16.5 km). Notable landmarks, including isolated boulders, 'fairy' thorn trees, bridges, fords and stone crosses were designated as waymarkers that enabled the traveller to find his or her way. They continued the tradition of earlier times, where cairns and standing stones marked the track. These monastic trackways are reliable routes characterized by moderate gradients, avoidance of hill-crests, and easy river crossings. Crosses mark sanctified stopping-places, where prayers and offerings were made. Between Tavistock and Plympton there are thirteen crosses, whilst between Tavistock and Buckfast there are twenty-three. Their names recall those things that ensoul the landscape. They celebrate innate numinousness, notable local historic events, celebrities and usages.

THE OLD STRAIGHT TRACK AND FAIRY PATHS

Some trackways in the Welsh border region are famous today because they were described in the 1920s by Alfred Watkins as *leys* or 'old straight tracks'. From his own knowledge of the landscape and the traditions of his native Herefordshire, he developed the concept that in former times there existed a dense network of straight traders' tracks across the landscape, defined by notable landmarks, such as hill-tops, mounds, standing stones, ponds, churches, crosses and groves of trees. These he found in abundance in his native region. The type of landscape Watkins studied is ideal for straight tracks, containing many features that are less common elsewhere. The complexity of each individual case makes it difficult to draw general conclusions. However, it is clear that the numerous mark stones that Watkins found on his travels are stopping-places comparable with those on the more common 'unstraight' tracks. Latter-day followers of Watkins have tended to play down their use for walkers, giving them a more mystical interpretation, visualizing straight tracks as ways primarily of spirit and light. As a traditional Gaelic maxim tells us: 'He who will not take advice will take the crooked track.'

Otherworldly thoroughfares called fairy paths are acknowledged in parts of the British Isles and Brittany. In the west of England, a straight line in the grass, a recognizably different shade of green from the rest of the meadow, is called a *trod*. People seeking relief from rheumatism will walk a trod, though animals are reputed to avoid them. It is essential to avoid them at times when otherworldly beings are using them. It is said that should a human being meet a supernatural procession on the fairy path at

Penwortham in Lancashire, it will prove fatal. Fairy paths in Ireland are said to take straight courses between raths, which may be situated a few miles apart. At certain times, as in Lancashire, the fairy procession will pass along this path, so disaster will befall anyone rash enough to build a house on such a line. But one can be built there if the path itself is not blocked. Wherever there is an unusual passage that takes the walker beneath or through an ancient building, then it is likely to be just such a right of way. In Scotland, this is called a *closs*. A remarkable example exists on Dartmoor, where at West Combe an ancient track known as the Mariners' Way passes through the central passage of a longhouse.

Irish fairy paths are not just lines on the landscape, however. They also exist under water, reminiscent of the secret causeways to crannogs and council islands. 'Sometimes the cave fairies make a straight path in the sea from one island to another, all paved with coral, under the water; but no one can tread it except the fairy race,' wrote Lady Jane Wilde in her *Ancient Legends, Mystic Charms and Superstitions of Ireland.* 'Fishermen coming home late, on looking down, have frequently seen them passing and re-passing – a black band of little men with black dogs who are very fierce if any one tries to touch them.' Beneath the waves is the otherworldly fairy kingdom, either completely separate from the human world or the remains of a lost age.

Otherworldly underwater tracks or causeways can sometimes be seen at low tide in Cardigan Bay. They are said to be the main roads of Cantref y Gwaelod – the 'Lost Lowland Hundred' – a land overwhelmed by the sea in the sixth or seventh century. The longest of these is Sarn Badrig, 'St Patrick's Causeway', a road and sea wall said to extend for 22 miles (35 km) from the coast half-way between Barmouth and Harlech. It was described in 1795 in *The Cambrian Register*, where the antiquary Robert Vaughan asserted that 'A whole Cantred or Hundred called Canter Gwaelod ... has been overwhelmed by the sea and drowned, and still a great stone wall, made as a fence against the sea, may be clearly seen.' According to legend, the lost land was divided by four main roads which can still be discerned at low tide.

THE SPIRITS OF THE ROADS

According to folk belief, the sovereign spirits of the roads possess a subtly different character from those that occupy special places on roads: the village boundaries, stopping-places, fords, tidal causeways, bridges, crossroads and mountain passes. In addition to protecting the actual path, road or track, folk traditions tell that the boundaries of a place and the roads leading to it possess their own supernatural guardians. Beliefs current in parts of Scotland and eastern England tell of the ward, a band of vigilant spirits that protect a village or town from internal troubles and external dangers. Each dusk, the sprites that comprise the ward first assemble at a certain stopping-place outside the settlement, then travel their respective fairy paths to their night-time watch-posts. These are ward hills, stones, crosses and gentle trees – the stopping-places along the roads and paths leading to the settlement. The ward forms nightly a ring of benevolent spiritual protection against harmful spirits. But once the sprites are driven from the landscape, the protection is no longer forthcoming and the settlement is open to psychic ills.

Ancient Celtic tradition possessed a system of *geassa* in which there are spirit-places that only divine or sacred persons can enter, the *locus terribilis*. Royal footprint stones are such places. Sometimes the *locus terribilis* appears as a bad place on the road where it is inadvisable to cross. Anyone who sets foot there will suffer unpleasant consequences. These include the phenomenon known as 'the hungry grass' and 'the stray sod'. In Ireland, the *fear gortach* ('hungry grass' or 'violent hunger') is said to grow at a place where an uncoffined corpse was laid on the ground on its way to burial. This affects the quality of the place permanently for the worse. Those unfortunate enough to step on such a spot are doomed to suffer insatiable hunger. An infamous place for the hungry grass was on a road near Ballinamote. It was activated so frequently that the woman of the house nearby kept a bowl of stirabout in a state of permanent readiness to feed passers-by who stepped on the fated ground. There are also other bad places near which no one should go willingly. In former times, a notorious place near Meigle in Perthshire was 'shunned as a pestilential spot'. The body of Vanora, one of King Arthur's queens who died barren, was reputed to lie there, and bad luck befell even those who merely looked at the spot.

More widely recognized is *foidin seachrain*, the 'stray sod'. Anyone unfortunate enough to step upon this piece of ground becomes disorientated. The classic example is the 'gateless field'. Travelling a footpath, an unsuspecting wayfarer climbs a stile and enters a field surrounded by an impenetrable thorn hedge and bank. Although the traveller knows his or her location perfectly well, the way out of the field cannot be found; neither can the entrance. Delay is guaranteed. Perhaps the wayfarer will have to spend the night sleeping on the ground before waking to find that he or she has slept next to it. Certain places are notorious. A rath or fort at Lismirraine is named 'the fort of the place where people are put astray'.

CROSSROADS

Places where tracks join, especially where they cross, are dangerous places occupied by special spirit-guardians. Crossroads are places of transition, where the cosmic axis between the underworld and the upperworld intersects with middle earth. They are places at which the distinction between the physical and non-material worlds appears less certain. Sacred to the gods of travel, commerce and growth, crossroads have always attracted ritual and performance. In classical times they were marked with a Herm, an ithyphallic image of Mercury, psychopomp of the dead and sovereign deity of the crossways. Frequently, the Herm was accompanied by a tree and an altar upon which wayfarers would make offerings. Julius Caesar tells that the principal god of the Gallic Celts was 'Mercury, of whom there are many images throughout Gaul: he is considered to be the originator of all of the arts; the god who indicates the right road and guides the traveller's footsteps; he is the great patron of trade and riches.' Caesar was writing of the Celtic god Lugh. In northern Europe, the crossroads divinity was the god of hanged men, among other attributes, for crossroads were especially sacred to the dead. In later times, the sacred cross of roads was given a newer interpretation as the Cross of Christ, another hanged god. Priests erected stone crosses at crossroads as prayerful stopping-places for devout travellers.

Until the eighteenth century, dismembered limbs and torsos of executed people were displayed at British crossways. A particularly notorious instance occurred in the aftermath of the Duke of Monmouth's defeat at Sedgemoor. The remains of executed rebels were hung at crossroads throughout western England to remind others of the consequences of disobedience. In addition to displaying such grisly remains, crossroads served as burial-places for those who, for some reason, did not qualify for interment in Christian ground. Until 1823, the law of England and Wales directed that anyone who committed suicide should be buried in the local crossroads with a stake of iron or ashwood driven through the heart. Others disposed of in this manner were the inhabitants of the liminal regions of society: witches, outlaws and gypsies.

PLACES OF PASSAGE: RIVER FORDS AND MOUNTAIN PASSES

A ford through a river is a liminal *locus terribilis*. In practical terms, ford-
ing a river is a dangerous thing to do, especially at times when the waters
are high and turbulent. Formerly, before bridges were universal, at the ford
the traveller was sometimes compelled to make the momentous decision
whether or not to take a life-threatening risk in order to continue her or his
journey. But there was help. Sometimes, the water level above which it was
unsafe to cross was marked in some way. A stone that stood formerly in the
River Teviot at Borthwick Mains had a fish carved on it to show when it
was safe to cross. There was also spiritual assistance. Traditionally, there
are two stopping-places, one on either side of the ford. The shrine before
the ford gives the wayfarer the spiritual support to go forward through the
waters, and that after the ford enables him or her to give thanks for a safe
crossing. At these shrines, the traveller can propitiate the dangerous spirits
of road and river, and remember the souls of those who have perished
there. In Irish tradition, fords are the residence of the phantom being
known as the Bean Nighe, 'the washerwoman at the ford'. To see her is to
receive an omen of death, perhaps of being taken from this life into the
otherworld. Crossing the river symbolizes a change in one's way of life,
perhaps in terms of a fundamental alteration of attitude or commitment.
Once one has crossed, one is in a new land and there may be no way back.
Mountain passes are another kind of *locus terribilis* where the traveller is
challenged in a similar way. Ancient Celtic passes across the Alps and the
Pennines were guarded by the goddess Brigida, and her consort Poeninus
was invoked for a successful journey through 'the notch'.

SACRED CIRCUITS

Sacred circuits involve the pilgrim in visiting specific sacred places in a certain order. They may be localized in a small area, or may be separated
widely around a longer route. They are an ancient tradition from pre-
Christian times. The *Capitularia Regum Francorum*, dating from the time
of Charlemagne, tells of the Gallic 'Pagan Trackway' called Yries, whose
stopping-places were marked with shoes and rags. In character, these
Pagan trackways were identical with the later Christian sacred circuits,
and it is probable that the Church assimilated many of them with only
minor alterations. Essentially, like labyrinths, they perform the function of

long pilgrimages in a small area, the pilgrims visiting a series of sacred places of different kinds, experiencing a wide variety of sacred landscapes in a small area. In Ireland, a series of stations at which prayers and other rites are offered is called a 'round'. When pilgrims do this *en masse* on a saint's day, it is known as the saint's 'pattern'. In Brittany this is called a 'pardon'.

When these take place, the spiritual content of the landscape is raised temporarily to a higher level by the presence of pious people performing their devotions. The pilgrim experiences a progressional series of stations, some of which bring new experiences, and some of which repeat and reinforce earlier ones. Each serves to heighten awareness, bringing archetypal spiritual qualities into consciousness. The pattern performed at the shrine of St Gobnat at Ballyvourney is a perfect example of this ritual walking through a sacred landscape. St Gobnat's temenos contains a series of hallowed stations situated in a remarkably small area. The beginning of the round is marked by a modern image of the saint. Next comes an ancient holy well from which the pilgrim must drink. The path leads onwards to a round enclosure, called St Gobnat's House, the ruins of a prehistoric building which excavation has shown to be a place of metalworking, whose deity, Gobniu, is recalled by the saint. A stone pillar stands at the centre, upon which pilgrims must use a stone to inscribe a cross. The next stage reaches the churchyard, sheltering a modern church and the ruins of an ancient one. At the eastern end of the ancient church, pilgrims must kneel in prayer and then inscribe a cross on a nearby stone. The next station is another holy well, adjacent to the south wall of the church. They then go to a mound near the churchyard gate, called St Gobnat's Grave, which they circumambulate sunwise on their knees. Crutches and walking-sticks are left behind on the mound. Finally, pilgrims pass through a stile below the churchyard to visit a third holy well and drink the waters. St Gobnat's image, which dates from the thirteenth century, is exhibited each year on 11 February and Whit Sunday, and these are the main days of pilgrimage.

Pilgrims attending the pardon at Locronan volunteer to undergo considerable hardships in their ritual walking. Commemorating the Irish St Ronan, the pardon is called 'La Trömênie' from the Breton *tro minihy*, said to mean either 'the monk's walk' or 'the walk through the mountains'. Every year, a 4-mile walk (6.4 km) is held, but every six years the Grande Trömênie (9 miles, 14.5 km) trudges the tracks that the saint used to walk, marking the boundaries of St Ronan's territory. Along them are forty-four stopping-places, which are decked with flowers for the occasion. On the second Sunday in July fasting pilgrims walk barefoot around the whole sacred circuit, climb the hill upon which St Ronan's Church stands and circumambulate the rock called Kador St-Ronan (St Ronan's Chair). When ritual walkers carry holy objects and relics in procession around the prescribed circuit, they serve to sanctify and protect the locality against all evil.

By their very nature, perambulations are transitory, entailing temporary dressing of permanent shrines, or even the construction of temporary stopping-places along the route. In former days at Tenby in Pembrokeshire, people erected a series of maypoles as stopping-places for the Maytide round-dance of the town. A report from the year 1858 recounts that 'May-poles were reared up in different parts of the town, decorated with flowers, coloured papers, and bunches of variegated ribbon. On May-Day, the young men and maidens would, joining hand in hand, dance round the May-poles and "thread the needle". ... A group from fifty to 100 persons would wend their way from one pole to another, till they had traversed the town.'

Another aspect of the ceremonial route is the lych way, the path taken by cortèges carrying corpses to their burial-place. In remote areas where churchyards were few, such as in alpine and moorland regions, special trackways were used to take the dead to consecrated ground. In flat country they tend towards straightness, but elsewhere they follow the contours in the skilful manner of ancient tracks. Thus, lych ways resemble the pilgrimage rounds, except that one of the participants never returns. Like the rounds, they take a specific route and involve characteristic rites at stopping-places. On the island of Mull, for example, funeral cortèges would halt for prayers and rest at the summits of steep hills or beside water. On leaving the stopping-place, every mourner would add a stone to the cairn that marked the stopping-place. The customary route finished with a circuit of the church or burial-ground. Shaw, in his *History of Moray* (1775), records the cortège going sunwise around the church three times with the coffin before entering the church for the funeral service. Similarly, in South Uist and Arisaig it is customary to make a sunwise approach to the graveyard.

Although they are no longer used in these days of motor hearses, several notable lych ways can still be traced. The Burnmoor Track can still be followed between Wasdale and Eskdale in Cumbria. In the days before consecrated ground for burials existed at Wasdale Head, coffins were carried by pony by way of this track to the Church of St Catherine at Boot. Another long route of the dead is the Lych Way on Dartmoor, which brought the dead across the moor to the churchyard at Lydford.

CELTIC ROYAL ROADS

The more adventurous apologists for Celtic culture frequently assert that the old road system of Britain, usually ascribed to Roman engineering skills, was actually in existence before the Roman conquest. They cite as evidence the ancient roads of Ireland, which was never ruled by Rome. There is some truth in the idea. Certain Irish routes do reflect a skill in road-building comparable with that of the Romans. In County Kerry, Brandon Mountain is linked with Kilmachedor church over bog and hill by a causeway over 7 miles (11 km) long called Casan na Naomh, 'The Pathway of the Saints'. However, it is uncertain whether these fine Irish roads predate the Christian religion, whose priests brought with them Roman techniques of building. Almost invariably they are named after Christian saints.

British traditional history tells of certain roads that were under the jurisdiction of the king's peace – the four royal roads of Britain. Bardic literature ascribes them to two pre-Roman kings of Britain, Dunwal Molmutius and his son Belinus. When they were ready, we are told, they were thrown open 'to all nations and foreigners'. All who journeyed along them were under legal protection, for roads had the same sanctity as rivers and sanctuaries, and free passage was guaranteed for all. 'There are three things free to a country and its borders – the rivers, the roads and the places of worship,' a bardic triad tells us.

The British bardic accounts are medieval and often dismissed as mythical, but there are historical parallels among the Celts of mainland Europe. In his *De Mirabilibus Auscultis*, the Pseudo-Aristotle informs us: 'From Italy as far as Celtia, in the territory of the Celtoligurians and the Iberians, there is a highway with the name of the Heraclean Way. Should a Greek or local man venture along it, the inhabitants ensure that no harm befalls him, as they would bear the penalty.' In essence, this Celtic assurance was identical with that traditionally ascribed to the royal roads of Britain. Sometimes this protection was afforded only to pilgrims. In 1427, the Scots King James I gave royal protection to all pilgrims going to the shrine of St Ninian at Whithorn, provided that they wore the prescribed badges to identify themselves.

Another strand of bardic tradition ascribes British roads to Elen, daughter of Eudaf, from whom the Cornish kings claimed their descent: 'Elen bethought her to make high-roads from one town to another throughout the island of Britain. And the roads were made,' *The Dream of Macsen Wledig* tells us. 'And for this cause they are called the roads of Elen Luyddog.' Whatever their historic origin, the British royal roads were confirmed later in better-documented reigns, including those of Edward the Confessor and William the Conqueror. Edward's roads were Watling Street, the Fosse Way, Icknield Street and Ermine Street. Because these roads were themselves sanctuary, the crossing-points were particularly significant stopping-places. Of the four crossings, three have considerable historical importance, Cirencester, Dunstable and Royston, all of which are small 'holy cities' in plan.

Medieval Ireland possessed five royal roads, radiating from Tara. They were Slige Midluachra, Cualann, Dála, Asal and Mór. Slige Mór, the Midwest Road, was an equinoctial sacred axis, linking the administrative centre of Tara with the sacred omphalos at Uisnech. There is a single royal road on the Isle of Man which is now called the Millennium Way. Like the British royal roads, it is connected with an ancient king named Orry. This royal road, like Ermine Street and the later pilgrimage way to Walsingham, is an earthly reflection of the starry path of the Milky Way in the heavens.

Places of Epiphany

DREAMS AND VOICES

MANY SACRED places come into being or are rediscovered through prophetic voices, dreams and visions in which some mysterious element of the landscape speaks to people through their unconscious. Through the medium of revelation, forgotten sacred places can re-manifest themselves. The Breton sanctuaries of Josselin and Rochefort-en-Terre commemorate miraculous rediscoveries of forgotten images of Our Lady, whilst in Lancashire the holy well at Fernyhalgh was discovered through revelation. In 1471, a merchant sailing from Ireland was caught in a storm, and when it seemed inevitable that his ship was doomed, he prayed that if he were saved he would found a shrine in thanksgiving. Coming ashore in Lancashire, he heard a voice telling him to go to a place where he would find an apple tree bearing coreless fruit next to a spring; there he must set up a chapel. He walked around looking for the place, and some days later came to Fernyhalgh, where he found the prophesied tree and fountain. There he rediscovered a forgotten image of Our Lady, for which he built a new chapel. Another chapel was built there in 1685, but although this is now a private house, an image of the Madonna and Child sanctifies the open stone-lined well.

Perhaps Glastonbury is the most visited of all ancient Celtic sacred places. One of its most numinous loci is the Chalice Well, which lies at the foot of Chalice Hill near to the much more impressive Glastonbury Tor. Little is known of its early history, but it has long been the focus of devotions. In former times it was known as Chilkwell, the 'chalk well', or as the Blood Spring, after its red waters. In 1750, Matthew Chancellor, a local man, dreamt that if he drank its water, his asthma would cease. He did so on seven successive Sundays and was cured. The news of his cure spread, and soon the well was the focus for visitors from miles around, eager for a cure for their ills. Through this well, Glastonbury became a minor spa in the new enthusiasm for taking the waters that swept England at that time.

Someone then rediscovered an old legend that told how the Holy Grail had been deposited there by Joseph of Arimathea. Christ's blood had supposedly coloured the waters, endowing them with healing properties. The well has been revered since then. The present guardians, the Chalice Well Trust, have laid out a wonderful garden of peace and tranquillity through which flow the red chalybeate waters from the well. The well-shaft itself is covered by a modern iron-bound lid bearing the mystical sigil of the Vesica Piscis, symbolizing the geometry of creation. Although it is no longer overtly associated with cures, it is one of the most perfect examples of a modern Celtic well-shrine and could profitably be emulated at other places.

APPARITIONS

Dreams and voices are never as impressive as visible apparitions, which cannot be so easily ignored. The greater number of such epiphanies are of feminine beings, and they have been happening for a long time. Around 500 BCE, Artemis appeared 'like a flame of fire' to the girl-princess Hagelochia of Sparta at her loom. Subsequent recorded apparitions have followed this pattern. The place of an epiphany is hallowed by the occurrence, and many important shrines have come into being in this way. Our Lady, the more recent manifestation of the goddess, has been pre-eminent over the last millennium. Her first recorded epiphany was at Little Walsingham in 1061. Richeldis, the lady of the manor, saw her in three separate apparitions. The shrine remains the most important centre of pilgrimage today in Britain. But although the predominance of the Christian religion caused some confusion over the identity of the apparitions, it did not prevent continued manifestations of Pagan goddesses. Venus manifested herself on the Hörselberg in 1398, and the Scottish *Ballad of Thomas the Rhymer* describes a medieval epiphany of the Elvish Queen to Thomas of Ercildoune:

> True Thomas lay on Huntlie Bank;
> A ferlie he spied wi' his e'e;
> And there he saw a ladye bright
> Come riding down by the Eildon Tree.
>
> Her skirt was o' the grass-green silk,
> Her mantle o' the velvet fyne;
> At ilka tett o' her horse's mane
> Hung fifty silver bells and nine.

True Thomas pu'd aff his cap,
And louted down on his knee:
'Hail to thee, Mary, Queen of Heaven!
For thy peer on earth could never be.'

'O no, O no, Thomas,' she said,
'That name does not belong to me;
I'm but the Queen o' fair Elfland,
That I am hither come to visit thee.'

Then the Elvish Queen takes Thomas on the 'third road' that leads neither to the hell nor the heaven taught by the Church, but to another place, the Celtic otherworld. Like others before him, Thomas later returns from the otherworld a transformed man – as a bard of the highest order.

Public rather than private apparitions seem not to have the same power of transformation. In 1879, a number of people witnessed a multiple apparition on the gable-end of the village church at Knock in County Mayo. 'On passing by the chapel, and at a little distance from it,' recalled Mary McLoughlin, one of the witnesses, 'I saw a wonderful number of strange figures or appearances at the gable, one like the Blessed Virgin Mary, and one like St Joseph, another a bishop; I saw an altar.' Another witness, Mary Beirne, gave an alternative version of the apparitions: 'Above the altar, and resting on it, was a lamb, standing with the face towards St John, thus fronting the western sky. I saw no cross or crucifix. On the body of the lamb and around it, I saw golden stars, or small brilliant lights, glittering like jets or glass balls, reflecting the light of some luminous body.' Curiously, only a small group of people witnessed the apparition, and they made no attempt to summon others to see what appeared to be a miracle. Despite significant inconsistencies in the witnesses' accounts, people began to visit Knock, and the influx of pilgrims has never stopped. Today, 750,000 people a year visit the shrine of Our Lady of Knock, whose Brutalist concrete basilica completely fails to acknowledge the *anima loci*.

PHANTOM LIGHTS

Closely related to apparitions of divine beings are formless lights. According to Celtic monks, certain highly developed individuals could produce spiritual flames, which were viewed as emanations of the Holy Spirit. Adamnan, who documented the saint's life, asserts that St Columba was especially gifted in this matter, and recounts several instances: 'St

Brendan saw a certain blazing and most luminous globe of fire burning over St Columba's head and rising up like a pillar as he stood before the altar consecrating the holy oblation.' On another occasion, as Virgno and Columba were praying at night, 'a golden light descended from heaven and filled all that part of the church.'

Occasionally people see lights of unknown origin, unconnected with human beings. There are many accounts of them, which are often embellished with explanatory myths. A number of recurrent forms of phantom light have been documented in recent times. Lights may manifest themselves as ground-based hemispheres; a sphere of light floating a few feet above the ground; a humanoid shape; a single pillar of light; or a column with cross-arms. Often, phantom lights contain shimmering, iridescent patterns. In 1940, a man digging his garden in Coventry suddenly saw a phantom sphere of light appear close by, which he described as being composed of 'a mass of writhing strings of light'. Light columns, too, resemble known geomantic features. They can take the form of a T-shaped Tau cross, a Celtic wheel-headed cross or the Germanic sacred world-axis column, Irminsul. St Trillo is said to have discovered his holy well on the seashore at Llandrillo-yn-Rhos when a shaft of light emerged from the ground there. Writhing strings of light recall the designs carved on ancient omphaloi. The Turoe Stone has similar patterns, and may reproduce in stone an ancient apparition.

William Lethaby, in his seminal book *Architecture, Mysticism and Myth*, tells of 'the all-embracing world-tree that carries the stars for its fruit in the dark heaven of night'. This is the jewel-bearing tree, a phenomenon where phantom lights appear amid the foliage, sparkling like gems. When I witnessed one in a German forest on May Day 1993, I beheld tiny shimmering pinpoints of white, red and green light. Reproductions of the tree illuminated by spirit are set up every year as Christmas trees with imitation lights significantly named 'fairy lights'.

In parts of Ireland, phantom lights on or above the ground are said to denote fairy land. They are the night-time manifestations of the 'fairy clans of the earth folk'. According to Irish folk observation, these phosphorescent lights appear over water, marshy ground or churchyards, often taking the form of dancing flames. There was a belief that places where inexplicable lights appeared were special. Tongues of flame have been observed over Loch Maree, where they were seen as a manifestation of the god Mhor-Ri, who was revered on a holy island there. Phantom lights over water were ascribed to the agency of spirits. Fairy lights appearing on holy islands in lochs, those mystic 'islands within islands', are considered to be divine in origin. When they were seen in 1912 in the ruined church on Church Island in Lough Beg, County Londonderry, witnesses regarded them as a spiritual sign. According to one Irish tradition, however, they are not from the heavenly realms, but appearances of the Water Sheerie, an elemental spirit that wears a garment of fire and carries a handful of burning straw. He can take many forms: flames dancing on a cart, fairy lights on the mast of a sailing ship or tongues of fire over water. There is only one way to drive away this dangerous fire-demon, which is to carry iron, preferably in the form of a knife or a cross. Like the 'good people', fire sprites are said to be earthbound souls that have been refused entry to either the upper or lower worlds.

Phantom lights are sometimes observed shining on the cemetery-island of Mun in Loch Leven. Traditionally, supernatural lights at burial-places are viewed as omens of impending death. It was widely believed that when the soul departed the body, it left in the form of a flame or light. When St Columba died, Adamnan tells us that his church filled with 'angelic light'. Bede reports that after his death in battle, a pillar of light stood over the recovered remains of the slain Northumbrian King Oswald 'stretching from the wagon to the sky'. It is believed in Wales that when a light appears at a certain spot, especially repeatedly, it foretells a death that is destined to occur there, though it does not necessarily mean that the witness will die. When phantom flames appear around buildings, they are said to signify forthcoming death within.

Corpse candles also appear when someone is about to die. A corpse candle is a flame or ball of light that is seen to travel closely above the ground from the graveyard to the dying person's house and back again in the other direction. It is said to take the route that the funeral cortège will use, disappearing at the place where the grave will be. They are reputed to be the manifestations of ancestral spirits residing in the churchyard, coming for their kinsperson. In western England, it is taken as a warning only to those who have relatives buried in the parish. If the dead cannot rest, the spirit manifests itself as a light that draws attention to the spirit's plight. Phantom lights also lead searchers to dead bodies. In his *Miscellanies*, John Aubrey wrote that when 'any Christian is drowned in the River Dee, there will appear over the water where the corpse is, a light, by which means they do find the body; and it is therefore called the Holy Dee.' There is the suggestion that Iona may have been considered especially sacred as a result of repeated apparitions of this kind.

SPIRITS OF THE LAND

The northern European folk tradition is particularly rich in the matter of the spirits and apparitions of the land. In Ireland, there are precise and detailed descriptions of each class of spirit. Although the Banshee and the Leprechaun are famed throughout the world, there are countless others, present in almost every element of the landscape and every aspect of traditional life. When treated properly, they bring prosperity to the farm and good catches for fishermen and hunters. But if they are ignored or insulted, then they may play tricks or bring disaster. The fairy folk of Ireland are the Daoine Sidh, 'the good people'. They are said to be either the remnants of the former inhabitants of Ireland, the Tuatha da Danaan, driven to the edge of the otherworld, or fallen angels, neither good enough to be saved nor bad enough to be lost. They live in ancient raths, travel along their own roadways and sometimes attack people or cattle with their fairy darts. They appear most frequently on the high days of the Celtic calendar: Beltane (May Eve), when they fight; Midsummer Eve, when they celebrate; and Lá Samhna (November Eve), when they dance with ghosts and mourn the coming of winter. As William Butler Yeats explains in his *Irish Fairy and Folk Tales*, when the Pagan gods of Ireland were robbed of their worship and offerings, they grew smaller and smaller in the popular imagination until they turned into fairies. Conversely, the Pagan heroes grew bigger and bigger until they turned into giants. But not all Celtic supernatural beings fit into these categories. Outside Ireland, the benevolent Breton being known as Yann-An-Ôd may sometimes be encountered on the seashore, lurking among the sand dunes. Like the ancients' Proteus, he has the habit of shape-shifting, changing from a giant to a dwarf at will.

On the Isle of Man it is customary to put out food, milk and water at night for the Mooinjer-ny-gione-veggey, the 'good little people'; the practice was formerly universal in Celtic lands. In general, the 'good people' are considered to be gregarious, but Celtic lore also knows other species of solitary, independent spirits. Some are helpful, but others are demoniacally dangerous. Leprechauns are the best known, and the most misrepresented. Strictly, they are fairy shoemakers, though the name is used somewhat indiscriminately today to describe any Irish fairy being. The Cluricaunes of Ireland and the Lutins of Brittany are household spirits which, although they will steal food and drink, have their good points, warning off any other potential thieves. The Manx Phynnodderee is a rather similar mischief-maker. In Ireland, the Fear Dearg, the 'red man', appears dressed in crimson. He shares many of the characteristics of the

German *Kobold* and the English hobgoblin, being attached to a locality or house rather than a family. According to Irish stories, this being has a voice that can be likened to the sound of the waves, the warbling of birds and the music of angels. If summoned, he will come to liberate human beings who are trapped in fairy land. The Gruagach is recognized in the north of Ireland and Scotland as a helpful spirit of the farm who tends to cattle, so long as he is placated by offerings of milk and food at his 'dobbie stane', a bullaun that stands at the entrance to the farm. If they are acknowledged appropriately and treated well, these spirits cause no trouble.

This cannot be said for the Fear Gorta, 'the man of hunger', the demonic personification of the *fear gortach* who is greatly feared in Ireland, for he appears during times of shortage or may actually be the bringer of famine. In more prosperous times his place is in the ground, where the hungry grass grows. Like all spirits, he can be placated by gifts of food, as can his Manx counterpart, the Glashten. Equally fearsome demons are the Dublachan, the dark phantoms who appear at places where a death is about to take place. For some reason, they are especially prevalent in Sligo. As night falls in Brittany, a similar being, the Bugul-Noz or 'Night Shepherd', warns the late homecomer to find shelter for the night. Those unfortunate enough to encounter the Breton Ankou or the Manx Keimach when they enter a graveyard have been served with a summons of their own impending death. Another ominous being, the Bean Si (Banshee) manifests as either an aged hag dressed in a winding-sheet or as a beautiful young woman, finely apparelled, aspects of the threefold goddess. She is believed to be an ancestral spirit who serves as a messenger of death for her family descendants, and may be named after the family. 'O'Neill's Banshee' appears at Shane's Castle, the ancestral home of the O'Neills near Lough Neagh. Each family has its own Bean Si, which appears on its own territory, emphasizing the hereditary nature of guardian spirits. Each Celtic family has a guardian spirit, which may or may not be the same as the Bean Si. It dwells in the ancestral homestead, and may be an ancestral spirit, or an otherworldly guardian that was never human. In Manx tradition this is called the Ihiannan-Shee.

The Irish Tash or Thevshi may appear in either animal or human form. Usually attached to a particular locality, it is said to be the spirit of a person who has died violently, either by suicide or at the hands of others. Thevshi are bound to the place, bringing attention to their plight as a lesson to others. In certain places, it was thought that, at New Year, freshly buried corpses would revive and roam the countryside seeking blood.

Cairns were raised on the graves of those suspected of being a Dearg-due or 'red bloodsucker'. The most feared Dearg-due of Ireland was the shade of a woman buried close to Strongbow's Tree in Waterford. In her hag form, the Bean Si is related to the horrible shape-shifting Morrigan and the Bean Nighe, 'the washerwoman at the ford'. This latter death-goddess is a deathly pale ghost-woman, whose apparition at fords washing blood-stained clothing presages violent death. The most terrible manifestation of this deity is as the war-goddess Badb, who haunts battlefields, often in the form of a raven, mutilating corpses.

Fascinating but fatal is the Leanhaun Shee, the 'fairy mistress', who is so hauntingly beautiful that men cannot fail to fall in love with her. If a man should meet her, then through his love for her he is inspired with the power of the bardic arts. However, she is a malevolent muse, for through loving her the Gaelic poets die young. She is restless and will not let them practise their art long on earth. Once a man has fallen for the Leanhaun Shee, there is no escape and the life-force is progressively sucked from his body. Only if another man should take his place can he escape death, but then he also loses his powers and is driven into exile. When one rejects the spirit of the land, one must leave one's own country and wander the world, lost and rootless. Sometimes, as in the case of Eodain, the court poetess of Eugene, king of Munster, the poetic spirit of the Leanhaun Shee comes through a living woman. In that case the poetess does not die, rather she is empowered by it.

Some otherworldly beings are associated with specific things, for example the Lunantishees, who dwell in and guard blackthorn bushes. Under no circumstances should ancestral spirits be disturbed. The Hogboy of Orkney inhabited burial mounds, where they were given offerings of food and drink. If a mound was disturbed in any way, especially by digging, then the Hogboy would cause the local cattle to die. It is a general belief that spirits forced out of their abode by human activity, whether accidentally or with malice, will travel to another suitable place, but only after perpetrating some act of revenge against the culprits. They remind us that, if we do not pay due respect to the earth upon which we live, dire consequences will result.

Images and Temples

The perfect temple should stand at the centre of the
world, a microcosm of the universe fabric, its walls
built foursquare with the walls of heaven.

William Lethaby, *Architecture, Mysticism and Myth* (1891)

EARLY CELTIC religion was both aniconic and atectonic. Deities were not housed in buildings, and there were few figurative images. Dating from the sixth century BCE and later, the Celtic sanctuaries at Entremont, Mouriès and Roqueperteuse had stone structures but were roofless. As late as 278 BCE, the Celts who sacked Delphi were astonished that the Greeks had the audacity to make statues representing the gods. But under first Greek and then Roman influence, both images and roofed buildings were adopted and the Celtic temple came into being. The roofed temple was adopted first by the Celts of Cisalpine Gaul. Livy and Polybius recorded the temples of the Boii and Insubres at Mutina and Milan. The Roman conquest of Gaul, western Germany and Britain led to the erection of temples in the temenoi of Celtic sacred places and in already existing cemeteries. The latter seem to have served as the prototype for Celtic churches which, almost invariably, were shrines of founder-saints or other ancestral heroes.

Although the design of most are known mainly through excavation of their remains in the ground, there are contemporary illustrations and descriptions. Typical Celto-Roman temples were either square, circular or polygonal. An altar of Nantosuelta from Saarburg shows two temples. In her hands the goddess holds two sceptres, one topped with a small square gabled temple, and the other with a circular building with a conical roof. A fine reconstruction of a 'Gallo-Roman' temple exists at the Freilicht-museum at Homburg-Schwarzenacker in the Saarland. It is of the square peripteral type with twelve columns. In certain places, these relatively simple temples were replaced by larger, classical ones, especially in the

Rhineland and the Lower Seine. This may have occurred when a new deity was installed at the Schönbühl at Augst, where the cultus of Cybele superseded the former Celtic divinity worshipped there. It happened again when the cultus of Christ was adopted.

THE PROCESS OF TEMPLE DEVELOPMENT

Things that remain completely unseen by us in our normal state of consciousness are nevertheless capable of exerting a noticeable influence upon the physical world. If we are to take account of this unseen world, we must acknowledge and venerate it. Places where we can contact the otherworld are those where the *anima loci* projects herself into the phenomenal world without the necessity of a special mediator. They can be recognized by sensitive or specially trained people, those to whom traditional society ascribes the power of second sight. But the presence of the divine is only fully accessible to everyone when it is represented by a visible symbol through which some of its mystery may be comprehended. By acknowledging sacred places, we show respect for the *anima loci*, focusing the consciousness on its divine ancestry and spiritual nature.

There is a well-established process of recognition and accretion by which shrines and temples come into being and develop. One of the basic beginnings in the process of recognition of the *anima loci* is the honouring of the sacred tree of life – the indwelling place of the god or goddess who manifests his or her presence there. Upon this tree, and at its foot, offerings were placed. Next, they were protected by a sacred enclosure, a fence erected around the tree. Within this, an offering table and other sacred objects, including aniconic and iconic images, were set. Ceremonies to keep the *anima loci* present were enacted, and the remains of these ceremonies on the material and psychic planes remained to empower the sacred place further.

A reconstruction of part of the Celto-Ligurian shrine at Entremont, Provence, France. The archway containing human skulls and mummified heads is a prototype of the later gateways and standing stones bearing carved human 'Celtic Heads'.

Devotees brought votive offerings to the sacred place and left them there. Animal skins, skulls, bones, horns and antlers, eggs, garlands of flowers, sheaves of corn, flowers and fruit, ropes, nets, tools and weapons were all deemed appropriate. These votive offerings and the remains of sacrifice are the fabric of ornament on temples. Almost every design component of the classical temple derives from one or other of these elements. The carved skulls and garlands reproduce in stone the real ones that hung on former buildings in earlier times. Fully developed temples preserved and revered the original sacred objects rather than abolishing them. The original rocks where rites were celebrated were left exposed within the new building. Temples were erected around stones that contained sacred virtue. The most famous of these in the Mediterranean was the aniconic image of Aphrodite, revered in the shrine at Paphos on Cyprus. It was a meteoric *baetyl* which still exists in the Cyprus Museum at Nicosia. When the places of the elder faith were appropriated by the Christian Church, many revered objects were retained but given a fresh interpretation more fitting to the newer doctrine.

Images of divinity were erected at special places, furthering the process of converting a natural sacred place into an artificial place of worship. Even when it contains no images, a temple houses the earthly manifestation of a divine principle. In a temple it is present permanently rather than sporadically. Once it exists and has been dedicated to a particular deity, that deity no longer needs to be asked to come. It is a place of presence. The development of a natural sacred place might continue with the erection of a holy building, a temple, to house the earthly manifestation of the deity. In its structure the temple should reflect the nature of the deity, so, in their form and symbolism, temples and churches embody the image of the tutelary deity, each of whom is a specific interpretation of the cosmic human being.

The custom of making votive offerings at the place was continued at the temple. The offerings that people left were appropriate to the deity who ruled there. Weapons were deposited in temples of war-gods and agricultural tools in those of field-deities. Small replicas of knives, axes and other symbols of the deity are common, as are ex-votos given in thanksgiving for answered prayers. But where there were no temples, people continued to cast pins and coins into holy wells and hammer nails into sacred trees and posts.

Celtic craftspeople insisted that sacred artifacts should be of sound construction, with a careful choice of materials and careful attention to

The west front of the Romanesque church at Belsen, near Tübingen, Germany, bears both Pagan and Christian symbols. Beneath a cross, the image of Béél, the Celtic god Belenos, is flanked by the heads of a bull, sheep and pigs, perhaps reproducing the appearance of Pagan shrines that displayed the real heads of sacrificial animals.

detailing and finish. Their intrinsic form encapsulated both their func-
tional needs on the material level and their symbolic qualities. Celtic
artists loved multivalent, ambiguous images that could be seen as one
thing from one angle and something else from another one. Here, interpretation depends on the observer's perception as much as the artist's
definitions. In the spiritual realm, this reflects the concept of aspectual
deity, where a single divine being may have many different forms and
appearances and is found in every branch of European Paganism. Celtic
deities have multiple forms and exist in aniconic or iconic forms,
depending on the context in which they are found or into which they
are brought. They may manifest themselves as natural phenomena or be
approachable through natural features in the landscape.

ASPECTS OF CELTIC DIVINITY

A sacred place may be honoured or recognized through the reverence of
various aspects of divinity. There are four general classes of divinity that
may be worshipped at a shrine. The most basic is the *anima loci*, which is
the spirit present in natural surroundings. The *anima loci* may be revered
as such, or may be interpreted through the medium of other archetypes.
Among these are the universal divinities, which include the elemental
powers of Earth, Water, Air and Fire, personifications of qualities such as
love and redemption, and conceptual deities. Imported deities may be
worshipped at a sacred place once recognized as sacred to something else.
These are the manifestations of the *animae* of other places, elements of
which are brought to other sites either by means of a transported sacred
object or by ritual. Those that do not conform with the *anima loci* are on-
lays, more or less in disharmony with the place. Finally, departed human
beings, whose lives were in conformity with a divine ideal, are celebrated
as gods, saints or heroes.

Ancestors, both human and divine, were fundamental to the Celts.
Here, there is no absolute dividing line between mythology and history. As
I noted in the Introduction, Celtic origin-myths are neither poetic inventions nor rationalizations of inexplicable phenomena by primitives. They
are best seen as primordial truths expressed at the highest level comprehensible to humans. We can try to understand them as they are, without
any ideological resolution. There can be no final exegesis, for they are
capable of being interpreted in different ways, all of which have their place.
From ancient times, gods or goddesses were seen as ancestors of families,

clans, tribes and nations, and their sacred places were especially significant to members of that stem. Widespread reverence was paid to the progenitrix, a mother goddess called by various but similar names: Ana, Anu, Danu, Dana or Don. Many rivers are named after her, the greatest of which is the Donau (Danube). In his ninth-century *Glossary* Cormac tells of this ancestral goddess: 'Ana is the mother of the gods of Hibernia, well she used to nourish the gods, from whom is said her name *anae*, that is, abundance, and from whom are called the Two Paps of Ana, west of Luchair [County Kerry], also Buanann, nurse of the heroes ... as Ana was mother of the gods, so Buanann was mother of the Fiann.' Just as the Anglo-Saxon kings counted Woden as their forefather, so Celtic monarchs claimed descent from the goddess Ana and her consort Beli.

Because she is described as the mother of the gods, Ana is clearly an aspect of the primal Great Goddess. In Christian mythology she is Anne, mother of Our Lady, and in English folklore Black Annis, the hag who rules wild country. However she may be named, she appears at different times as one of her three aspects, virgin, mother and old woman or hag, reflecting the three stages of the life of woman. Sometimes these aspects are portrayed as three separate individuals. The Celtic pantheon has three sister goddesses, the Deae Matrones or 'Mother Goddesses'. In Wales, the fairies, from whom inspired people gained esoteric knowledge, are still known by the same name, Y Mamau. Celtic and Celto-Roman representations of the Deae Matrones usually depict them as three women bearing images of growth and fruitfulness such as baskets of apples or horns of plenty. Images from Celtic Pagan shrines of this era include threefold goddesses in the form of the Proximae (kinswomen), the Dervonnae (oak-sprites), and the Niskai (water nixies). They are particularly plentiful in the Rhineland.

The threefold goddess has a place in the British literary tradition. Holinshed's *Chronicle* of 1577, the source for Shakespeare's *Macbeth*, tells of 'three women in wild apparel resembling creatures from an elder world'. Further on, he states that these were none other than the 'Weird Sisters, that is ... the goddesses of destinie'. In *Macbeth*, Shakespeare downgrades the goddesses to the three horrible witches. In general, all triune deities symbolize the basic triadic nature of all processes. Any goddess can be viewed as an aspect of the Great Goddess, among them Brigid, who passed straight into Christian hagiography as a virginal aspect.

Irish myths also recall a father god, called the Daghda, whose by-name, Eochaid Ollathair, means 'All-Father'. His attribute is a cauldron of plenty which signifies the renewal of life. It may have been to him that Julius Caesar was referring when he wrote, 'The Gauls claim, on the authority of the Druids, that their whole race is descended from Dis, lord of the underworld', for the cauldron is a significant symbol of the underworld. Other gods, who again may be viewed as aspects of the All-Father, rule over the weather, warfare, travel, trades and crafts. Under Roman influence, every Celtic deity was equated with some or other variety of the Mediterranean deities with whom they shared common qualities. But until their legends and attributes were recorded in written documents, the goddesses and gods of the Celts were flexible and ungraspable. Once written texts defined the myths, then their stories and attributes became fixed and they entered a literary pantheon. Today, the Celtic divinities have that status, with an extensive literature of description and interpretation. In parallel with this is the non-literary, oral tradition, which today feeds on and feeds into the literary one.

ANCESTOR WORSHIP

If it were not for our forebears we would not exist, so recognition of the fundamental importance of ancestors is the foundation of all religions that have not divorced themselves from physical reality. Ancestor-worship usually involves the preservation and veneration of things considered to be relics. Regardless of the variations in religious doctrines, the consensus on what composes a relic is quite consistent. First, a relic is part of the material remains of a holy person after her or his death, and respect should be shown to it. Second, his or her clothing, and objects such as weapons, tools and utensils used by the holy person may be preserved as relics. Third, objects placed in contact with bodily relics also become empowered. To the early Church, the official definition of an altar was a tomb containing relics. The deposition of a relic or relics was obligatory in the consecration of churches before the Reformation, and in non-Protestant churches this condition still applies. The practice continues the Pagan tradition of making foundation-deposits, either animal or human. In former times, all ancestral human remains were deemed sacred, containing some essence of the personality of the deceased. This remains in the Breton language in the word *relegou*, which means all human bone remains, not just those of saints. Because the bones are the dwelling-place of an aspect of the ancestral spirit, the tomb that enshrines that spirit is a place of worship.

Throughout the world religions assimilate departed worthies into some part or other of the pantheon. The process whereby a human becomes a worshipful divine being has continued from antiquity to the present day. Greek and Celtic kings and Roman emperors became gods, as later Christian priests and heroes became saints. Today, there are many contemporary manifestations of the process, evidence that human society still needs such heroes. The traditional Celtic landscape preserves the knowledge of ancestral goddesses and gods, tombs of mortal ancestors, heroes and priests. A special virtue resides in the presence of the ancestor from whom the local people were descended, or the hero or deity upon

The mounted image of King Gradlon on the cathedral at Quimper in Brittany, which continues the Celtic tradition of ancestor-worship, enshrining notables in sacred places. In Pagan times, the King would have been assimilated into the pantheon as a divine being.

whom they were dependent. Often, they are sited in or overlooking places of communion and decision, with their votive offerings on view. The names and locations of sacred places were rendered in poetic form for retention in the memory, as in the *Black Book of Carmarthen*. Performing one of the main bardic functions, that of record, it contains 'The Verses of the Graves' which recounts the place of burial of around two hundred warriors, kings and famous people of early Britain. Thus, in the Celtic world the physical landscape coincided with the country of the mind, the internal cosmos reflecting the outer one.

In later times, ancestral figures were acknowledged on a more official level. Until the French Revolution, a sculpture of King Gradlon on the Cathedral of St Corentin in Quimper was acknowledged annually. Each St Cecilia's Day the King was sent a drink. A man would climb up the outside of the cathedral to the statue, offer it a drink, and, when the King refused, drink it himself. The glass was then thrown down to the watching crowd below. Anyone who could catch it would be rewarded with a prize. It is said that no one ever did. In the nineteenth century, the influence of Romanticism led to a renewed acknowledgment of ancestral heroes. In 1865 the local authorities erected Millet's gigantic statue of Vercingetorix on the hillside overlooking Alise-Sainte-Reine in commemoration of the Battle of Alesia, where Caesar defeated the Celtic alliance.

VOTIVE OFFERINGS

Closely related to ancestral relics are votive offerings. These may include natural materials, produce, the spoils of hunting, livestock, weapons and craftsmen's tools. The tradition is best known from the Pagan epigrams that record the texts of votive offerings to ancient Greek temples, but it was also a Celtic tradition. Philippus of Thessalonica tells how a retired tradesman deposited his tools in the temple appropriate to his craft. Going blind with age and no longer able to work, Demophon the goldsmith dedicated his tools to Hermes: the bellows that stoked his forge, the file with which he scraped the gold, his double-clawed fire tongs and the hare's pads that picked up the valuable gold-dust. Over four thousand bone slips, many bearing Celtic patterns and believed to be craftsmen's trial-pieces, were deposited at a neolithic chambered tomb at Lochcrew. Once such items had been deposited at a sacred place, they were the property of the deity and could never be used again. Deposition of worn-out military flags and banners in churches continues this practice at the present day.

Celtic Heads. Left: Wakefield, England, medieval. Centre: Halifax, England, 1660. Right:
Holzgerlingen, Germany, c. 500 BCE.

Trophies are another kind of votive offering that left their mark on the landscape. 'Before battle the Gauls generally vow all their spoils to Mars,' wrote Julius Caesar; 'after victory they sacrifice the captured animals and collect everything else together. In many states, on consecrated ground, one sees trophies built of such material; and it is rare that anyone dares to go so far to ignore the claims of Heaven so as to conceal the spoils of war at home or to take them away from a trophy: the sacrilege is punishable by death under hideous torture.'

In Pagan times there was no relic considered unfit to be deposited at a shrine. But once the Christian religion was dominant, certain relics and sacred objects were excluded, especially those things believed to emanate from the otherworld. But to their guardians, ancestral sacred objects are considered no less sacred than those revered by the Church. They are preserved at other ancestral places of keeping, family seats such as castles and manor houses. Dunvegan Castle, for instance, houses three ancestral objects: the twelfth-century Rory Mor's drinking horn, the fifteenth-century Dunvegan Cup, and, most precious of all, the eleventh-century Fairy Flag of the MacLeods.

ORAL AND LITERARY IMAGES

To the modern observer, Christian images differ in an important way from those of Celtic Paganism. The vast majority of Christian images are illustrative of literary texts, whether biblical or liturgical. Pagan images, however, reflect the myths and beliefs of a non-literary society where the mythological narrative was part of oral culture. By definition, in oral culture there can be no fixed version of a narrative. The search for a reliable, fixed version of scripture and thus of myth lies behind literate attempts to define orthodoxy. Oral myth lives in action, word and image. In the oral tradition, mythic image is not an illustration of a literary or ritual text as it is in Christian and later iconography. Here, each image is an independent, individual example or variant of the myth. Pagan images, then, represent the pictorial language of myth, whilst Christian ones are an outgrowth of a literate structure.

Moreover, there is no real distinction between Pagan and Christian images. Throughout the Celtic lands we find a juxtaposition of elements from various sources, each of which reinforces the archetype of sacredness that may be identified with a specific character from Christian mythology. Traditional Celtic images with forerunners in La Tène times mingle with representations of Christian priests and themes from Christian mythology.

A sheela-na-gig from Seir Keiran, County Offaly, Ireland, which has been bored into in the most magical part of the genital region by people seeking curative stone-dust.

159

Countless ancient churches contain within their fabric or churchyards quite remarkable images, of which but a few can be mentioned here. On the island of Inishkeen in Upper Lough Erne, St Fergus's cemetery contains the stone head of a Celtic divinity with antlers. In Caldragh churchyard, we can find a Janus with a stoup for water between the heads, and at Rougham in County Clare is a Tau cross with faces on the upper side. A collection of images on Boa Island, lined up in a roofless twelfth-century church, comprises seven stone figures from around the year 900. They include a sheela-na-gig, a seated man holding a book, and an abbot or abbess with a bell and crozier.

Sometimes the images are called openly by their Pagan names. On the Isle of Man, Kirk Conchan, the church of Onchan near Douglas, has an image depicting the Manx deity, Conchem (identified with St Christopher), as a dog-headed man. Images on the west front of the twelfth-century church at Belsen, near Tübingen, are known in local lore as Little Béél and Big Béél. Little Béél is situated immediately above the west door, whilst Big Béél is higher up, accompanied by the heads of cattle and sheep and a cross. The church stands on an ancient Celtic holy hill north of a venerable linden tree and a *Viereckschanze*.

Perhaps the most obvious continuity of all lies in the sheela-na-gigs, female figures dramatically exposing their genitals. Although many conflicting theories have been expounded about their meaning, images of the female generative and sexual power are not part of traditional Christian iconography, and continuity of Pagan usage is more plausible. Until the Revolution, many French churches of Celtic origin possessed phallic images representing the generative power of man. One of the largest phalli was revered at Toulouse Cathedral. The Church of St Eutrope at Orange displayed a leather-clad wooden phallus, which was resorted to by women wishing to become pregnant. In the Auvergne, the stone of St Foutin at Chapaulieu de Clermont was the focus of the phallic cultus of the saint. His cult was characterized by the display of male and female sex organs made of wax. He was a popular saint, with shrines at Varailles (Provence), where phallic ex-votos were suspended from the chapel ceiling, and at Verdre (Bourbonnais), Viviers (Bas-Languedoc), Bourgdun near Bourges, and at Brest. But because of prudery, many phallic beings and sheelas succumbed to destruction, leaving us today with only a few remaining.

POPULAR SHRINES

Until the traditions were crushed by Protestant puritanism, Celtic people in Great Britain would visit shrines to worship the local spirit. In Ireland and Brittany, as well as in Wales and Scotland, the old gods and goddesses were often worshipped through the medium of Celtic saints – none officially canonized by the Pope in Rome – and revered according to ancient tradition. Most were barely authorized by the Church, for they retained many Pagan or non-Christian characteristics. The sort of religion practised at these shrines was a version of traditional Paganism that had assimilated just enough Christian elements to make it acceptable to the local Church authorities. The theological status of the entities being worshipped was often unclear. Acts of pilgrimage and worship were more matters of ceremonial action than religious theory. At Llanderfel, the deity called Darvel Gadarn was revered in an image 'in which the people have so greate confidence, hope and trust, that they come dayly a pilgrimage unto hym, some with kyne, other with oxen and horses'. His cultus was suppressed in 1538, when the image was confiscated, transported to London and publicly burned at Smithfield. In 1589, John Ansters reported that bullocks were being sacrificed 'the half to God and to Beino' in the churchyard at Clynnog Fawr on the Lleyn Peninsula. Cattle born with 'the mark of Beino' on their ear were literally earmarked for sacrifice at his sanctuary. The custom fell into disuse in the nineteenth century. But this was not the end of popular devotion, for the ancient sacred places of the landscape, such as standing stones, hills and holy wells, were still widely spoken of as shrines of certain goddesses and gods.

Vigorous attention to the spirits of the land flourished in Scotland after the break-up of the Catholic Church. The focus of popular worship at shrines was suppressed, and so people resorted in greater numbers to the older sacred places that had never been taken over by the Christian religion. In the region of Gairloch, the 'old rites' of the divinity Mhor-Ri, 'The Great King' (also known as St Maree, Mourie or Maelrubha), were observed until the nineteenth century. In 1656, officials of the Dingwall presbytery attempted to suppress the observances of Mhor-Ri, 'findeing, amongst uther abhominable and heathenishe practices, that the people in that place were accustomed to sacrifice bulls at a certaine tyme upon the 25 of August, which day is dedicate, as they conceive, to St Mourie, as they call him … and withall their adoring of wells and uther superstitious monuments and stones.' The rites included 'sacrificing at certain times at the Loch of Mourie … quherein ar monuments of Idolatrie', and also the 'pouring of milk upon hills as oblationes'. The cultus was important far beyond the Gairloch region, for strangers and 'thease that comes from forren countreyes' were reported as participants in the 'old rites'. But the presbytery was unable to suppress this popular deity. Writing in 1860, Sir Alexander Mitchell tells us that the 'people of the place often speak of the god Mourie'. Another writer of the same period tells of the god's holy hill, called Claodh Maree, which was the Scottish parallel of Iceland's Helgafell, whose benevolent power was active wherever it could be seen. 'It is believed … that no-one can commit suicide or otherwise injure himself within view of this spot.'

On the island of Maelrubha in Loch Maree, the sacred oak tree of Mhor-Ri was studded with nails to which ribbons were tied. Buttons and buckles were also nailed to it. The oak grew close to a healing well, to which patients suffering from insanity were brought from far and wide. As described on page 73, Thomas Pennant visited Loch Maree in 1774 and witnessed the proceedings in which the derilans, the officiating Pagan priests on the island, had sufferers drink water from the well before they were 'thrice dipped in the lake'. The well is now dry and the island is privately owned.

Parallel with Christianity, worship of the mother-goddess was continued under several names. Until the seventeenth century there were shrines in Brittany kept by old women known as Fatuae or Fatidicae, who taught 'the rites of Venus' to young women. In Wales, the goddess of heaven or mother of all human beings was known as Brenhines-y-nef, who, whilst assimilated with Our Lady, retained the special characteristics of the goddess. In their monumental work, *The Lives of the British Saints*, Baring-Gould and Fisher tell us that in Brittany, the cult of St Anne 'stepped into the place of one of the Bonae Deae, tutelary earth goddesses ... themselves representing the Celtic or pre-Celtic Ane, mother of the gods.'

During the periodic persecutions of vernacular piety, many images were buried. The images singled out for burial were those which, whilst not being totally heretical, were the foci of cults considered dubious by Church officials. In 1640, the Bishop of Tuam ordered the wooden image of St Macdara, considered to work powerful magic at the saint's island on the edge of County Galway, 'to be buried for weighty reasons'. Gwen Teirbron, three-breasted patroness of nursing mothers, an aspect of the bounteous goddess of the earth, was revered particularly in Brittany. Nursing mothers would visit her shrines and offer a distaff and flax to secure a proper quantity of milk for their babies. A major shrine was at the

Image of the three-breasted saint Gwen Teirbron, with her three saintly children. Known in England as St Candida or St White, Gwen Teirbron is a Christian aspect of the bounteous threefold earth mother goddess. From the Church of St Venec, Brittany.

Chapel of St Venec between Quimper and Châteaulin. Unfortunately, in the 1870s most of her images were removed by the priests, 'who have buried them, regarding them as somewhat outrageous and not conducive to devotion'. In Britain, churches dedicated to St Candida, St White and St Wita are sites of former devotion to this singular deity.

Because sacred images were usually buried rather than being burned or broken up, there is always the possibility that they will re-emerge at a time when they can be revered once again. Unearthed images account for a number of important refoundations. Symbolically, when the ground gives up a special stone or an ancient sculpture, it is a real gift from Mother Earth, demanding reverence. In Brittany, there are instances of rediscovered Pagan images of Bona Dea being restored to sanctity and revered as St Anne, the Christian version of Ana, mother of the Celtic deities. In 1625, whilst working in a field at Keranna in the parish of Pluneret in Morbihan, a farmer named Yves Nicolazic had a series of visions of a white lady or a phantom light. He saw them as a sign to dig at the place where they appeared, and unearthed a statue. It was identified as St Anne by the local Carmelites, zealous advocates of the cult of the Mother of Our Lady, who constructed a chapel for the image, which was recarved to be more in keeping with the sensibilities of the time. An annual pilgrimage was instituted, which was most successful. The image was subsequently destroyed by the Revolutionaries, but the annual pilgrimages continue to Sainte-Anne d'Auray, where a basilica was built in the 1870s. Today it is the major shrine of Brittany, where up to twenty thousand people go on the pilgrimage, accompanied by as many as eighty thousand spectators.

The ancient image of Our Lady in the Lady Chapel in the Church of Notre-Dame at Granville in Normandy was found on the shore of Cap Lihoo. It was set up in its own chapel, and is still the focus of a pardon on the last Sunday in July, the 'Grand Pardon des Corporations et de la Mer'. But, at other times and places, the fate of the discovered image was not so fortunate. In 1726, it was reported at Botriphine in Scotland that a wooden image of St Fuomac was honoured annually in May at the local holy well, when its guardian, an old woman, would wash it ceremonially. But around 1800 the image was swept away by a flood of the River Isla. It was washed ashore at Banff, where the local Presbyterian minister had it burned publicly as 'a monument to superstition'.

Sometimes images from the elder faith have continued to be revered without reinterpretation. One that is still revered is the 'Vénus de Quinipily' near Lorient in Brittany. Local lore tells that this female stone figure (6 ft, 1.8 m) is an ancient Pagan image that stood formerly on a holy hill nearby. In the seventeenth century, Christian priests overthrew the image and cast it into the River Blavet. But it was retrieved by the local squire, who re-erected it in 1695 over a fountain. It was recarved in the 1700s, when its prominent buttocks were reduced in size. Until recently, the 'rude stone image' at Inishkea, County Mayo, was dressed in flannel each New Year's Day. It possessed weather-magic powers to produce calm or storm, and honouring it in this way was held to produce good weather for the coming year.

Continuity in the Celtic Church

*The Bards believed that all things were tending to
perfection; when, therefore, they embraced Christianity,
they must on their own principles have viewed it
as a stage in advance of their former creed.*

Rev. J. Williams ab Ithel, *Barddas* (1862)

NOTHING IN this world springs fully formed from nowhere, and
Celtic monasticism is no exception. Despite its seeming isolation,
the Celtic Church was cosmopolitan, incorporating ideas from
the Egyptians Anthony and Pachomius, the Greek Basil and Cassian the
Frank, as well as elements of Celtic and classical Paganism. Celtic monks
travelled widely. They undertook regular visits to the Mediterranean
region, and founded many of the most famous monasteries of mainland
Europe in the old Celtic heartlands. Following the Pagan tradition of
bardism, the Celtic monks laid great store by learning. In the sixth century,
outside the disintegrating Western Empire the Irish schools were the most
famous in Europe. Their pluralistic teachings were quite different from
those of modern fundamentalism, for they did not exclude classical or
indigenous learning as 'Pagan'. Columbanus, whom John of Tritheim
called the 'Prince of Druids', was a lover of the works of Ovid and composed poetry in Greek. Their understanding of geometry was masterful,
evident in the interlace and spiral designs of illuminated manuscripts,
metalwork and stone-carving. Here, the Christian tradition did not extirpate the earlier Pagan vision, but continued and developed it.

It is sometimes assumed that everything altered radically when the
Christian religion was introduced, but this was not the case. Many of the
founding saints of Celtic Christianity were of upper-class birth, just the
sort of people who, in earlier generations, would have become druids or
temple-priests. It was natural that the leaders of the new religion should
have the same career path as their Pagan predecessors. The Celtic perception of the landscape remained unaltered; traditional tribal and clan

territories were maintained. Hunting, animal husbandry, agriculture, transport, building techniques, the punishment of crime, and the arts of warfare did not change.

Neither were the ancient, traditional sacred places altered much. They were in a real sense private property, the inviolable hereditary preserve of the families that owned them. Holy men who became Christians maintained their hereditary rights over the places of their ancestral cults. Like all traditional crafts, Pagan priesthood was hereditary, and the Celtic Church largely maintained the custom, though women were now excluded from many of their traditional religious roles. These holy loci gradually acquired a patina of the newer creed, whilst retaining the essence of the older faith. A syncretic 'dual faith' came into being, in which an official Christian liturgy was supplemented by vernacular Pagan customs and usages. Localized legends of the old gods and heroes were reinterpreted as episodes in the lives of saints. When Christianity was established, the worship of founder-priests, universally called saints (although never canonized by the Roman Church), was added to traditional ancestor- and hero-worship. Their names were remembered in the landscape at locations where they had founded churches, drawn water from the earth, sat in judgment and had slain dragons. With the arrival of Christianity, Celtic sacred places underwent the process of gradual accumulation and change that is history. A few external changes took place, such as stone buildings being erected, and shrines acquiring new names, crosses and an augmented iconography. Tribute was given to the church, and wealth accumulated there instead of being deposited in sacred lakes as before.

The earliest Celtic churches were probably wooden structures. It seems likely that temples, where considered appropriate, were rededicated to the newer religion. Ancient Irish accounts tell of very small buildings with a width-to-length proportion of 2:3, the musical fifth. In the Scilly Isles and Cornwall, the double square is more common. The source of these dimensions can be found in Mediterranean sacred geometry. The *cella* of the Jewish temple in Jerusalem was of this proportion, and Vitruvius wrote that the 'length of a temple must be twice its width'. Because the ground-plan of the church represents the body of Christ, that is, the cosmic human, it is a symbolic manifestation of the Hermetic maxim, 'as above, so below'. In Ireland there are a few ancient stone oratories approximating to this pattern. About a dozen survive in the West, the best preserved of which are the Oratory of Gallerus and that on St MacDara's Island. The former church is a corbelled structure in the tradition that stretches back

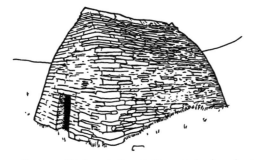

The corbelled drystone Oratory of Gallerus in County Kerry, Ireland, evokes the archaic roots of Celtic Christianity.

to megalithic times, whilst the latter has elements that imitate timber-frame construction.

Owing to the relatively impermanent nature of their material, no ancient timber churches have survived. But it is clear that they existed. *Landnámabók*, the settlement book of Iceland, recounts that one of the Norse settlers, Örlygr Hrappson, was Christian, having been fostered under Patrick the bishop in the Sudereys (Hebrides). *Landnámabók* gives us a rare glimpse at Celtic church foundation customs. When Örlygr went to settle in Iceland, Patrick gave him timber for the church, a plenarium, an iron bell, and also consecrated earth to be laid under the main posts. The church, which was probably prefabricated in the manner of all timber-framed buildings, was dedicated to St Columcille.

The typical Celtic monastery was a circular enclosure containing a number of oratories or churches, traditionally seven. Monastic places where this form can be seen still include Clonmacnois and Glendalough. In addition to places where the sacraments were celebrated, Celtic monasteries contained a number of supplementary structures including clocháns (circular corbelled beehive huts), a holy well, a cross or two, perhaps a bullaun and a round tower. Clocháns or beehive huts are typical of the early monastic settlements. Among the best preserved are found on the Dingle Penisula and Scelig Mhichil. In later times, clocháns and corbelled oratories were superseded by more sophisticated buildings, but the technique was not lost. Henhouses and pigsties, and the Irish baths (sauna-like sweat-houses), were constructed by this technique until they, too, were superseded by modernity. Round towers are the most characteristic structure of Irish Celtic monasteries. Among the best examples are those at Antrim, Ardmore, Cashel, Devenish and Glendalough. They are considered to be primarily defensive in nature, yet they are also significant

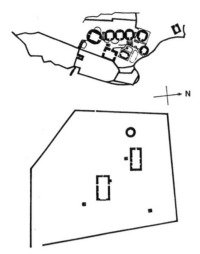

landmarks and serve as geomantic structures that link special places on earth with the heavens.

When the Celtic Church lost its unequal struggle with Rome, the Celtic style of building was replaced by an alternative type of church with apsidal eastern ends after the Roman fashion. As such, organizational and constructional principles from mainland Europe superseded the insular Celtic ones, with the result that the larger churches that survive are either the result of rebuilding on earlier sites, or completely new foundations selected according to the preferences of one of the monastic orders. With this, the Celtic tradition of church building can be deemed to have ended. But, despite this, Catholicization did not

Plans to the same scale and orientation of the Celtic monasteries of Scelig Mhichil and Monasterboice. The first, built on a rocky island, preserves the more organic forms of the drystone clocháns, whilst rectilinear Roman planning and orientation, which finally supplanted the older forms, are apparent at Monasterboice.

affect the ancillary structures, crosses, wells and stopping-places, or most of the practices associated with them.

GEOMANCY IN THE CELTIC CHURCH

Every traditional society in Europe used some form of augury to determine sacred places. The members of the Celtic Church were no exception. Continuing earlier customs, they practised magic and divination. Animal augury was used to discover new sacred places; customary oracles and curses were worked at holy wells; fairy ground and sacred ways were recognized and acknowledged. Even Pagan sacred images were reinterpreted according to Christian canons. The Celtic priests were inheritors of a syncretic tradition that included elements of Jewish, Egyptian, Graeco-Roman and pre-Christian Celtic practices. The *Lives* of many early Celtic priests tell of the magical techniques they employed to discover appropriate sites for new churches, monasteries and burial-places. Foundation was symbolic of sowing or planting anew, and it seems most churches were not, at least in the early days, places of Pagan sanctity. If they had been, signs would not have been needed. New sites need signs. Prominent among the signs sought for the location of new churches or graves was the appearance or behaviour of certain animals. Traditions from the sixth century tell of insects, birds, swine, cattle and deer playing their part as omen-bringers. Some legends are squarely within divinatory practice, whilst others incorporate episodes bordering on the supernatural, or even involving direct divine intervention.

The Breton legend of St Samson tells of the messages that can be read from nature. Wandering around looking for a place to found a new settlement, he came across a spring with a bramble bush on which a number of locusts had settled. He saw the Latin name *locusta* as the omen *locus sta*, 'stay in this place', and founded the monastery there at Dol. On one level, this can be considered a witticism, but on a deeper, symbolic level it is clear that such an event can be taken seriously as an authentic message from the otherworld. And on a third level, it reflects the ancient Greek tradition, where the insect denoted nobility, that is, the ownership of land. Most legends have more than one version, and a similar story is told by Paulus Diaconus of St Gregory the Great.

Many foundation legends contain the symbolism of sowing the earth. When St Carannog arrived as a missionary at Carhampton in Somersetshire, he borrowed a spade from a peasant and began to dig the earth preparatory to building a church. He also carved a pastoral staff from the local wood. A wood-pigeon flew out of a tree, picked up some of the wood-shavings and carried them off. Carannog followed the bird and discovered that it had dropped all of the wood-chips at a certain place in preparation for nest-building. This was the place where he built his church, 'the City of Carrov'. St Dyfrig owned land in south Wales called Inis Ebrdil and sought there for the proper location for his new monastery. On thorn-covered land in a meander of the River Wye he came across a wild white sow with her piglets. This was the omen. As such, he built there the monastery of Mochros, 'the swine-moor'.

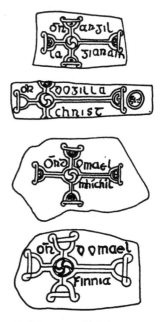

Eighth-century Christian grave-slabs at Clonmacnois, bearing texts that invoke the reader to pray for the soul of the departed.

The wild pig is a symbol of fruitfulness, since in autumn it tramples the seeds into the earth. The boar, which lives in solitude, symbolizes the power of self-reliance in the role of the male warrior in human society. But it is secondary to the sow as a sacred animal. The sow is a symbol of motherhood; she gives birth to many young, and lives wild in matriarchal clans, ruled by the oldest and most intelligent female. Like the earth, the sow also devours her own young. Before the Christian religion was adopted, the sow was sacred to the goddess of vegetation as the divinatory animal of Cerridwen. Emulating their patron, the monkish followers of the ascetic cultus of St Anthony of Egypt were enthusiastic pig-keepers, and in Celtic monastic legend the tradition easily merged with the earlier Pagan swine-cultus. The monks claimed that 'St Anthony's pigs' were special because they could detect hidden sacred objects. They were especially effective in seeking buried bells with the power to ward off evil spirits that caused fires and bad weather.

Occasionally, the omen was given by supernatural agency. St Patrick's disciple, St Ieuan Gwas Padrig, was advised by an angel not to found his church on his own land at Llwyn in Ceinmeirch, but to travel southwards until he saw a roebuck, and to build on the place where he saw it rise. At Cerrig y Drudion he came across the roebuck, and the church was built. Like the sow, the roebuck was the therioform manifestation of a Celtic deity, the lord of the forest, Cernunnos, later known as Herne, patron of hunters. Sometimes unusual animal behaviour was taken as indicating a sacred place. An unusual incident during stag hunting occasionally led to a supernatural encounter, or to the discovery of a sacred place, which was then honoured. To the Pagan Norse, dwarfs sometimes took stag form during the hours of daylight, and the same belief may have existed in Celtic society. In Welsh legend, whilst chasing a deer, Pwyll, prince of Powys, is led to Arawn, lord of the underworld (Annwn). Conmore, count of Poher, was hunting in the parish of Desault near Carhaix, when the stag he was pursuing stopped at the grave of St Hoiernin, and the hounds refused to kill it. The Count ordered a church to be built there in commemoration of the miracle, clearly acknowledging a sacred place of Cernunnos. A comparable legend accounts for the foundation of the two main churches of Zurich, the cathedral (Grossmünster) and the monastic settlement on the other side of the River Limmat, Fraumünster. An image of the stag is carved over a door at the latter. Also in Switzerland the city of Bern, now the capital, was founded after a supernatural hunting incident. In the twelfth century, a knight beheld a miraculous apparition of a bear.

The four sides of the magnificent tenth-century cross at Nevern, west Wales, display the several aspects of non-figurative Celtic art. There are echoes of anthropomorphism in its shouldered form.

This was a therioform apparition of divinity, for to the Pagan Celts the local deity was Artio, a bear-goddess. Somehow, the foundation was blessed by the Church, and bears are kept at Bern to this day, being the 'luck' of the city.

The cattle-cults of St Cornely in Brittany and St Beuno (or Beino) in Wales are among the last remains of a former universal reverence for cattle in Celtic lands. The Cornish nun, St Endelienta, seems to have been a devotee of cows, for she lived only on their milk. In his *Lives of the Saints*, Nicholas Roscarrock recounts how her grave-site was divined: 'When she perceived the day of her death drew nigh, she entreated her friends after her death to lay her dead body on a bed, and to bury here there where certain young stots, bullocks and calves of a day old should of their own accord draw her, which being done they brought her to a place which at that time was a mirey waste ground, and a great quagmire on the top of a hill, where in time after there was a church built dedicated to her.'

In former times, oxen were essential draught animals, and sometimes they were allowed to divine sacred locations. Saints Cadoc, Dunwyd and Tathan resolved to found a church, so they yoked up oxen to the wagon on which they carried their building materials and let them pull it wherever they would. Where the oxen stopped of their own accord was to be their church site. They stopped on an elevated place between two groves. After his conversion, King Gwynllyw the Warrior also resolved to build a church and sought an omen. When he saw a white ox with one black spot on its forehead, he resolved to build there on the high point where it stood. The ox was called Dutelich, and on the place where it stood was erected the Church of St Wooloo (an Anglicization of Gwynllyw).

A similar use of animals is recorded in the search for appropriate burial-places for princes and prelates. When King Clydog of Ewyas was murdered by a rival in love, his body was placed on a cart. Two oxen were yoked to it, and they were driven towards the River Monnow. But when the cart reached the river bank, the yoke snapped and the oxen would go no further. This was the sign that the King should be buried at that place, and the tomb-chapel of Clodock was founded. In a battle at Tintern Ford against the Saxons, Tewdric, the eremitical ex-king of Glamorgan (Morganwg), was mortally wounded. Although his men wanted to take him elsewhere, he forbade them to move him, expressing the wish to be buried on the island of Echni (Flat Holm) in the Severn estuary. The next morning a miraculous wagon drawn by two stags appeared. The dead King was put into the wagon, which carried him to the banks of the Severn, where it stopped. There, at Mathern, below Chepstow, his son Meurig built a tomb-oratory.

Not all churches were built on previously unrecognized places. Indeed, there are numerous instances of Christian priests appropriating Pagan places of worship. Patrick, bishop of the Hebrides, ordered that a church should be built wherever upright stones existed, and throughout Western Europe Pagan temples were readily expropriated from their priesthoods. The Imperial Cathedrals of Germany at Aachen and Speyer are built on major Celtic shrines. Aachen Cathedral stands over the hot springs of the god Grannos, whilst Speyer, the crowning-place of the Holy Roman Emperors, lies over a temple dedicated to the goddess Nantosuelta, at which the threefold goddesses Einbeth, Wilbeth and Barbeth were also venerated. There are numerous other instances. Santyves, in his *Corpus de folklore préhistorique en France*, lists 134 places in Brittany alone where this happened. There are even a few places where converted megalithic structures can still be visited. The Dolmen de la Chapelle at Confolens is still a place of Christian worship. The Chapelle des Sept Saints at Plouaret, also in Brittany, is a Christianized megalithic gallery-grave. In the Channel Islands, the church fabric at Catel, Guernsey, contains megaliths that resemble parts of a megalithic tomb, whilst the passage-grave at La Houge Bie on Jersey has two chapels built on top of it.

SPIRITUAL ESSENCES

Because they are archetypal qualities, spiritual essences are 'otherworldly': their existence is implicit rather than explicit in the material world. Nevertheless, they are real: events, thoughts, ideas, physical objects and places can be understood in terms of these essences. When an individual approximates in her or his life to one of these archetypes, in a real sense he or she is an actual embodiment of that essence. Such a person can become assimilated with that essence in people's minds to such a degree that the essence becomes identified with the historical personage. Thereby a saint or divine human comes into being: finite humanness is transcended, and the historical being enters the realm of timelessness. In this way, the names, beliefs and rituals of the elder faith were conserved through considerable change. Often, in this age of literalism, such beings are mistaken for the actual original of that essence, or the myth is viewed as a deliberate and fraudulent attempt by the Church or others to personify a deity of the elder faith. Neither interpretation is satisfactory.

The cultus of St Brigid of Kildare is the epitome of this process, encapsulating every aspect of Celtic religion. Brigid was a threefold light-goddess, whose festival was Imbolc (1 February). Cormac's ninth-century *Glossary* tells that Brigid was 'A goddess whom the poets worshipped, for very great and noble was her perfection. Her sisters were Brigid, the woman of healing, and Brigid, the smith-woman.' When monotheism was introduced, her attributes were transferred to the saint of the same name. It appears that an individual priestess of Brigid became identified mythically with the goddess herself. Having adopted Christianity, the priestess became the focus of devotion rather than the more abstract female deity. The essences once ascribed to the goddess Brigid were now ascribed to St Brigid, whose sacred places were maintained as Christian shrines. The coming into being of St Brigid was a remarkable accommodation of polytheism in a monotheistic framework, permitting the continuation of women's mysteries under the aegis of patriarchal monotheism.

There were many Brigids, all in some ways aspects of the archetypal Brigid. Christian hagiography lists numerous St Brigids, of whom a not inconsiderable number were the disciples of St Brigid of Kildare, and probably converted adherents of the cultus of the goddess. Traditionally, Brigid is welcomed in at her festival by the symbolic rekindling of the hearth fire after the house has been spring-cleaned from top to bottom. In County Kildare, Brigid's shrine had a sacred flame, tended by a college of women rather like that of the Vestal Virgins in Rome. The flame was kept burning into historical times, being extinguished finally at the dissolution of the monasteries. There have been attempts to rekindle it in the 1990s.

ANCESTRAL CULT-PLACES AND SACRED OBJECTS

Following Greek Pagan tradition and the Christian veneration of the cave of the nativity at Bethlehem, the reputed birthplaces of saints are worshipful locations. At Fouchart, County Kildare, the birthplace of St Brigid is celebrated at a shrine-complex that contains the usual array of sacred places: a holy well, a chapel, a Calvary hill and a rock with an impression said to be that of the saint's knees. The temenos was laid out in 1933 to enshrine a fragment of her head, continuing the ancient Celtic tradition of head-veneration. South-west of the ruins of the old church is the source of St Brigid's Stream, a well where votive rags are hung on the posts and barbed wire that enclose it. Trees and bushes close to other shrines of the Fouchart complex are similarly bedecked with rags.

The act of preserving heads as oracles was practised throughout the ancient Mediterranean, but it is most associated with the Celts. The heads of several gods or heroes feature in Celtic myth, for the skull is the container of the personality, the essential aspect of the dead person. Diodorus Siculus tells us that the ancient Celts used to nail 'these depressing trophies to the door of the house and mummify the heads of the most illustrious enemies'. Similarly, Pliny recounts: 'They used cedar oil to preserve the heads of enemies they held in high regard, and exhibited them to strangers, and they would not agree to return them even for a ransom of their weight in gold. But the Romans ended these customs, as well as to everything connected with sacrifices and divinations that are against our practices.' The sanctuary of the Saluvii at Entremont contained skulls which were embalmed and nailed up as trophies. It was destroyed by the Romans. But in unconquered Scotland and Ireland, this custom continued into the Middle Ages. Giraldus Cambrensis tells of the two hundred Anglo-Norman heads piled before Dermot, the Irish king; and over two centuries later, in 1396, six score heads of a defeated Anglo-Irish force were piled before the ruler, O'Toole. In 1879, a mound dug up at Donnybrook in Dublin revealed that it was a heap of skulls covered over with earth.

The Welsh *Mabinogi* of Branwen tells of Bendigaidvrân, whose severed head was preserved with herbs and carried round Britain for a number of years. Each evening it was set up in a tent, where it spoke oracles. Finally it was returned to the earth at the White Mount, where the Tower of London stands, guarding Britain against invasion. Later, this mythical King was revered by the Church as St Brán Fendigaid, 'the first that brought the Faith in Christ to the nation of the Welsh'. Although this claim has been called 'the most impudent forgery in Welsh literature', it is typical of the change from polytheism to monotheism that the older gods and heroes should be assimilated into the newer pantheon. Another Welsh legend tells of the giant Ysbaddaden, who was slain and whose head was set up on a stake.

Until the present day, the Church has continued the characteristic Celtic head-cultus, albeit in modified form. The presence of the ancestral guardian soul in the head is still recognized today in the West African tradition as well as the Celtic. Because saints are ancestors, both literally and in the spiritual sense, it was natural to continue the preservation of heads of ancestral beings. Head-shrines in Catholic churches in Celtic and former Celtic lands perpetuate the practice of preserving and venerating the heads of ancestors and heroes. An early record of Christian head-veneration was of that belonging to St Piran, which was preserved in a chapel at Perranzabuloe, Cornwall. According to common practice, Piran's body was buried intact beneath the altar of his oratory. But in the tenth century, when the oratory was covered with wind-blown sands, a new chapel was built a mile (1.6 km) away. Then the founder's head was disinterred and taken to the new place to be enshrined as a relic. At the Reformation, the head was removed from its shrine and reinterred with the body. In 1835, the oratory was dug out of the sands once more, and the bones were scattered.

Before they were dispersed at the Reformation, there were several celebrated head-shrines in Celtic lands. Among the most venerated in England were the head-shrine of the Celtic saint, Chad, at Lichfield, and the shrine of the head of St William of York in the Minster. In Wales, St Elios's head was preserved at Llandaff Cathedral, and the head of St Martin of Tours at Cochem in the Rhineland. Among the more grisly examples of this cult we can see today are a group of mummified heads with jewels in the eye sockets that stare from the Baroque altar of the cathedral at Constance in Germany, close to the Celtic holy island of Reichenau. An ancestral relic in the form of a cast of Robert the Bruce's skull is preserved as a national icon in the Scottish National Portrait Gallery. It was made in 1819 when Bruce's tomb at Dunfermline Abbey was opened. An even more modern Celtic head-shrine can be seen in St Peter's Church, Drogheda. The mummified head of Oliver Plunkett, archbishop of Armagh, executed at Tyburn in 1681, is preserved visibly in a gilded glass reliquary. He was made a Roman Catholic saint in 1975.

Another typical Celtic sacred object is the hand-bell. Although they had been put to use at Pagan shrines in France, the typical Celtic bells were copied from those employed by the Egyptian Christians, who had taken them from the monks of Isis. The earliest ones were not cast as bells are today, but fashioned from pieces of bent sheetmetal riveted together. The thirteenth-century tale *Perlesvaus* records their exotic origin, reporting that they were brought to Britain during the Arthurian period. It describes Arthur's amazement on hearing a bell for the first time: 'at this time there were no bells, neither in Greater Britain nor in Lesser; but people were summoned by a horn, and in many places were sheets of steel, and in other places, wooden clappers. King Arthur was amazed by this sound, because it was so clear and sweet. It seemed to him that it came on behalf of God, and he longed to see a bell.'

But the primary function of bells was to drive away spirits. Aubrey, in his *Miscellanies*, tells us that 'the curious do say that the ringing of bells exceedingly disturbs spirits'. This is clear from another passage in *Perlesvaus* which tells how Arthur, Gawain, Launcelot and their squire spend the night in a decayed house which is the target of nightly assaults by demons. The knights are compelled to fight against the evil spirits: 'And when they were in the thick of battle, they heard a bell sounding, and immediately the demons of the night fled rapidly.' Celtic bells are divine instruments of sacred power. Priests used them to drive away unwanted spirits from sacred places, and to attract worshippers. Metal breaks harmful magic, and noise drives away demons. The evil spirits that flock around the dying and dead are kept at bay by ringing the 'passing bell'. Solemn oaths were sworn on bells, and they also empowered curses and exorcisms.

All sacred Celtic objects remain the property of the family whose ancestor was the original owner. Where the family has not died out or abdicated its duties, the office of maer, coarb or dewar, the hereditary keeper, is maintained. In former times, ancestral land was deemed to be the property of the object, and, in return for the solemn duty of bell-keeping, the maer received the income from the land. Sadly, there are few hereditary keepers still with bells, most famous ones now being in museums. The bell of Cumasnach is still in the possession of its keepers at Roscommon. The career of Clog-an-Eadbacta Phatraic, 'The Bell of St Patrick's Will', is typical. Originally, it was buried with St Patrick, but was disinterred after sixty years. Until 1441, the hereditary keepers were the O'Mellans. It is now kept in the National Museum in Dublin. Another celebrated Celtic bell is the Skellat in the Municipal Museum in Dumbarton. Ancient Celtic bells are extant in France, Ireland, Germany, Scotland and Switzerland. Most of them are now in museums, though a few, such as St Gwynhoedl's at Llangwnnadl church, are still retained in their proper keeping-places.

THE BREAKDOWN OF SANCTITY

Paradoxically, it was not Celtic or even Catholic Christianity that led to the comprehensive destruction of Celtic sacred places, rather it was the Reformation. When the Roman Catholic Church was suppressed in Britain, sacred places were deliberately destroyed for being alleged objects of superstition. Both Catholic and Pagan observance were extirpated together. A Scottish Parliamentary Act of 1581 epitomizes the attitude of the Puritans:

> The Dregs of Idolatry yet remain in divers Parts of the Realm by using of Pilgrimage to some Chapels, Wells, Crosses, and such other Monuments of Idolatry, as also by observing the Festal days of the Saints sometime Named their Patrons in setting forth of Bon-Fires, singing of Carols within and about Kirks at certain Seasons of the Year.

The process was protracted and thorough. In 1802, a Welsh bard lamented the effect of evangelical religion on folk culture. 'The sudden decline of the national Minstrelsy, and Customs of Wales, is in a great degree to be attributed to the fanatic impostors or illiterate plebeian preachers, who have too often been suffered to over-run the country, misleading the

Left: Panel from the shrine of St Mogue. Right: The eleventh-century shrine of the bell of St Cuilleann, formerly kept in a hollow tree in the parish of Glenkeen, County Tipperary, Ireland, was used until the eighteenth century as a sanctifier of oaths.

part of the common people from their lawful Church; and dissuading them from their innocent amusements, such as Singing, Dancing and other Sports and Games,' wrote Edward Jones in *The Bardic Museum*. 'I have met with several Harpers and Songsters, who actually had been prevailed upon by those erratic strollers to relinquish their profession, from the idea that it was sinful. The consequence is, Wales, which was formerly one of the merriest and happiest countries in the World, is now one of the dullest.'

Fortunately, the coherence of family and bardic traditions was a check against cultural genocide. Traditional Celtic society was underpinned by hereditary *aos dana*, 'men (and women) of art' – poets, musicians, craftsmen, navigators, lawyers and healers – whose knowledge of everything from the land to the law was essential. Relics of Celtic saints and certain sacred places were often private property on loan to the Church, and passed back to the heir of the saint to whom they belonged. Christian relics, such as croziers, bells, books and even bones, went back from Church ownership to the ancestral family. In many localities, guardian families had preserved Pagan and non-Christian sacred objects and places. To them were added the relics and sacred places abandoned by the Protestant Church, producing a syncretic, vernacular religion composed of various elements. It is this religion with no name that exists today in local tradition and custom wherever it continues in the Celtic lands.

POSTSCRIPT

Out of the Wasteland

THE DOWNGRADING and destruction of the sacred landscape is one of the less attractive results of modernity. Aesthetically, it is deplorable, but this is only the outer aspect of a more serious problem. Psychologically, sacred landscapes are humane places that support the human psyche. When they are damaged or destroyed, a significant part of human life is erased. In symbolic terms, the medieval Arthurian story *The Elucidation* tells us much about this problem. At certain sacred stopping-places, holy wells and hills called *puis*, there lived maidens who would refresh tired travellers with food or drink. One had only to go there and ask, and it would be brought out in a golden bowl. But then a king called Amagons abused the privilege. He raped one of the maidens and stole her bowl. At once, everything changed. Every stopping-place became deserted and the bounty ceased. But that was not all, for the whole land went to waste: nothing would grow or thrive and the bonds of human society were dissolved. King Arthur's knights took upon themselves the task to rediscover the vanished *puis* and to restore the land. They prayed to God to re-establish them and thereby revive the country, but it was useless. The land remained waste; nothing would grow or thrive. At its roots the destruction was spiritual, and the only way that the *puis* could be re-established was by rediscovering the Holy Grail, which, if brought to the right place, would through its divine power revivify the *puis* and hence restore the land and people to their former flourishing condition.

Although this legend originates in remembrances of the historic 'Ruin of Britain' in the mid-fifth century, when in a generation, from being a prosperous Roman land of peace and plenty, the country was laid waste by famine, plague and invasion, the archetype of the Wasteland can be understood at a deeper symbolic level. The Wasteland comes when the spiritual is abandoned in favour of the material. Inner nature is rejected and eternal truths are forgotten. When respect for the old ways is lost, it is rarely replaced with something of equal value; rather, it erodes the very fabric that sustains life. Much of modern science and technology ignores our place within the natural order; continual encroachment threatens to disrupt the delicate balances upon which life on this planet depends.

This dislocation is recognized by the increasing number of people who are attempting to reclaim a harmonious relationship with the world. But it is a mistake to deny the reality of the modern world by making some vain attempt to reconstruct the lost past. Attempts to reclaim the Wasteland by re-creating bygone times cannot succeed, for they demonstrate a lack of recognition of the nature of present conditions. Once traditional ways are destroyed, they cannot be restored from the outside, for the essential conditions that once sustained them exist no longer. If the sacred landscape is to be re-created in those places where it has been destroyed, a new tradition must develop whose inner essence expresses itself in ways appropriate to existing conditions. Spirituality is inherent in nature. It has not gone away; it is still there for anyone who seeks it. Where it continues in existence, the Celtic sacred landscape serves to remind us that there are viable alternatives to the spiritual Wasteland.

Throughout the millennia, the ever-flowing patterns of Manred have continually brought new forms into being, and they will continue to do so as long as the spirit that informs them remains vital.

Gazetteer

of Notable Celtic Sacred Places

IT IS NEITHER possible nor desirable to list every known Celtic sacred place in a gazetteer. However, this list contains significant places in the landscape of present-day Celtic countries, and also in territories formerly inhabited by Celtic people. In this book I have presented an overview of Celtic sanctity in the landscape, but this list of places is not intended to imply that there is some kind of transcendent overall 'structure' connecting them all together. Such a viewpoint is the result of a certain kind of human perception, not an objective reality: in terms of immediate experience, no place is more important than any other, for all are images of paradise.

Although it is inherent in the nature of national and international organizations to list and categorize, designating certain places to be so-called 'heritage sites', complete with reference numbers, it is meaningless to compare the essentially unquantifiable manifestations of sacredness with one another in some sort of 'league table' of importance. Large and impressive complexes need not have more value spiritually than small oases of sanctity. Unfortunately, the hierarchical structure of established religions often imparts elevated importance to such places as 'great centres' of worship as compared with 'minor shrines'.

Occasionally, on visiting a Celtic sacred place, one may find that it has been desecrated or destroyed. Modernity, to which nothing is sacred, knows no means of distinguishing the sacred from the profane, and if a sacred thing or place is 'in the way', then it is obliterated. Sacred places which, in some way, have become famous escape obliteration, but their fate is equally bleak, for fame often destroys that which it celebrates. The way in which rocking stones were destroyed is typical. There is an ever-present danger that, once a place becomes famous, the pressure of visitors causes it to lose its more subtle qualities, and it is reduced to a spectacle.

A spectacle is created when people focus their consciousness upon a single aspect of reality, disregarding all else. Spectacle lays an unbalanced emphasis upon the relevance of what is being viewed. Once a sacred place is treated as a spectacle, people will go there to see it as an object that they do not experience. All too often, visitors arriving at a so-called 'ancient monument' are drawn straight to the information signposts at the entrance rather than to the place itself: their perceptions and impressions are moulded by what they read. By visiting the place unmindfully, they have no relationship with its individual character. Their experience is primarily visual: they have not partaken of the spirit of the place. They have not been participants in its mysterium.

It is clear that, to prevent their destruction, certain places should be left alone by outsiders, to be visited only by their guardians and local devotees. A vast influx of tourists can easily destroy for ever a sacred atmosphere, as has been demonstrated by the popularization of Stonehenge almost to the point of destruction. It is evident that, when people go to a sacred place for non-spiritual reasons, there is a great probability that they will not respect it appropriately. Their behaviour is quite different from that of someone who does respect the sanctity of the place. It is important to treat all sacred places with respect, to visit them in a respectful frame of mind, for these are places of spirit. When we go to a sacred place, we should not be intrusive, but should approach it with due reverence, in harmony with the *anima loci*.

All grid-references are from the Ordnance Survey map of the relevant area.

Ireland

Ahenny, Kilkenny, X 2413. At the monastic settlement of Kilclispeen are two eighth-century high crosses. The damaged North Cross is a remarkable sun-wheel with five prominent bosses, a finely carved wheel and a conical omphalos-like capstone.

Altadeven, south-east of Augher, Tyrone, H 2635. In Favour Royal Forest are the chair and well variously dedicated to St Brigid or St Patrick. The chair is a large rock carved into a seat. The well is below it. Until recently this was a site of Lammas celebrations.

Ardboe, Tyrone, H 2937. Cross with biblical figures, reputed to be the finest high cross in the north of Ireland.

Ardmore, Waterford, X 2107. South-east of Ardmore is the complex of St Declan's monastery. Dating from the sixth century, his original oratory still stands. There is a holy well, the saint's grave, cathedral ruins and a twelfth-century round tower (88 ft, 29 m tall). At the southern end of the beach is St Declan's Stone, a 'mother-stone' (puddingstone boulder) that in legend came from St David's in Wales.

Armagh, Armagh, H 2834. Seat of both Catholic and Protestant archbishops of Ireland, Armagh is named after the fourth-century BCE legendary Queen Macha, whose fortress, Ard Macha (Macha's Height), was here. The Pagan sanctuary of Emania, seat of the Ulster kings for more than six hundred years, is at Navan Fort, 2 miles (3.2 km) west of the Protestant cathedral.

Athleague, Roscommon, M 1827. Two miles (3.2 km) north-west of Athleague is the Castlegrange Stone, a boulder carved with La Tène-type spirals.

Augher, Tyrone, H 2535. Queen Baine of Clogher is said to be buried in a chambered cairn at Augher in Knockmany Forest.

Ballineaning, near Ballyferriter, Kerry, Q 0310. East of the oratory ruins is St Molaga's Well.

Ballinskelligs, Kerry, V 0406. Killerelig, the remains of a classical anchoritic monastery, stands inside a ring-ditch. It comprises the remains of a corbelled oratory, two clocháns, a souterrain and cross fragments.

Ballymoreagh, west of Dingle, Kerry, Q 0410. A complex including St Manchán's holy well, oratory and grave.

Ballynacarriga, Cork, W 1205. The castle at Ballynacarriga, near Dunmanway, built by Randal Og O'Hurley in 1585, has a sheela-na-gig on an external wall.

Ballynana, Kerry, Q 0310. The Oratory of Gallerus is one of the most perfect remains of Celtic Christianity. It is a dry-stone building with a corbelled roof rising directly without break from the walls. It has a door at the west end and a small window to the east.

Ballyvourney, Cork, W 1107. The sacred complex at St Gobnat's contains the holy well, St Gobnat's Grave, a sheela-na-gig, three ogham stones, and the remains of a pre-Christian building, St Gobnat's House. Crutches and offerings are left at the grave, whilst the well has its annual pattern. St Gobnat is the Christian version of the Pagan deity of metalworking, Gobniu.

Banagher, Londonderry, H 2640. In the churchyard is the House of the Dead, the tomb of St Muirdeach O'Heney, from which the famous curative Banagher Sand is obtained.

Blarney, Cork, W 1607. Three miles (4.8 km) north-west of Cork, beneath the battlements of Blarney Castle, is the Blarney Stone. To receive its gift of speech, one must kiss it.

Boa Island, Lower Lough Erne, Fermanagh, G 2136. In the graveyard of Caldragh at the west end of the island is a Pagan Janiform stone figure and another image called 'The Lusty Man'. Lined up in a roofless twelfth-century church is a collection of seven stone figures from around 900. They include a sheela-na-gig, a seated man holding a book, and an abbot or abbess with bell and crozier.

Brandon Mountain, north of Dingle, Kerry, Q 0411. A holy mountain (3127 ft, 1025 m) sacred to St Brendan, whose oratory and holy well can be reached by footpath from Tiduff. Stone circles indicate the earlier Pagan sanctity of the mountain.

Brideswell, Roscommon, M 1926. A pattern is held at Bride's Well here on the last Sunday of July, when a perambulation visits several stopping-places. The waters are accessible in a ruined bathhouse, constructed in 1625 for Sir Randall MacDonnell, whose wife was made fertile by the holy well.

Brugh na Boinne, Meath, O 3027. In a meander of the River Boyne is an area of great sanctity, in which are fifteen neolithic passage-graves, including Dowth, Knowth and Newgrange, places revered by the later Celts and resorted to for rites and ceremonies on the holy days of the Celtic year.

Bullaun, Galway, M 1622. To the west of Bullaun is the celebrated La Tène-style omphalos known as the Turoe Stone.

Burial Island, off the Ards Peninsula, Down, J 3636. One of the numerous Celtic cemetery-islands, Burial Island has the privilege of being the most easterly part of Ireland.

Burt, Donegal, C 2342. Near Bridge End on the N13 is the church of St Regnus at Burt. Consecrated in 1967, it follows the circular plan of Grianán of Aileach, a hill-fort directly above the church. Labyrinths are present as doorhandles, and also on a free-standing wall there are plaques with a labyrinth and sacred images.

Cardonagh, Inishowen, Donegal, C 2444. West of Cardonagh is the Donagh Cross, otherwise called St Patrick's Cross, thought to be the oldest low-relief cross still standing in Ireland.

Castlebaldwin, Sligo, G 1731. The enormous Heapstown Cairn near Castlebaldwin is reputed to be the burial-place of a Pagan king.

Castledermot, Kildare, S 2818. Castledermot, named after St Diarmuid, who founded the monastery here around 800, possesses two fine high crosses, the north one having particularly fine spiral carvings on its 'holy mountain' base.

Castlekieran, Meath, N 2627. St Ciarán's Well is visited at midnight on the first Sunday in August. Pilgrims use lights to glimpse the supernatural trout, visible only at this time.

Churchtown, Antrim, J 3038. On the shore of Lough Neagh, east of Cranfield Church ruins, is St Colman's Well, the source of the much-prized amber-like Cranfield Pebbles, which are believed to have the power to save women from danger in childbirth and to prevent men from drowning.

Clogher, Tyrone, H 2535. Clogher is so named as the keeping-place of Clogh-Oir, the 'Gold Stone', a gold-covered Pagan image. In the sixth century it was the centre of the kingdom of Oriel.

184

Ireland

Behind the cathedral is the hill-fort of Rathmore, inauguration-place of the kings of Oriel.

Clonmacnois, Offaly, N 2023. The most celebrated place of the Celtic Church in Ireland, founded by St Ciarán in 548 on royal ground given by King Dermot. The temenos contains two round towers, several churches, several fine Celtic high crosses and a cathedral. There is a holy well, near which is a thornless hawthorn tree upon which pilgrims hang offerings. A pattern is held on the first Sunday in September.

Cloughballybeg, Cavan, N 2628. East of Virginia is St Kilian's Well, the birthplace of the seventh-century St Kilian, founder of the monastic city of Würzburg in Bavaria.

Coolineagh, near Coachford, Cork, W 1407. A Celtic well-stone complex containing St Ólann's Well, north-east of the ruined church of Aghabulloge. It is in a well-house overshadowed by a thorn tree. Nearby is the stone called St Ólann's Cap and also a rock with incised footprints. The pattern of St Ólann's Well is held every 5 September.

Craggaunowen, Clare, R 1417. Three miles (4.8 km) east of Quin is the castle of Craggaunowen, whose grounds contain a modern reconstruction of a typical Celtic hill-fort and crannog.

Creeslough Church, near Letterkenny, Donegal, C 2141. This is an example of modern reflective geomancy. It has a roof whose form imitates that of the hill which overlooks it.

Croagh Patrick, Mayo, L 0928. Off the R335, west of Westport, is Cruach Phádraig (2510 ft, 765 m), Ireland's primary holy mountain, topped by a chapel. It is the focus of pilgrimage on St Patrick's Day, either from the church of Leckanvy or from Murrisk Abbey.

Cushendall, Antrim, D 3242. Tieveragh Hill, a volcanic plug near Cushendall, is reputed to be a powerful 'gentle' place, the local fairy hill. West of the A2 is Ossian's Grave, the reputed site of the Celtic hero's grave.

Devenish, Fermanagh, H 2234. Daimh Inish, the island of Oxen in Lower Lough Erne, is the holy island associated with St Molaise. It contains several interesting ruins including the House of St Molaise and Teampull Mór, as well as an unusual cross and a monastic museum.

Downpatrick, Down, J 3534. St Patrick's grave is marked by a monolith of Mourne granite in the cathedral churchyard. At the Wells of Struell, 1½ miles (2.5 km) east of Downpatrick, is a notable well-complex comprising four curative holy wells. Today, there is a circular drinking well, a quadrangular eye-well, a ruined church and separate bath-houses for women and men. It is a place of pilgrimage every Midsummer Eve and Eve of Lammas.

Drumcliff, Sligo, G 1634. The grave of William Butler Yeats is in the churchyard here.

Dungiven, Londonderry, C 2641. South of Dungiven is the priory church, close to which is the Wart Well, a bullaun beneath a rag-bearing whitethorn.

Durrow, south of Kilbeggan, Offaly, N 2323. North-east of Durrow Abbey is a tenth-century high cross and the holy well of St Columba, whose pattern is on 9 June.

Dysert O'Dea, R 1218. A church, with a high cross with interlace and zoomorphic figures, and a stone representing St Tola, the eighth-century founder.

Fahan, Buncrana, Donegal, C 2343. Four and a half miles (7 km) south of Buncrana at Fahan is St Mura's Cross, a stele with striking interlace and human figures, and another cross-slab built into a roadside wall.

Fallmore, Mayo, F 0631. A complex of St Derivla lies at the southern end of the Mullet Peninsula. It includes a church, 975 feet (300 m) south of which is St Derivla's Vat, a holy well, and St Derivla's Bed.

Faughart, Louth, N 2929. A shrine set up in 1933 to commemorate the legendary birthplace of St Brigid in the fifth century.

Fenagh, Leitrim, H 2130. At Fenagh, three miles (4.8 km) south of Ballinamore, is the site of St Caillín's monastery where *The Book of Fenagh*, now in Armagh Library, was compiled by Tadg O Roddy, of the family that were the coarbs of St Caillín's bell.

Ferns, Wexford, T 3015. A monastic enclosure. Outside the churchyard is the nineteenth-century well-house of St Mogue's Well. Older Celtic heads from Clone are incorporated into the stonework, making it a head-well.

Finglass, Dublin, O 3123. The chalybeate holy well of Fionn-Ghlais, a remedy for eye ailments, was an important resort in the eighteenth century.

Fore, Westmeath, N 2527. Next to the church, the holy well, Tobhar Féichin, comes from an underground stream flowing from Lough Lene.

Glendalough, Dublin, T 3119. The Vale of Glendalough is a classic Celtic sacred landscape, 'The Valley of Two Lakes'. Around the lakes are many sacred buildings associated with the sixth-century monastic settlement of St Kevin. They include a round tower (108 ft, 33 m), ruins of a cathedral and several churches, St Kevin's Cross (*c.* 1150), St Kevin's Kitchen, a two-storey oratory with a uniquely Irish roof construction. Near the confluence of streams east of the

Lower Lake is a bullaun. To restore one's health, one should visit the Deer Stone on the Sunday, Tuesday and Thursday of the same week, and circumambulate it sunwise on bare knees seven times on each occasion. Like some Christian holy islands, when it was a monastery women were forbidden to enter. St Kevin's Road (formerly marked by the labyrinthine Hollywood Stone) runs to Glendalough from Hollywood for 14 miles (22.5 km) through the Wicklow Mountains. Part of it is followed by the L107 road.

Glen of Aherlow, Tipperary, R 1913. At Ardane on the southern side of the Glen of Aherlow is the ovoid sacred enclosure called St Berechert's Kyle. It contains two ancient crosses, a bullaun, the saint's holy well and over fifty cross-slabs set on the drystone walls.

Gortahork, Donegal, B 4319. The sacred boulder, Cloch Cheannfaoladh, is in the grounds of Ballyconnell House at Gortahork. Like the stone of Beuno at Clynnog Fawr, it contains a red vein, said to be the blood of Faoladh, who was beheaded here by Balor of the Evil Eye.

Grianán of Aileach, Londonderry, C 2341. A concentric hill-fort with three stone ramparts stands on top of a hill (803 ft, 244 m). It was the capital seat of the O'Neills, kings of Ulster.

Holywell, Belcoo, Fermanagh, H 2034. A mile (1.6 km) north of Belcoo is Holywell (Temple Rushin), site of pilgrimages around Lammas. There are a number of sacred stopping-places, a bullaun, a holy well of St Patrick and an ancient cross.

Inishcealtra (Holy Island), in Lough Derg, Clare, R 1618. Another 'Holy Island', occupied by St Caimin in the seventh century, it is a fine example of an old Celtic monastery. A round enclosure contains the remains of four churches and the Cross of Cathasach (*c.* 1094). There is a round

tower and two enigmatic buildings, the Temple of the Wounded Men and the Anchorite's Cell, probably Pagan in origin. Boat access is from Mountshannon.

Inishkeen, in Upper Lough Erne, Fermanagh, H 2233. Three miles (4.8 km) south-east of Enniskillen in Upper Lough Erne is the island of Inishkeen. St Fergus's cemetery contains an antlered stone head of a Celtic Pagan divinity.

Inishmurray, Sligo, G 1535. Uninhabited since 1948, the island of Inishmurray is named after St Molaise and contains numerous remains of Celtic religion. Here is a Pagan cashel (133 x 169 ft, 41 x 53 m), showing how a Celtic monastery was made at an older site. It contains a clochán and 3 oratories, Teach Molaise (ninth century), Teampull Molaise and Teampull-na-Teinidh (The Temple of Fire), 3 pillar-stones, 2 holy wells and 2 bullauns.

Inishtooskert, Blasket Islands, Kerry, Q 0210. This uninhabited island contains the ruins of a church of St Brendan the Navigator, 4 clocháns and 3 stone crosses.

Kells (Ceanannas Mór), Meath, N 2727. The remains of a famed monastery founded by Columba around 550. Devastated by raiders on six occasions, the monastery was dissolved in 1551. In the marketplace is a high cross, substantially intact in its original socket, a good example of the proper geolocation of the cross at the omphalos of the town. The churchyard contains a slab with an ancient sundial marked to show the eight tides of the day, also a round tower, close to which is a Celtic cross with a Latin inscription. Next to the church is another Celtic cross, of interest because it is unfinished and shows the crosswright's technique. Up the hill is St Columba's House (c. 807), a prime example of the unique Irish-style roof construction using vaulting and corbelling.

Kilcolumb, Kilkenny, S 2612. Close to the ruins of Kilcolumb Church, 6 miles (10 km) north-east of Waterford, is Cloch Cholaim, a boulder with bullauns said to be the imprints of the head and knees of the praying St Colm. Water from these depressions is used to treat headaches.

Kildare, Kildare, N 2721. Site of the fire-shrine of St Brigid of Kildare (Cill-Dara, 'the Church of the Oak-Grove'). Her sacred fire was tended here, with few interruptions, by a college of nuns until the Reformation. The foundations of the 'fire-house' can be seen to the north-west of the cathedral.

Kilfenora, Clare, R 1119. An eleventh-century cross, which, with that at Dysert O'Dea, is a prime example of the type where a full-length Christ is carved on the cross, making the Celtic cross into a crucifix.

Killabuonia, Kerry, V 0407. St Buonia's Well is part of a sacred complex, near a cairn and the Priest's Grave. There is a pattern which includes a ninefold perambulation of the holy well.

Killaloe, Limerick, R 1717. St Flannan's Oratory at Killaloe is one of the few examples of a church with the unique Irish roof construction using barrel-vaulting overlaid by a corbelled roof. In the churchyard is Thorgrim's Stone (c. 1000), a cross-shaft with an inscription both in runic and ogham. Beside the Catholic church is the reconstructed oratory of St Moluaig, removed from Friar's Island during hydroelectric work in 1925, when the lough's level was raised.

Killeany, Inishmore, Aran Islands, L 0820. South of Killeany on the island of Inishmore (also called Aranmore) is the sixth-century church of Teampull Bheanáin (Benen – St Benignus). The church contains many large stones which indicate its location on a former megalithic site. The Aran Islands contain over forty Pagan and early Christian remains.

Killinagh, near Blacklion, Cavan, H 2033. The monastic settlement at Lough Macnean Upper is a good example of the Celtic sacred landscape, which brings together elements of Pagan, Christian and vernacular religion. At Killinagh is a megalithic tomb called St Brigid's House; St Brigid's Well (Toberbride); and St Brigid's Stones, cursing stones in bullauns.

Killycluggin, Cavan, H 2231. Three miles (4.8 km) south of Ballyconnell is a stone circle with the remains of a phallic megalith with La Tène-type incised work. It is possible that this was the Pagan sacred place of Crom Crúaich, profaned by St Patrick.

Kilmacduagh, Galway, M 1420. The remains of one of Connaught's premier monasteries, founded by St Colman MacDuagh in circa 600, containing a cathedral, several churches and a round tower.

Kilmacrenan, Donegal, C 2142. The Rock of Doon was the inauguration-place of the O'Donnels. South of it is the Doon Well, dedicated to St Columba, who founded the church at Kilmacrenan. At the well is an ex-voto pile of walking-sticks and crutches.

Kilmanagh, Kilkenny, S 2315. The ruins of the monastery contain St Nadán's Well. The ancient wooden image of the saint is preserved at St Kieran's College in Kilkenny.

Kilronan, Roscommon, G 1931. West of Drumshambo, to the east of Lough Meelagh, close to the ruins of the church, is Lassair holy well. Beside the stream that issues from the well is St Ronan's Holy Font, in which pilgrims wash before drinking water from the holy well itself. The blind bard Turlogh O'Carolan (1670–1738), composer of the melody to

which were later added the words of 'The Star-Spangled Banner', is buried in Kilronan churchyard.

Knock, Mayo, M 1428. A concrete basilica serves the pilgrims who flock to the site of multiple apparitions in August 1879 in search of revelation or cures.

Knockainy, Limerick, R 1316. Cnoc Áine, the holy mountain of the goddess Áine, overlooks Knockainy. Until 1879, men carried *cliara*, burning brands of hay and straw on poles, to circumambulate the three summit tumuli, Mullach an Triúir, sunwise. Also, the Aoinach Áine, a fair to celebrate the commencement of harvest, was held here.

Knockgraffon, Tipperary, S 2012. Near Cahir is the motte, the 'Throne of Majesty' holy hill that was the crowning-place of the kings of Munster.

Knocknarea, Sligo, G 1633. The cairn at the summit of this holy hill is reputed to be the burial place of Queen Maeve of Connacht. Nearby is a stone labyrinth constructed in 1988.

Lemanaghan, Offaly, N 2122. East of the church at Lemanaghan, north-east of Ferbane, is St Manchán's Well, linked to the 'abbey' ruins by an ancient holy road or causeway.

Limerick, Limerick, R 1515. The town contains the Treaty Stone, an ancient stone of agreement, at which the Treaty of Limerick was authorized.

Lough Gur, Limerick, R 1614. A ritual landscape dotted with dolmens, menhirs, cairns, passage-graves, stone circles and other stone structures. The lake contains several crannogs. The Lios, Ireland's largest stone circle, is here.

Loughrea, Galway, M 1622. Four miles (6.4 km) north-east of Loughrea is the Turoe Stone, a phalloid omphalos-stone bearing La Tène-style carvings.

Mám Eám, Galway, L 0825. The holy well of the mountain pass, resorted to at Lughnasa, and the rock-cut St Patrick's Bed are here.

Monasterboice, Louth, O 3028. A Celtic monastery founded by St Buithe (Boethius), containing 2 churches, 3 crosses and a round tower. Muirdach's Cross is one of the most celebrated Irish high crosses (*c.* 923), a crucifix-sunwheel with 'world mountain' base and 'heavenly house' top-part. The north and west crosses are also particularly noteworthy.

Moone, Kildare, N 2719. In the grounds of Moone Abbey is the Moone Cross, over 16 feet (5 m) tall, whose base bears a Crucifixion scene, whilst the sunwheel head has a fourfold spiral pattern.

Naas, Kildare, N 2922. Nás na Riogh, 'The Meeting-Place of the Kings', formerly the capital of the kings of Leinster at a rath close to the present town.

Navan Fort, off the Caledon to Killylea Road, close to Armagh, Armagh, H 2834. It was occupied between around 700 BCE and 332 CE as the stronghold of the kings of Ulster. Emain Macha, Queen Macha's Palace, crowned the summit, where there was a Pagan temple measuring 120 x 40 feet (39 x 13 m).

Nendrum, Strangford Lough, Down, J 3536. The remains of the monastery of St Mochua (from the seventh century) in a cashel enclosure include part of a round tower and an eighth-century church with sundial.

Omey Island, near Claddaghduff, Galway, L 0525. On Omey Island is St Fechín's Well at the north shore of the bay on the western side of the island. It is adorned with offerings of wooden crosses and smooth pebbles.

Pallas Green, Limerick, R 1714. The names of the villages of Old and New Pallas Green preserve the names of the sun-goddess Grían, one of whose holy mountains is the nearby Cnoc Gréine.

Peakaun, Tipperary, M 1819. At the base of Gaulty Mountain is the monastic ruin of St Béagán of Peakaun. There are 2 bullauns, 4 stone crosses, 30 ancient tombstones and a holy well.

Rathcroghan, Roscommon, M 1828. Many ancient monuments in this area recall the royal, sacred nature of the place. The cave at Oweynagat (The Cave of the Cats) is an entrance to the otherworld, with two ogham inscriptions.

Rathmore, Meath, N 2724. Inside the south wall of the ruined church of St Lawrence there is a carved stone labyrinth, probably dating from the fifteenth century.

Rossinver, Leitrim, G 1935. Close to the church ruins (St Tigernach) at the south shore of Lough Melvin is the holy well of St Mogue. Close by is the Black Pig's Race, a border earthwork erected by the Ulstermen in the third century.

Saul, north-east of Downpatrick, Down, J 3534. Mearing Well, with a bullaun carved from the living rock, is next to the road at Saul, 975 feet (300 m) west of the church.

St MacDara's Island, near Roundstone, Galway, L 0722. The ancient church here is notable for its stone construction which imitates timber-frame technique.

St Mullins, Carlow, S 2713. Seven and a half miles (12 km) north of New Ross is the sacred locus of St Moling (d. 696), containing St Moling's Well, a ninth-century high cross and the remains of a round tower.

Scattery Island, Clare, Q 0915. Scattery Island, in the estuary of the River Shannon, contains the monastic remains of St Senan's settlement, Temple Senan,

189

Ireland

his holy well and the Moenach inscribed stone. Nearby are the remains of four other churches, including the ninth-/tenth-century cathedral, with oratory and round tower, the oldest in Ireland (125 ft, 38 m). This was an island where women were prohibited (cf. Iona, Caldey and the inland monastery of Glendalough). Access is by boat from Cappagh Pier near Kilrush.

Scelig Mhichil (Skellig Michael), Kerry, V 0206. An early Celtic monastery, situated on a spectacular rock in the Atlantic, accessed by boat from Portmagee or Waterville.

Shillelagh, Wicklow, S 2916. The remains of the great forest of Shillelagh, whose oaks were plundered in the medieval period for building works in Dublin and London, adjoin the village. The cudgels used in the Irish martial arts traditionally come from this forest.

Sliabh na Caillighe, N 2527. Three peaks on which stand a group of more than thirty chambered cairns. The Witch's Chair, a giant-sized rock seat, is part of one of the cairns.

Station Island, Lough Derg, Donegal, H 2037. Near the southern edge of Lough Derg is Station Island, the focus of the pilgrimage to St Patrick's Purgatory, a celebrated cave of visions whose entrance is barred. An octagonal church in Byzantine style and a hospice cater for the penitent pilgrim, mainly in the period between 20 July and 15 August each year.

Stepaside, Dublin, O 3122. At the foot of the Three Rocks Mountain are Jamestown Holy Well and Cross, north of Stepaside Farm.

Tallaght, Dublin, O 3022. The monastery of the Culdee founder St Máel-Rúáin is represented by St Maelruan's church on the site of its medieval predecessor, but the ancient stone basin, called St Mulroon's Losset, and his cross remain in the churchyard.

Tara, Meath, N 2925. Tara of the Kings (Teamhair na Riogh), first the capital of the kings of Meath, later became the capital of the island of Ireland, seat of the *Ard Rí* (high king). Cursed by St Ruadhan in 563, Tara was nevertheless used until 1022. Befitting a former geomantic centre, Tara contains numerous significant features, most notable of which is the pillar-stone called Lia Fáil, believed to be the inauguration-stone of the high kings. From Tara ran five ancient roads. To the north ran Slige Midluachra, which took the traveller to Emain Macha near Armagh, via Navan, Drogheda and Dundalk. To the south was Slige Cualann, which linked Tara with the Hostel of Da Derga at Bohernabreena, south of Dublin. Slige Dála was the south-western highway to Tipperary, whilst the north-western road was called Slige Asal. It connected Tara with the Shannon. Slige Mór, the Midwest Road, links Tara with Uisnech, the navel of Ireland, then continues to the west coast at Galway.

Teltown, Meath, N 2827. A mile and a half (2.4 km) west of the church of Donaghpatrick is Ráth Dubh, a hill-fort where the Aonach Tailteann Festival took place each Lammas (1 August), at which games were held in honour of departed spirits. Teltown Marriages, lasting a year and a day, were formerly celebrated here.

Temple Cronán, north of Killinaboy, Clare, M 1219. Two holy wells, St Cronán's Well and the Eye Well, are located in fields south of the church ruins.

Tory Island, Donegal, B 1844. There are many cross- and slab-fragments, including the famous cursing stones, in the ruined monastery.

Tullylease, Cork, R 1311. The ruins of the monastery contain St Berechert's Well, a bullaun and the Berechtuine Stone, an eighth-century cross-slab with geometric and spiral Celtic sculpture.

Tulsk, Roscommon, M 1828. Tobar Ogulla, in which St Patrick is said to have baptized Irish royalty, has a pattern on the last Sunday in June.

Tynan, Armagh, H 2734. The area of Tynan Abbey, west of Armagh, has four ancient crosses, probably dating from the eighth century. Both the Village Cross and the Terrace Cross were taken in 1844 from Egish churchyard, whilst the Well Cross and Island Cross come from Glenarb, so despite their artistic and symbolic splendour they are not in their proper locations.

Uisnech, Westmeath, N 2325. The Hill of Uisnech (Ushnagh) (602 ft, 183 m), the druidic centre. To the south of this is the hill of Knockcosgrey (557 ft, 169 m), the geographical centre of Ireland.

Valencia Island (Oiléan Dairbhre), Kerry, V 0307. Linked to the mainland by a bridge, this holy island contains a number of interesting remains, including monastic sites at Kilmore and Feaghmaan West. Tobar Ula Bhréanainn, a holy well of St Brendan, is at Coarhabeg.

White Island, Lower Lough Erne, Fermanagh, H 2135. The ruined church here contains seven remarkable stone figures, of dual-faith nature (Pagan/Christian), including a sheela-na-gig.

Wales

Abbey Cwmhir, Powys, SO 0571. A whitethorn tree in the ruins of Abbey Cwmhir marks the grave of Llewelyn ap Gruffydd, the last Welsh Prince of Wales, slain in 1282 at Cilmeri, 13 miles (21 km) to the south. For his megalith there, see below. The abbey ruins are in a field next to the Clywedog stream.

Bardsey Island (Ynys Enlli), Gwynedd, SH 1222. Off the tip of the Lleyn Peninsula, the site of a Celtic settlement where twenty thousand saints are said to be buried. It was the end of a pilgrimage route that began at St Beuno's shrine at Clynnog Fawr. Bardsey is one of the legendary places where Merlin sleeps in a cave or invisible house of glass.

Bridell, Dyfed, SN 1742. In the churchyard stands a megalith inscribed with an ogham text, which, translated, reads: 'Nettasagrus, son of the descendant of Brecus.' On one side is a cross within a circle, added in the ninth century. Many later tombstones here resemble doors that lead to the next world.

Bristol Channel. Somewhere in the Bristol Channel, between Devon and Dyfed, are the otherworldly Green Meadows of Enchantment, evanescent islands of faerie, seen only occasionally by favoured people. The 'good people' of the islands were sometimes reported to have visited the market at Laugharne (SN 3011), the place that inspired Dylan Thomas.

Cader Idris, south of Dolgellau, Gwynedd, SH 7013. This is a holy mountain, 'The Chair of Idris', named after a giant who observed the heavens from this vantage point. Anyone who spends a night on the Craig Lwyd, the summit, will be either dead, mad or a poet by morning.

Caerwys, Clwyd, SJ 1272. A modern replanting of the bardic sycamore tree stands opposite the old eisteddfod place.

Cardigan Bay. There are four causeways in Cardigan Bay, said to be the old roads of the lost land of Cantref y Gwaelod. They are: Sarn Ddewi, 'St David's Causeway', aligned with the church at Llan Ddewi Aberarth (St David's) at the mouth of the River Arth; Sarn Bwch, 'The Goat's Causeway', which extends 1½ miles (2.4 km) from Aberdysini; Sarn Cyngelyn, 'Cymbeline's Causeway', extending into the sea for 7 miles (11 km) from Gwallawg; and Sarn Cadwgan, 'Cadogan's Causeway', half a mile (800 m) south of Sarn Ddewi. The causeway, said to be the former sea wall Sarn Badrig (St Patrick's Causeway), which is 22 miles (35 km) long, runs from the coast between Harlech and Barmouth. Parts may be discerned at low tide.

Carew, Dyfed, SN 0403, beside the A4075, close to the castle entrance. Broken and reassembled sixth-century cross, commemorating King Maredudd ap Edwin, who ruled Deheubarth (the kingdom of south-west Wales) from 1033 until 1035.

Carn Ingli, near Nevern, Dyfed, SM 0838. The holy mountain where St Brynach communed with angelic beings, visible from Nevern churchyard.

Carn March Arthur, Gwynedd, SN 6598. A rock overlooking the Dovey estuary, on a hill above the A493, bears a depression of the hoof-print of Arthur's horse.

Carreg Cennen, Dyfed, SN 6619. South-east of Ffairfach, east of Trapp and signposted off the A483, there is a ruined castle with a holy well at the end of an underground passage.

Cilmeri, Powys, SO 0051. A granite megalith (15 ft, 4.6 m) commemorating the death-place of Llewelyn ap Gruffydd, the last Welsh Prince of Wales (d. 1282), stands at the west end of Cilmeri, south of the A438.

Clynnog Fawr, Gwynedd, SH 4149. The shrine of St Beuno (or Beino) is at Clynnog Fawr, 9 miles (14.5 km) south-west of Caernarfon. The church and tomb-chapel of St Beuno stand on mega-liths, one of which protrudes through the nave floor. On view in the church is 'Cyff Beuno', Beuno's money chest, hewn from a single oak. The bard Eben Fardd (d. 1863) is buried in the churchyard. Ffynnon Feuno is located south of the church on the opposite side of the road. This well is associated with the incubation cures of epilepsy, where patients would bathe in the well before sleeping on St Beuno's tombstone.

Conwy, Gwynedd, SH 7777. In Lancaster Square stands a Celtic ancestral hero-column commemorating Llewelyn the Great (1167–1240), sculpted by E.O. Griffiths in 1898.

Craig-y-Aderyn, Gwynedd, SH 6406. 'Bird Rock', as it is called in English, towers over the flat land of the Dysynni Valley, 4 miles (6.4 km) inland of Tywyn. It was a special place because only here did the cormorants – sea birds – nest inland.

Craig-y-Dinas, Mid Glamorgan, SN 9108. The Rock of the Fortress is at the head of the Vale of Neath, above the confluence of the rivers that form the Neath. It is the legendary site of a cave containing Arthur and his knights.

Cwm Bychan, Gwynedd, SH 6431. From the coast at Llanbedr runs a mountain road along the course of the River Antro to the mountain lake of Llyn Cwm Bychan. Beyond the lake is an ancient flight of stone slab steps, the Roman Steps, that lead up to the Rhinogs. In legend, they are linked to Harlech Castle by a tunnel.

Devil's Bridge, Dyfed, SN 7376. A threefold bridge over the River Mynach gorge, at the junction of the A120, B4343 and B4574 roads, which is reputed to have been built by the Devil in the hope of taking a human soul as reward.

Dinas Emrys, north of Beddgelert, Gwynedd, SH 6049. The hill-fort where Merlin revealed fighting dragons to King Vortigern.

Ffestiniog, Gwynedd, GR 701413. In the valley of the Cynfal below Ffestiniog is a rock island resembling a pulpit, known as Huw Lloyd's Pulpit-Stone after the seventeenth-century wizard-bard who communed with the *anima loci* there. It is signposted and can be reached by a track to the left of the chapel south of the town.

Ffon y Cawr, south of Penmaenmawr, Gwynedd, SH 7371. There is a standing stone called the Giant's Staff or Picell Arthur (Arthur's Spear), which is said to have been thrown by a giant at an inefficient sheepdog.

Holywell, Clwyd, west of Chester, SJ 1876. St Winefride's Well, the finest medieval holy well in Britain, one of the few sites of unbroken religious continuity from at least the seventh century until the present. Located next to the church, beside the B5121. Admission is charged.

The Landsker, Dyfed, is a line that separates Welsh-speaking north Pembrokeshire from the 'Englishry' in the south. It runs from Amroth, east of Tenby, to Newgale on the west coast. The landscape south of the Landsker, with its small fields, hedgerows and church dedications, has a different character from that of the Pembrokeshire 'Welshry'.

Llanafan, Dyfed, SN 7273, Maen Arthur (Arthur's Stone) in Maen Arthur Wood.

Llandanwg, Clwyd, SH 5728. This medieval church is a stopping-place on a pilgrimage route to Bardsey. Being on the seashore, it is always in danger of being overwhelmed by sand dunes.

Llandegla, Clwyd, SJ 1952. St Tegla's Well here was once the resort of epileptics. The patron saint was the Welsh equivalent of St Thecla, whose chief shrine was at Seleucia in Isauria, where, as a Christianized Greek chthonic deity, she healed people through incubation.

Llandeilo Graban, Powys, north of the B4595, south-east of Builth Wells, SO 0944. The church tower is reputed once to have held the nest of a dragon that was killed by the local blacksmith.

Llandough, South Glamorgan, SS 9972. The churchyard of St Dochdwy contains a pillar cross, the Stone of Irbic. It has a 'holy mountain' base with a carving of a horseman. Recent building-works north of the church have uncovered a Romano-British graveyard.

Llandrillo-yn-Rhos, Clwyd, SH 8380. On the foreshore is the chapel of St Trillo, containing his holy well. Until recently, the remains of a monastic fish-weir were visible nearby. It is a place of votive prayer, where notes of petition and thanks are left on the stone altar-slab in the chapel over St Trillo's Well.

Llandrindod Wells, Powys, SO 0561. Nine wells of mineral water once flowed here. During the nineteenth century the sacred element of taking the waters dwindled, and a fashionable resort with medical overtones replaced it.

Llandudno, Gwynedd, SH 7584. At the Great Orme, north of Llandudno, are a number of sacred places associated with St Tudno, after whom the town is named. The church on the Great Orme is close to a number of healing wells, and the former rocking stone, Maen Sigl (St Tudno's Pulpit or Cradle), is now cemented in place to prevent it from being overturned! The Great Orme is best climbed by tram from Victoria Station, signposted from the eastern promenade.

Llanfair Caerinion, Powys, SJ 1006. Ffynnon Fair, St Mary's Well, between the church and the river in a stone-walled temenos of its own. Once bathed in against rheumatism, the water was used as a prophylactic against harmful magic.

Llangammarch, Powys, SN 9347. Over the door of the church porch is a fragment of a ninth- or tenth-century sunwheel-cross, with a human figure and a spiral, perhaps a serpent, below.

Llangelynin, near Henryd, Gwynedd, SH 7573. Ffynnon Gelynin, St Celynin's Well, is situated at Llangelynin Old Church, along steep and narrow lanes from Henryd, then across rocky fields. Ffynnon Gelynin is to be found in the south-western corner of the churchyard, beneath a tree.

Llangollen, Clwyd, SJ 2044. A stone cross-shaft known as the Pillar of Eliseg is in a railing enclosure close to the Cistercian abbey of Valle Crucis. It contains a genealogy of Eliseg, a ninth-century worthy. It was overthrown by Puritans in the sixteenth century but re-erected in 1779.

Llangorse Lake, Powys, SO 1326. The largest natural lake in south Wales, in which oracular red and green currents were once observed. Nowadays it is covered with motor boats, and access is through car parks and a leisure complex. It contains a tree-covered crannog, a ninth- or tenth-century artificial island with monastic and royal connections.

Llangybi, Gwynedd, SH 4241. Five miles (8 km) north-east of Pwllheli, at Llangybi, is Ffynnon Gybi, St Cybi's Well. Patients resorted to the well for the cure of warts, blindness, scrofula, scurvy, rheumatism and lameness.

Llangynhafal, Clwyd, SJ 1363. Seven miles (11 km) west of Mold, in the orchard of Plas Dolben, a farm off the lane leaving the village to the north, is Ffynnon Gynhafal. It is a wart-well. Patients should prick their wart with a pin and then throw it into the well.

Llangynog, Dyfed, SN 3316. This church is a perfect example of a circular *llan* at a trivium of roads, continuing the Pagan tradition of sacred sites at crossroads and road junctions.

Llanidloes, Powys, SN 9584. This town is laid out according to the 'holy city' plan. The timber-framed Old Market Hall stands at the town's omphalos, the focus of four straight streets pointing in the four directions. Several houses here have pavements with pebble-patterns intended to prevent the ingress of evil spirits or bad luck.

Llanlawer, south-east of Fishguard, Dyfed, SM9836. In a field close to Llanlawer Church is a holy eye-well, whose well-house was restored in the 1980s.

Llanrhaeadr, Clwyd, SJ 0863. Two miles (3.2 km) south-east of Denbigh, behind the church, is a steined pool, formerly inside a building. This well was the cure for 'scabs and itch'.

Llanrwst, Gwynedd, SH 7961. In the riverside Gwydir Chapel, situated off the main square, is the empty sarcophagus of Llewelyn ab Iorwerth, who died in 1240.

Llansannan, Clwyd, SH 9365. In the village street is the gilded bronze statue known as 'The Girl', a monument to five Welsh bards, Tudor Aled (d. 1526), William Salesbury (*c.* 1520–*c.* 1584), Henry Rees (1797–1867), Gwilym Hiraethog (1802–83) and Iorwerth Glan Aled (1819–67). North-east of Llansannan, off the B5382 at SH 9667, is Bwrdd Arthur or 'Arthur's Table'. This is a circle made up of twenty-four impressions cut artificially into a rocky hillside.

Llansteffan, Dyfed, SN 3409. Seven miles (11 km) south-west of Carmarthen is Llansteffan, where St Mary's Well is in an arched niche in the wall of the garden of Well House. St Anthony's Well can be found at St Anthony's Bay.

Wales

Llanthony Abbey, Powys, SO 2827. From the ruins of the priory run several trackways. Three enigmatic parallel straight paths run up the hillside to the south, whilst others, defined by hill-crest notches, link the monastery with other religious sites in adjoining valleys.

Llantrisant, Mid Glamorgan, ST 0483. In the Bull Ring stands sculptor Peter Nicholas's statue of the bard William Price (1800–93), druid and the innovator of modern cremation.

Llantwit Major, between Bridgend and Barry, South Glamorgan, SS 9678. On the B4265, Llantwit, founded by St Illtyd in 500, is the site of one of the former perpetual choirs of Britain (like Glastonbury and Amesbury), where relays of monks sang round the clock. Amid a jumble of stacked chairs is a collection of ancient Celtic crosses, including that of Hywel ap Rhys, king of Glywysing, who died in 886, and a remarkable serpent's head. The churchyard contains a fine perron, and there is a 'death road' called Burial Lane which leads to the churchyard.

Llanwrtyd Wells, Powys SN 8746. Y Ffynnon Ddrewllyd, 'The Stinking Well', gives out blue-coloured malodorous waters. This sulphur well was resorted to for cures.

Llowes, Powys, on the A438, west of Hay-on-Wye, SO 1941. St Meilig's Cross in the church is better known as the Malwalbee Pebble, sacred stone of the demoness Malwalbee, who built Hay-on-Wye Castle by magic. It is a Christianized menhir, taken into the church from the churchyard in 1956.

Llyn Cynwch, east of Llandelltyd, Gwynedd, SH 6511. A lake in which dwelt a Nwyvre that burnt all with its basilisk-like stare. The place where it was killed by a shepherd is marked by Carnedd-y-Wiber, 'The Cairn of the Nwyvre'.

Llyn Dywarchen, in the Nantlle Valley, off the B4418 from Rhyd Ddu, Gwynedd, SH 5652. According to Giraldus Cambrensis, this holy lake contained a floating island, 'which belonged neither to the earth nor to the waters', but was a spirit-island carried by the winds.

Llyn-y-fan Fach, Dyfed, SN 8021. This is a fairy lake from which came a 'lady of the lake' who, by marrying a local farmer, founded a dynasty of doctors, the Physicians of Myddfai, renowned throughout medieval Wales. The lake is reached through Llanddeusant, south of Llandovery, by way of a footpath which begins where the metalled road ends.

Maenclochog, Dyfed, SN 0717. Ten miles (16 km) south-east of Fishguard, on the lane west of Maenclochog, is Ffynnon Fair (St Mary's Well), once reputed to cure rheumatism. Close by are some megaliths from a wrecked cromlech.

Maesyronnen Chapel, Powys, SO 1740. Forbidden worship, whether of the elder faith or of newer, heretical sects, was carried on in secret places. The remote chapel at Maesyronnen, founded in 1696, a mile (1.6 km) from the A438 between Llowes and Glasbury, was a secret place of dissenters' worship in the days when Nonconformism was proscribed by the Church of England.

Margam Stones Museum, The Old School House, Margam, West Glamorgan, SS 7887. A valuable collection of ancient Celtic crosses and slabs from the early days of the Christian religion in Wales. It includes the sixth-century Bodvocus stone. In the ninth and tenth centuries there was a school of cross-sculptors at Margam, and the Conbelin wheel-head cross displayed here is a fine example of their work.

Mathern, near Chepstow, Gwent, ST 5291. Close to the church is St Tewdric's

195

Wales

Well, named after the King of Glamorgan whose mortal wounds were washed in the well after the battle at Tintern Ford in 470 CE. The church nearby was built as his shrine.

Mold (Yr Wyddgrug), Clwyd, SJ 2363. In Maesgarmon Field, off the Gwernaffield Road, stands the Alleluia Stone, erected by Nehemiah Griffith in 1736 to commemorate St Germanus's army's victory over Saxon and Pictish forces in 429 CE. Also on the A494 at SJ 2062 was Maen Arthur, a stone bearing the impression of King Arthur's horse's hoof-print.

Wales

Nevern, east of Newport, Dyfed, SN 0839. The churchyard contains a phallic stone and a Celtic cross 12 feet (3.7 m) in height, dating from the tenth or eleventh century. Inside the church are ancient cross- and ogham-stones. The churchyard also contains bleeding yew trees and the grave of the bard Tegid (the Reverend John Jones), which is geomantically located on the only place in the graveyard from which Carn Ingli is visible.

Newton Nottage, Porthcawl, Mid Glamorgan. There are two holy wells here, St David's and St John's. St John's Well is at SS 8377, on the south side of Newton Church. About a mile (1.6 km) away to the west is The Cross at Nottage. In nearby Moor Lane is St David's Well at SS 8278.

Ogof Arthur, west of Llangwyfan, Anglesey, Gwynedd, SH 3270. A cave on the foreshore, reached by a turning off the A4080 between Aberffraw and Llanfaelog; accessible at low tide. It is one of the caves associated with the legend of the sleeping King Arthur and his knights.

Ogof Myrddin, north-west of Brechfa, Dyfed, east of Alltwalis. There is a cave behind a waterfall at SN 5230, a reputed imprisonment place of the wizard Merlin.

Partrishowe, north-east of Crickhowell, Powys, SO 2722. At the foot of the hill, where the road crosses a stream below the church, is St Ishow's Well.

Penegoes, Powys, SH 7600. In a field next to the A489, a mile (1.6 km) east of Machynlleth, are the two Health Wells next to each other. Curiously, one is warmer than the other.

Penmaenmawr, Gwynedd, SH 7176. A stone circle called Y Meini Hirion, 'The Druids' Circle', stands on the moor above Penmaenmawr. A stone at the centre was a place where newborn babies were placed to ensure a fortunate life. Access is by a rough track 2 miles (3.2 km) long, misleadingly signposted.

Penmon, Anglesey, SH 6380. Close to the priory, whose church contains cross fragments and a sheela-na-gig, is St Seiriol's Well. It is at the foot of impressive rocks and is reached by a footpath next to the pond opposite the notable dovecot.

Pennard, Gower Peninsula, West Glamorgan, SS 5388. The Fairy Ring stone labyrinth, constructed in 1972, is a continuation of the Welsh tradition of making *Caerdroia*. It measures 31 x 29 feet (9.4 x 8.8 m).

Pentre Ifan, east of Fishguard, Dyfed, SN 0937. A megalithic structure, also known as the Womb of Cerridwen, reputed to be a place of initiation, now the haunt of Y Tylweth Teg, the fairy folk.

Pistyll Rhaeadr, north-west of Llanrhaeadr-ym-Mochnant, Powys, west of the B4396, SJ 0729. The highest waterfall in Wales was the haunt of a Nwyvre, defeated by locals using an iron-spiked standing stone.

Porth Oer, Gwynedd, SH 1630. A beach on the Lleyn Peninsula known for its magical sand which whistles when one walks upon it.

Rudbaxton, north of Haverfordwest, Dyfed, SM 9818. On the hill called The Rath is Fons Leonardis, 'St Leonard's Well'. An eye-well, it formerly accompanied a Hospice of St Leonard, now destroyed. It is 2 miles (3.2 km) north of Haverfordwest. A mile (1.6 km) to the north of this, outside the wall of Great Rudbaxton Church, is St Madoc's Well.

Ruthin, Clwyd, SJ 1258. Maen Heuil, 'Hueil's Stone', a megalith in the market place near Exmew Hall, commemorates a warrior who fought against King Arthur and who is said to have lost his head at this place.

St David's (Menevia), Dyfed, SM 7525. One of the 'Three Tribal Thrones of Britain', St David's is the holy city of Wales, containing the shrine of the effective founder of the Welsh Church. Possibly the earlier sacred site from which the cathedral and bishop's palace complex developed is the curative holy well of St Non, St David's mother; it is signposted above St Non's Bay, a mile (1.6 km) south of St David's. It is overlooked by a niche containing her image. There are many megaliths in the surrounding fields. Nearby is a Catholic chapel, built in 1934 as part of St Non's Retreat, where votive prayers are left.

St Govan's, south of Bosherston, Dyfed, SR 9792. A chapel in the rocky cliff to the west of St Govan's Head. The pathway from the cliff-top to the beach passes through the building – a typical fairy path. To the left of the altar is a niche in the rocks in which can be heard ethereal noises. Further down the beach is a dried-up curative holy well, which is blocked with a boulder. Signposted south of the B4319; access is denied sometimes by the military.

St Tudwal's Island East, SH 3426, a mile (1.6 km) east of the Lleyn Peninsula. It contains the thirteenth-century chapel of St Tudwal and the remains of the Augustinian monastic settlement of 1410. It also contains the ruins of the monastery founded in 1887 by Balie Hughes. It failed, was abandoned and the buildings were bombed by the Royal Air Force in the Second World War for practice.

Skenfrith, Gwent, SO 4520. The church here has a stone Celtic head over the south porch, said to represent St Bridget.

Strata Florida Abbey, Dyfed, SN 7465. Ruined Cistercian abbey which once held the Cwpan, a wooden chalice carved from a fragment of the True Cross. An ancient yew tree in the churchyard marks the grave of the bard Dafydd ap Gwilym. The abbey is signposted to the east of the B4343, south of Devil's Bridge.

Sudbrook, Gwent, ST 9744. The ruins of St Tegla's Chapel and Holy Well lie on a rocky islet that can be visited at low tide. They are located close to the entrance of the Severn railway tunnel and junction 23 of the M4.

Swansea (Abertawe), West Glamorgan, SS 6593. A commemorative statue of the bard Dylan Thomas (1914–53) stands at Dylan Thomas Square, South Dock Marina.

Tinkinswood, Gwent, ST 0874. South of the A48 near St Nicholas is a megalithic structure, with the largest capstone in the British Isles (14 x 10 ft, 4.3 x 3 m). It possesses the legend that the capstone turns three times at Midsummer Eve.

Trelleck, Gwent, SO 5005. A nexus of Celtic sanctity, with an alignment of three menhirs, Harold's Stones. Just outside the village is the Virtuous Well, sacred to the Earth Mother, St Anne. Outside the church is a stone cross, standing on a stepped 'world mountain' base, erected by an early medieval King of Wales.

Tremeirchion, Clwyd, SJ 0872. Three miles (4.8 km) east of St Asaph, half a mile (800 m) south of Tremeirchion

197

Wales

beside the B5429, is Ffynnon Beuno, a bathing pool enclosed in a stone wall.

Waun-y-Pound, Ebbw Vale, Gwent, SO 1611. On Sirhowy Top, four inscribed limestone megaliths commemorate the socialist politician Aneurin Bevan (1897–1960). Access is from the A4047.

Whitford, Clwyd, SJ 1477. Maen Ach-wyfan, 'The Stone of Lamentations', is a late tenth-century wheel-head cross-slab with designs related to Northumbrian cross-decoration, including spirals and interlace.

Worm's Head, south-west of Rhossili, West Glamorgan, SS 3887. A seaside rock-formation with a blowhole through which the waves make a strange sound, said to be that of the Nwyvre or the Devil.

Scotland

Aberlemno, Tayside, NO 5255. Alongside the B9134 road in Aberlemno are three Pictish 'symbol stones'. In the churchyard to the east of this road is the Aberlemno Stone, an eighth-century stone with incised cross with beasts and hunting or battle scenes.

Alves, Grampian, NJ 1362. The south slope of the Knock of Alves is said to be the place where Macbeth met the Weird Sisters.

Auchencrow, Borders Region, NT 8560. Two 'witch-stones' exist here, one built into a cottage wall at the junction of the B6438 with the main street, and the other, the Peg Tode Stone, in the main street near the beginning of the southbound footpath. Both stones are reputed to have been carried and dropped by witches during their night ride, but they are likely to be stones of former Pagan sanctity.

Auchenmaig, Dumfries and Galloway, NX 2749. On the A747 4 miles (6.4 km) south-east of Auchenmaig is Chapel Finian. In the ruins is a holy well formerly resorted to on the closest Sundays to the four Celtic fire-festivals (February, May, August and November).

Avoch, Highland Region, NH 6753. On the north shore of Munlochy Bay is the Craigie Well. Located on a tree-covered bank, it is marked by the rags tied to nearby bushes. Its water is reputed to be protective against harmful magic and evil spirits. For this purpose, it should be visited on the first Sunday in May.

Balbeggie, near Abernyte, Tayside, NO 1629. Just south of here are the Sidlaws of Shian Hill, a powerful fairy hill, reputed to be the major stronghold of otherworldly beings in the district.

Borthwick Mains, Borders Region, NT 4314. According to local lore, the Pictish stone in the private garden of the farm on the B711 4 miles (6.4 km) west of Hawick once stood in the River Teviot. Incised on the stone is a fish, whose tail marked the level of water at which it was safe to cross the ford.

Burghead, Highland Region, NJ 1069. The wall of the old cemetery at the top of Burghead contains a deep-hollowed stone slab called the Cradle Stone, used formerly for obscure ceremonies. At the end of King Street is the Roman Well (also called the Pictish or Bailey's Well), rediscovered in 1809. In an underground chamber cut from living rock is a cistern fed by springs with a walkway around it.

Burwick, Ronaldsay, Orkney, ND 4484. In St Mary's Church is the Ladykirk Stone, a boulder with incised footprints, reputed to be those of St Magnus, who crossed the Pentland Firth on the stone.

Campbeltown, Kintyre, Strathclyde, NR 7620. The votive painted cave containing images of the Crucifixion is on the seaward side of Davaar Island in Campbeltown Loch, approachable at low tide along a rocky causeway.

Chapel of Garioch, Grampian, NJ 7124. A high cross shaft (12 ft, 3.7 m) called the Maiden Stone stands half a mile (800 m) beyond the village.

Clackmannan, Central Region, NS 9191. In the churchyard stands a phallic megalith that was an inauguration-stone for Pictish rulers. Next to it is a stepped perron.

Clickhimin, near Lerwick, Shetland, HU 4013. The causeway leading to this famous broch has a stone bearing a pair of footprints.

Coldstream, Borders Region, NT 8539. A classic liminal place of passage is the bridge over the River Tweed at Coldstream. Its mid-point is the border between Scotland and England. An old toll-house stands at the Scots end, where runaway marriages from England were celebrated until 1856.

Coll, Strathclyde, NM 1655. The name of a burn that flows into Loch Breachacha on the island of Coll is Struathan nan Ceann, 'The Stream of the Heads'. This is an example of a place-name that recalls a notable incident, being the site of a battle in 1593 between the MacLeans of Coll and the invading Duarts, who were defeated and massacred. Their severed heads filled the stream so that ducks swam in their blood.

Comrie, west of Crieff, Tayside, NN 7722. The rock called St Fillan's Chair sits on Dunfillan, the hill above Comrie. It was resorted to by sufferers from rheumatism and spinal problems. Close by is the holy well of St Fillan, visited each Lammas.

Craigmillar Castle, NT 2870, close to Edinburgh, contains the only surviving

ancient labyrinth carving known to exist in Scotland.

Cromarty, Highland Region, NH 8067. Fiddler's Well lies on the shore 2 miles (3.2 km) east of Cromarty. It was discovered as a result of a dream.

Crosskirk Bay, Highland Region, ND 0269. A stream enters the bay close to the ruins of St Mary's Chapel. At the head of the stream is the holy well of St Mary. Crosskirk has a Pictish stone.

Culloden, Highland Region, NH 7245. The Clootie Well (St Mary's Well) can be found in Culloden Wood, surrounded by trees on which rags are tied. Close by is the Well of the Dead, beside which the fallen clansmen from the 1746 battle are buried in the Mounds of the Clans.

Drumelzier, Borders Region, NT 1333. The confluence of Powsail Burn and the River Tweed is one of the reputed graves of Merlin, who, hunted as a wild man, died the threefold death of hanging, impaling and drowning.

Dunadd, Mid-Argyll, NR 8393. Erstwhile capital of the former country of Dalriada. There is an imprint of a foot 11 inches long and 4½ inches wide (28 x 11.5 cm), with a carving of a wild boar facing the footprint. In 736 Fergus brought the Stone of Destiny here.

Dunfermline, Fife, NT 0887. There is a holy well in the nave of Dunfermline abbey (as there is in Glasgow Cathedral).

Dunning, south-west of Perth, Tayside, NO 0114. On the road to Milhaugh, west of Dunning, is a perron-cross on a rough stepped-stone base, said to be a memorial to Maggie Wall, who was burnt there as a witch in 1657.

Dunvegan, Isle of Skye, Highland Region, NG 2547. Dunvegan Castle contains the Fairy Flag, a silken banner given to the fourth Lady MacLeod by a fairy woman clad in green. Two miles (3.2 km) east of Dunvegan is Fairy Bridge.

Durness, Highland Region, NC 4367. East of Durness on the coast is Smoo Cave, a three-chambered cavern, reputed to be a portal to the otherworld. Legend tells how Donald, the Wizard of Reay, encountered demonic forces there.

Edinburgh, Lothian, NT 2773. In Holyrood Park, next to the remains of St Anthony's Chapel, is St Anthony's Well. It is a Beltane (May Day) custom to wash in the dew on Arthur's Seat and then wish at the well. Nearby is the Well of the Holy Rood, covered by a stone well-house that formerly sheltered St Margaret's Well at Restalrig. Also at Restalrig is St Triduana's Well in a hexagonal well-house next to the parish church. At Liberton, in the private grounds of St Katherine's House opposite Mortonhall Crematorium, is St Katherine's Well, whose oily water has curative virtues.

Ednam, north of Kelso, Borders, NT 7337. West of the village is the Piper's Grave, a Pictish tumulus and fairy hill. Its legend tells that once a would-be piper entered the fairy kingdom here to learn the craft of piping, never to return.

Eilean na hUamhaidh (The Isle of the Cave), in Loch Caolisport, Strathclyde, NR 7576. Three miles (4.8 km) from Achahoish, facing the first bay on the shore of Loch Caolisport, is the celebrated fairy cave.

Findhorn, Grampian, NJ 0564. The Findhorn Foundation, at the end of the B9011, is one of the most celebrated New Age places. In its work with otherworldly beings it perpetuates the fairy faith of the Celtic countries in a new form.

Fingal's Cave, Staffa, Strathclyde, NM 3335. On the island of Staffa is the 'Melodious Cave' named after the hero Fingal, who, in giant form, hewed it from the rock. One of the natural wonders of Scotland, it penetrates the basalt rocks for 250 feet (76 m), being 100 feet (30 m) in height. It is most easily reached by boat from Iona, but it is a risky place to land.

Forres, Grampian, NJ 0358. A witch-stone is built into the southern retaining wall of the A96, opposite the police station. It is a macabre stopping-place where someone was murdered during the witch-craze. Elsewhere in Scotland are similar stones, all said to mark the death-place of supposed witches (cf. Spott). The tenth-century Sueno's Stone, over 20 feet (6 m) high, is carved with scenes of hunting and battle.

Fortingall, Tayside, NN 7247. The Iron Well, next to the road in Glen Lyon, 1½ miles (2.4 km) west of Fortingall, is a wishing well whose ferruginous waters are said to be curative.

Glamis, Tayside, NO 3847. Situated in woodland near the church is the Lady Well. It has a dual dedication, as St Fergus is also commemorated.

Glasgow, Strathclyde, NS 6065. In the south-east corner of the cathedral crypt is St Mungo's Well (cf. Dunfermline). There is a Mungo's Well in Selkirk.

Glasserton, Dumfries and Galloway, NS 4238. In St Ninian's country, south-west of Whithorn, north-west of the ancient church, is the shore-well of St Medan, once used to cure whooping cough. St Ninian's Cave is 4 miles (6.4 km) from Whithorn, Cumbria (at NX 4236), marked by a sign on the A747.

Glenkiln, Dumfries and Galloway, NX 8477. On hillside locations in the Glenkiln estate, north-west of Shawhead village, stand sculptures by Rodin, Epstein and Moore. Here, one can experience the modern aesthetic of the landscape and compare it with the traditional.

Glen Moriston, Highland Region, NH 2210. The memorial cairn near the head of the glen commemorates Roderick Mackenzie, killed in 1746 by government soldiers who mistook him for Bonnie Prince Charlie. Another cairn further down the glen commemorates a 'miracle' in 1827, where an itinerant preacher insisted that the ground would be his witness. His footprints, made on that day, can be seen next to the cairn.

Handa, Highland Region, NC 1348. Until the late nineteenth century, the twelve families of Handa were ruled by a matriarchy. The eldest widow, who presided over all decision-making, was the queen of Handa. Today, the island is a bird reserve, reached by boat from Tarbet (NC 1648), north of Scourie.

Innerleithen, Borders Region, NT 3336. Robert Burns described Innerleithen as a famous spa. Its fame came from the Dow Well, a holy well now dedicated to St Ronan, celebrated in the Cleikum Ceremony; its sulphur-bearing waters are considered effective against eye complaints.

Invergarry, Highland Region, NN 3099. Next to the A82 at Loch Oich is Tobar-nan-Ceann, 'The Well of the Heads', named after an event in the 1660s when seven men were beheaded for murder and their heads were washed in the well before being displayed before MacDonell of Glengarry. A monument with Celtic heads was set up in 1812.

Inverness, Highland Region, NH 6343. To the south of Inverness, overlooking a modern cemetery, is the wooded holy hill of Tomnahurich. Here, according to local legend, the Fairy Queen Nicniven holds court. The famed bard Thomas the Rhymer is said to be buried here.

Iona, Inner Hebrides, Strathclyde, NM 2726. St Mary's Abbey, established by St Columba in 563, is one of the holiest shrines of the Celtic Church, but an old Gaelic name for Iona is Innis na Druineach (The Isle of the Druids). Before the Reformation there were 350 or 365 Celtic crosses on the island. Only the fifteenth-century Maclean's Cross, and the tenth-century St Martin's Cross, near the abbey, remain. Forty-eight kings of Scotland, eight Norse and four Irish kings are buried on the island. There are many other magically significant features including the Well of Age and the Well of the South Wind. It is considered lucky to ascend Dun-I (300 ft, 91 m), the only hill on Iona, seven times. On top is the Well of Healing, which is reputed never to have run dry, even in times of drought. Green (serpentine) stones from Iona make powerful amulets. Access to Iona is by sea from Fionnphort on the Isle of Mull.

Islay, Strathclyde, NR 2974. A stone labyrinth, constructed in 1986, stands on Ardnave Point.

Keil, Kintyre, Strathclyde, NR 6707. At Keil, situated 1 mile (1.6 km) south-west of Southend, is a nexus of three sacred things. In the cliff-face north-west of the ancient Keil Chapel is the Holy Well, and on a rock nearby are two carved footprints, St Columba's Footsteps.

Kempock, Strathclyde, NR 2678. The Granny Kempock Stone (The Longstone) stands on the headland near the A770 west of Greenock, to the north of St John's Church. Six feet (1.8 m) in height, it is considered fortunate for seafarers and betrothed couples to honour it.

Kilbarchan, west of Paisley, Strathclyde, NS 4063. The Celtic tradition of commemorating bards is displayed here on the north face of the Steeple Tower, where a bronze statue of the piper Habbie Simpson (1550–1620) is set.

Kildalton, Islay, NR 4550. The tenth-century wheel-headed Celtic cross in Kildalton churchyard, 4 miles (6.4 km) from Ardbeg, is the finest in Scotland.

Kilmacolm, Strathclyde, NS 3869. Next to the church ruins, one mile (1.6 km) on the road to Houston from Kilmacolm, is St Fillan's Well. In former times, to cure children of rickets, they were bathed in it and rags were tied to nearby thorn bushes.

Ladykirk, Borders Region. It contains five holy wells, some of which were ascribed oracular powers. Fairies' Well, at NT 8844, is beside the river footpath. St Mary's Well (NT 886466) is 650 feet (198 m) east of Nun's Well, which is marked by an obelisk at NT 887467. To the west of this on a hillside at Home Farm is Monk's Well (NT 885465). Sybil's Well, in the grounds of Ladykirk House, has dried up (NT 889463).

Lindores, Fife, NO 2716. One hundred and sixty-three feet (50 m) from the A913 on the Pow Burn that flows from the Loch of Lindores into the Tay east of Newburgh at Parkhill, there is one of the only three surviving Celtic eel-houses in Great Britain (one is in the grounds of the mansion house at Elie, south Fife, and another on the Lannan Burn in Angus). It is of stone and turf, measuring about 12 x 10½ feet (3.7 x 3.2 m), with a turfed roof rising to a height of about 6 feet (1.8 m). The door has a marriage lintel with the inscription 'LA 17♥87 AIB'. To catch eels, a fyffe net is set inside the building, and the net remains in the water, trapping the fish. Fish-traps play their part in Celtic legend, for instance in the discovery of the baby Taliesin.

Linlithgow, Lothian, NS 9977. A well-house dated 1807 in the square south of the palace covers the Cross Well.

Linton, Borders Region, NT 7726. Linton Kirk stands on a strange sandy hillock, Wormiston, which, according to legend, was made by the Linton Worm, a Nwyvre whose coils squeezed the earth into this shape.

Lochan Uaine, Highland Region, NJ 0010. In the Pass of Ryvoan, this 'Little Green Loch' is a fairy lake, accessed by a 2-mile path (3.2 km) starting from the information centre in the Glenmore Forest Park.

Loch Maree, east of Gairloch, Highland Region, NG 8076. The loch and its island Eilean Maree (NG 7292) were the centre of the vernacular religious cult of Maree (Maelrubha). The holy island (which is private) contains the holy well once served by derilans who administered healing rites for madness. Surrounding hills and the Stopping-Places of Maree are notable features.

Loch na Beiste, Highland Region, NG 8894. One of several lochs in Scotland with legends of water monsters. In the 1840s the local laird attempted to drain the loch to catch the 'beastie'. When this failed, he had numerous barrel-loads of lime dumped into the loch to kill the monster.

Munlochy, Highland Region, NH 6453. Next to the A832 just north of Munlochy is the Cloutie Well, dedicated to St Boniface. It is a remarkable rag-well, said by those who keep score to have over fifty thousand rags around it.

Orton, Highland Region, NJ 3255. In the wall of a chapel to the east of the B9015 is St Mary's Well, the water of which cured eye troubles, whooping cough and troublesome joints. It was formerly the focus of a pilgrimage.

Pittenweem, Fife, NO 5402. Pittenweem means the 'Place of the Cave', and in Cove Wynd there is the entrance to a cave-complex, the seventh-century hermitage of St Fillan. Inside the cave are a holy well and the altar used by the Celtic monk. In 1935, after years of neglect, the cave was reopened, and today it is used occasionally for religious services.

Rannoch Moor, Tayside, NN 4050. On the slopes of Schiehallion, 'The Fairy Hill of the Caledonians', at the eastern end of Rannoch Moor, are the remains of a holy well. In former times, it was visited at Beltane (May Day) by white-clad girls who left offerings of garlands for the *anima loci*.

Rhum, Highland Region, NM 3496. The island is the possession of the Nature Conservancy Council. At Harris, on the west coast 4 miles (6.4 km) south of Kinloch by the seashore, is the mausoleum of the Bullough family. It is a temenos defined by a double fence, an outer one of posts and an inner one of pillars. Within this is a classical temple, the mausoleum itself.

St Andrews, Fife, NO 5016. Laid out in 1144 by the royal *locator*, Mainard, St Andrews has three streets radiating from the cathedral, site of a Culdee monastic settlement. The omphalos of St Andrews, the Blue Stane, has been moved twice. Originally at Magus Muir, it was taken to West Point, and is now situated inside the railings of Kate Kennedy Bar, opposite the Hope Park Church.

Scotlandwell, Tayside, NO 1801. Close to Loch Leven in a fine Victorian wooden well-house in the middle of the village is the holy well of Scotlandwell. It has a royal connection, for it is reputed to have cured Robert the Bruce's leprosy. Mary Queen of Scots and King Charles II also made special visits to the well. It is signposted from the A911 road to the west of Kinross.

Selkirk, Borders Region, NT 4728. To the south of Selkirk is Mungo's Well in the Deer Park west of the junction of the A699 and A7 roads.

Silverwells, north of Arbroath, Tayside, NO 6442. The Silver Well, after which the village is named, is in the grounds of a garden centre. It is so named after the silver material that floats on its surface, though offerings of silver were left there in former times.

Skye, Highland Region. Dunscaith crowns a rocky headland in the north side of Ob Gauscavaig Bay, commanding the entrance to Loch Eishort (NG 5913). Rising 40 feet (12.2 m) above the ocean, it is the legendary fortress of Scáthach nVanaind, daughter of Airdgeme, tutor and lover of the Ulster hero Cú Chulainn. Once it was connected to the island by a natural bridge of rock. On the shore beneath Dunscaith is a grass-topped rock, Clach Luach, where Cú Chulainn tied up his hound Luath on his return from the hunt. There are three notable holy mountains on Skye. South-west of Dunvegan are two classic flat-topped holy mountains, Healabhal Mhor (Big Holy Mountain, 1535 ft, 468 m, NG 2245), and Healabhal Bheag (Little Holy Mountain, 1601 ft, 488 m, NG 2342). South-west of Portree is Beinn-na-Gréine (The Mountain of the Sun), NG 4642.

Spott, Lothian, NT 6775. South of the village, on the road to Chesters Fort, is Spott Loan, where a 'witch-stone' marks the place where witch-hunters killed people. Marion Lille, the last woman to be burnt as a witch south of the Forth, was murdered there. West of the churchyard is a holy well, formerly visited each St John's Day (Midsummer) with a ritual procession through the churchyard and church.

Storr, Isle of Skye, NG 5152. The freestanding rock stack known as the Old Man of Storr, which can be seen to the west of the A855 on the east of Skye, is said to be a giant who was turned to stone by the magic eye of Balor of the Evil Eye.

Thurso, Highland Region, ND 1168. Thurso Museum has a fine collection of Pictish stones, among them the eighth-

203

Scotland

century Ulbser and Skinner Stones, with crosses and 'this-worldly' and other-worldly beasts.

Traquair, Borders Region, NT 3533. On Minch Moor, 2 miles (3.2 km) by the footpath south-east of Traquair, is the Cheese Well. It was a stopping-place on the drove road, at which wayfarers would leave a piece of cheese in the water as an offering.

Troqueer, south of Dumfries, Dumfries and Galloway, NX 9572. South of Islesteps, St Queran's is a rag-well where offerings of coins are made in the hope of cures.

Whitehills, Grampian, NJ 6665. In a fine circular well-house is the Red Well, a chalybeate spring of healing virtue.

Whitekirk, Lothian, NT 5981. Our Lady's Well is to the north-east of Whitekirk. In 1297 the chapel was erected on the instructions of Black Agnes, Countess of Dunbar, as an offering of thanks to the waters for curing her pain. In 1309 a shrine of the Madonna was added and an annual pilgrimage instituted.

England outside Cornwall

Ashburton, Devon, SX 7569. In a park near Totnes Road is the eye-well of St Gudula, the patron saint of Brussels Cathedral.

Bath, Avon, ST 7564. The Roman Baths here are the remains of a Celto-Roman sacred complex dedicated to Sul, with baths, a temple and other features. In myth, the thermal springs were discovered by the Celtic King Bladud, who was cured of leprosy by the waters. The Gorgo and lunar images that once graced

the temple can be seen in the museum. It is likely that Bath Abbey lies over a Celto-Roman sacred place.

Beetham, north of Carnforth, Cumbria, SD 5173. West of the church is a footpath leading to the Fairy Steps, which are cut into a rock crevice. If anyone can make the ritual ascent without touching either wall, then he or she will be granted a wish by the good folk.

Breamore, Hampshire, SU 1420. The turf-cut Mizmaze, the typical medieval version of the *Caerdroia*, 87 feet (26.5 m) in diameter, is located in a secluded spot near Breamore.

Buckland St Mary, Somerset, ST 2713. This village is reputed to be the last place where the red-clothed fairies could be seen in Somerset. They were expelled from the county after losing a struggle with the Piskies, who now rule everywhere west of the River Parret. Most of the red-clothed spirits departed to Ireland, though a few went to Dorset and Devon.

Carrawbrough, Northumberland, NY 8671. The site of the Roman fort of Brocolitia contains a temple of Mithras and the holy well of the *anima loci*, Coventina, rediscovered in 1876. In former times, the spring was covered by a Celto-Roman temple. An image of the goddess, reclining on a leaf, and votive offerings, including 13,487 coins, were found here. These are displayed in Chesters Fort Museum at Humshaugh, 3 miles (4.8 km) to the east.

Cerne Abbas, Dorset, ST 6701. One of the best-preserved chalk-cut hill figures is the Cerne Abbas Giant, a club-wielding, ithyphallic man cut into the hillside. Above the giant is a rectangular earthen enclosure called 'The Trendle', where it was formerly the custom to erect a may-pole. The churchyard contains a wishing well.

Cinderford, Forest of Dean, Gloucestershire, SO 6515. In woodland north of Cinderford is St Anthony's Well, visited in May at the rising of the sun. Access is by trackways leading from Jubilee Road in the town.

Compton, Surrey, SU 9547. The Watts Mortuary Chapel is a remarkable symbolic chapel in Celtic Arts and Crafts style, designed by the Scottish artist Mary Tytler Watts and built by local people in 1896. Made entirely from local materials, it is a masterly example of location in the landscape in the Celtic tradition, containing symbolic elements including labyrinths and trees of life.

Dalby, North Yorkshire, SE 6271. A classical turf labyrinth, 'The City of Troy', is cut in the roadside verge by the B1363. It measures 26 x 22 feet (8 x 6.7 m), and was recut in 1900 to replace another with the same design close by.

Dartmoor, Devon. The monastic trackway between Tavistock (SX 4774) and Buckfast (SX 7367) is a classic sacred way that can still be walked. Its stopping-places are marked by crosses: Tavistock Abbey, Green Lane Cross, Pixies' Cross, Warren's Cross, Huckworthy Cross, Walkhampton Church House Cross, Yannandon Cross, Lower Lowery Cross, Lowery Cross, Lether Tor Bridge, Clazywell Cross, Newleycombe Cross, Siward's Cross, Nun's Cross, Goldsmith's Cross, Childe's Tomb Cross, Mount Misery Cross, West Ter Hill Cross, East Ter Hill Cross, Skaur Ford Cross, Horse Ford Cross, Horn's Cross, Two Thorns Cross, Play Cross, Hawson Cross, Buckfast Abbey.

Dinedor, Hereford and Worcester, SO 5376, west of the B4399. An ancient earthwork on a visible alignment discovered by Alfred Watkins, giving a sight of Hereford Cathedral and the spire of All Saints' Church. The earthwork is on a track south of the village.

Donington, Salop, SJ 8004. In wooded parkland close to the church is the eye-well dedicated to St Cuthbert.

Dunmail Raise, Cumbria, NX 0212. On the A591 between Ambleside and Keswick, at the pass between Steel Fell in the west and Seat Sandal in the east (832 ft, 256 m above sea level). It is a classic cairn, variously the marker of a battle in 945, the boundary between Scotland and England and between Westmorland and Cumberland.

Durham, County Durham, NZ 2742. The site of this cathedral was given by the omen of a dun cow, whose image may be seen carved on the outside of the present building.

Fernyhalgh, Lancashire, SD 5534. North of Preston, between Grimsargh and Broughton, is the holy well whose site was given in a vision in 1471, followed up by the discovery of a lost Madonna image. The well is in a private garden, but it can be seen from the public lane nearby.

Frensham, Surrey, SU 8441. St Mary's Church at Frensham contains an object from fairyland, a cauldron 3 feet (1 m) in diameter called 'The Fairies' Kettle'. It was borrowed from the fairies who lived on nearby Borough Hill and never returned.

Glastonbury, Somerset, ST 4938. Reputed to be the place where the first Christian church was built in Britain, Glastonbury is a centre of 'the Mysteries of Britain', and for this reason is significant in the New Age movement. The Tor (ST 5138) is the holy mountain of Gwynn ap Nudd, master of the entrance to the underworld. Near the foot of the Tor is Chalice Well, whose gardens are a haven of peace. The holy thorn tree on Wearyall Hill, *Crataegus oxycantha*, is a species of hawthorn that blossoms at midwinter. Another in the churchyard of

St John's in the town gives a flowering branch to the reigning monarch each Christmas.

Great Asby, south of Appleby, Cumbria, NY 6813. Four miles (6.4 km) south of Appleby is a spring that fills a basin. Its water is reputed to have great healing virtues.

Hardknott, Cumbria, NY 2402. Below Sca Fell, to the north-east of Ravenglass, are the ruins of a Roman fort which is the Cumbrian equivalent of an Irish fairy rath. Here, the Fairy King, Eveling, holds court.

Hartland Point, Devon, SS 2328. The former name of this feature was the Headland of Hercules, after the legend that Hercules landed here, defeated British giants in combat and ruled the land. Here was the hermitage of St Nectan, a head-well visited every 17 June, when foxgloves are offered to the *anima loci.*

Hempsted, Gloucestershire, SO 8117. West of Gloucester, access to Lady's Well at Hempsted can be gained from St Swithun's Church. The well-house stands on a rise in the middle of a field reached by paths to the right of the church's main entrance.

Hereford, Hereford and Worcester, SO 5040. The self-styled 'Site of St Ethelbert's Well' is in a wall close to the cathedral. In legend, it is associated with the last King of an independent East Anglia, Ethelbert, beheaded here in 792, when, in classic Celtic fashion, a spring arose at the place where his head fell.

Higher Penwortham, Lancashire, SD 5128. A Fairy Path, comparable with those in Brittany and Ireland, runs through Penwortham Wood. If one should be unlucky enough to encounter the Fairy Cortège, it is deemed an omen of death.

Holybourne, north-east of Alton, Hampshire, SU 7341. The church here is located above the source of the Holy Bourne, a sacred stream which flows from a pond beside the church. It is a good example of a Christian takeover of a Celtic source-shrine.

Holy Island (Lindisfarne), Northumberland, NU 1442. Bishop Aidan came to Northumbria in 634 and established Lindisfarne as a Celtic monastic settlement. From here, in 664 St Cuthbert made a new settlement on Hobthrush Island (St Cuthbert's Isle) and in 676 another on Farne Island to the southeast. Access to Lindisfarne is across Holy Island sands, on a causeway marked by posts. Called the Pilgrims' Way, it leaves the shore at Beal and reaches the island at Chare End. It is possible to walk from Holy Island to Hobthrush at low tide, when the ruins of St Cuthbert's Chapel are visible.

Ilton Circle, Masham, north of Ripon, North Yorkshire, SE 2280. Constructed according to esoteric principles, this megalithic structure was erected in 1820 by William Danby as a 'Druid Circle'. It can be reached from the road from Masham to Ilton.

Kirkby Lonsdale, Cumbria, SD 6178. The Devil's Bridge on the A65 over the River Lune is one of several places that bear the legend that the Devil agreed to build the bridge on the understanding that, in payment, he could take the soul of the first being across. Of course, a dog was sent across first, thwarting the fiend's plan.

Kirkoswald, north of Penrith, Cumbria, NY 5540. At the western end of Kirkoswald Church is found the well of St Oswald.

Lichfield, Staffordshire, SK 1210. St Chad's Well is in the churchyard at Stowe, in the north of the city. Formerly, the well was dressed on Ascension Day.

Marden, Hereford and Worcester, SO 5147. Inside the church at Marden, 4 miles (6.4 km) north of Hereford, is the holy well of St Ethelbert. Like the well at Hereford, this marks a significant place in the legend of St Ethelbert, king of East Anglia, whose imprisonment and execution at Hereford were followed by miracles and canonization. Here, a shrine was built over the spring next to which he was buried.

Meriden, West Midlands, SP 2482. One of the traditional places of the centre of England (or Britain), with a cross which has been in the present position since 1952. The remains of the holy well of St Lawrence are at the western side of the village, and its pond is said to have two outlets, one of which is the source of the Humber and the other of which flows westwards, eventually into the Bristol Channel.

Nine Standards Rigg, Cumbria, NY 8206. On a hill overlooking the Vale of Eden, close to the border between Cumbria and North Yorkshire, is Nine Standards Rigg, so named after the alignment of nine cairns on the hill-top. Formerly, the boundary passed through them.

North Brentor, Devon, SX 4881. A location-legend tells how it was intended to build a church on level ground, but that each night the building materials were lifted mysteriously to the summit. Eventually, the church was built on top of the holy hill. North Brentor is signposted west of the A386.

Okehampton, Devon, SX 5993. South of Okehampton is Fitz's Well, a stopping-place on a pilgrims' path on the edge of Dartmoor. In former times, the well was resorted to on Easter Sunday for divinations.

Patterdale, Ullswater, Cumbria, NY 3915. As one approaches the Glenridding boat-landing from the Patterdale direction, beside the main road at the southern end of Ullswater (a lake sacred to the Norse god of winter) is the well of St Patrick.

Penrith, Cumbria, NY 5130. St Andrew's churchyard contains a strange array of stones called the Giant's Grave. It is reputed to be the grave of the giant Isir, who resided in a cave near Eamonth Bridge.

Rothbury, Northumberand, NU 0601. At Holystone, Rothbury, is Lady's Well, found as a result of an apparition of Our Lady. It was used by the missionaries Ninian and Paulinus to baptize converts to Christianity.

Rudston, Yorkshire, TA 0967. A millstone grit pillar, the largest megalith in Britain associated with a church, stands in the churchyard here.

St Briavel's, north of Chepstow, Gloucestershire, SO 5504. The holy well of the Forest of Dean, St Bride's Well, is in Lower Road, close to the church. St Briavel's Castle was a major centre of arms manufacture in the medieval period.

St Herbert's Island, south of Keswick, Cumbria, NY 2720. The wooded island of St Herbert was a retreat of a kind better known in Ireland.

Southam, Warwickshire, SP 4161. The holy well here has a half-moon-shaped pool whose water issues from the mouths of three 'Celtic heads' into a trough accessed by steps from both sides.

Stoke, near Hartland, Devon, SS 2324. One of several wells dedicated to St Nectan – an appropriate name for a water guardian – St Nectan's Well is downhill from Stoke's main street in a small well-house.

Stoke Edith, Hereford and Worcester, SO 6040. St Edith's Well is a strongly flowing holy source close to the church. It is said to have sprung up when Edith, who was building a church, prayed for water.

Sutton Coldfield, West Midlands, SP 1296. The park, reputed to have been a seat of the Archdruid, and later a royal and episcopal park, contains three holy wells: Druids' Well, Keeper's Well and Rowton Well.

Todmorden, West Yorkshire, SD 9326. The Bridestones, on the moors near Todmorden, have a name redolent of the Celtic goddess-saint. This array of stones is resorted to for natural magic. One, the Balancing Stone, has a carved head of a horned figure, called the Devil, but equally the horned god Cernunnos.

Uffington, Oxfordshire, SU 3089. The Vale of the White Horse is so called from the white horse of Uffington, a Celtic Iron Age hill-figure, dated to the first century. Close by is a *locus terribilis*, Dragon Hill, where dragon's blood is said to have made the ground barren. It was formerly the site of a chapel, probably dedicated to St George, because of which the hill-figure is said sometimes to be a dragon.

Wells, Somerset, ST 5445. The city is named from the seven holy underground streams that well up in the garden of the Bishop's Palace.

Whitchurch Canonicorum, near Lyme Regis, Dorset, SY 3995. The north transept of the church of St Candida and the Holy Cross contains the shrine of St Candida (in English, St White), who is the three-breasted Celtic deity Gwen Teirbron. Ex-voto prayers are pushed into the niches of her shrine.

Winwick, north of Warrington, Cheshire, SJ 6092. The church was located by means of a pig which carried masonry

from an earlier site to the present one, reputed to be the place where St Oswald expired in 642.

Woolston, Salop, SJ 3224. St Winefride's Holy Well at Woolston is covered by a timber-framed building that once served as a courthouse. The practice of appealing to the water-spirits for judgment may be reflected in the legends of beheadings at holy wells.

Cornwall

Altarnun, SS 2281. The church and holy well are dedicated to St Non, St David's mother, probably a version of the Celtic Earth Mother deity, Ana. Her 'home' well is at St Non's in west Wales; another is at Pelynt in Cornwall. Insane people were immersed in the Altarnun water to cure their malady, then carried into the church for a Mass to be said over them.

Blisland, SX 0974. The ruined Treganna Chapel is in a wooded valley at Blisland. It contains a holy well. The field above carries the prohibition that it should never be ploughed.

Bodmin, SX 0767. St Guron's Well, once resorted to as an eye-well, is to the west of St Petroc's Church.

Boleigh, SW 4325. Five miles (8 km) west of Penzance is Rosmerryn House, in whose private grounds lies the Boleigh fogou. It has a passage 40 feet (12 m) long, with a short side-branch near the entrance. One stone is carved with the upper part of a human figure holding a spear and a diamond-shaped object, which some see as a snake's head.

Boscastle, SX 1192. The Witchcraft Museum contains a number of items relevant to Celtic folk traditions, the most significant of which is the Troy Stone, a slab of slate with a carved labyrinth pattern.

Callington, SX 3769. Dupath Well is on a farm a mile (1.6 km) east of Callington. It is an early sixteenth-century building, the largest well-house in Cornwall, surmounted by a pinnacled niche.

Cardinham, SX 1269. The church has a fine Celtic cross, and a few hundred yards north of the church is the stone-lined Trezance Well, amid the ruins of a former well-house and oratory.

Carn Euny, SW 4028. Two miles (3.2 km) west of Sancreed in the village centre is the fogou of Carn Euny. It is a passage 66 feet (20 m) in length, with a circular chamber part way along.

Cheesewring, Bodmin Moor, SX 2571. The Devil's Cheesewring is a remarkable natural rock-formation that is a good example of a place of natural sanctity in the landscape. Access is gained by a track north of Minions, signposted to the west of the B3254. Close by are the remains of the shelter of Daniel Gumb, an eighteenth-century stonecutter who, in the bardic tradition, carved geometric designs upon the rocks.

Chysauster, SW 4734. The fogou in this ancient ruined village is almost roofless, with only two remaining lintels.

Dozmary Pool, Bolventor, Bodmin Moor, SX 1777. Of several lakes said to be the resting place of Arthur's sword, Excalibur, Dozmary Pool is the most popular. Considered to be bottomless until it dried up in 1869, it is the reputed haunt of the Lady of the Lake. In 1994, talismans empowered magically by being 'washed in Dozmary Pool' were advertised in *Old Moore's Almanack*.

Duloe, SX 2457. Close to Duloe stone circle, the well-house of St Cuby's Well is located beside the B3254, south-east of Duloe, 4 miles (6.4 km) south-west of Liskeard. The basin formerly serving the well is now in Duloe church.

Fowey, SX 1152. The Tristan Stone, a pedestal bearing a sixth-century stone with an inscription commemorating Drustanus, perhaps Tristan, Iseult's lover; it is on the A3082 before Fowey. It is not on the original site, having been moved in 1971 from the Four Turnings crossroads near Menabilly.

Germoe, SW 5829. A medieval shrine in the churchyard is said to contain St Germoe's Chair, from which the saint preached.

Golant, north of Fowey, SX 1255. Next to the church porch is St Samson's Well, reconstructed in 1938 but dating from at least the sixth century. The well has a black image of the saint.

Halligye, SW 7123. In the grounds of Trelowarren estate at Halligye is a fogou.

Helston, SW 6728. Beside a stream near Trelil Farm is the holy well-house of St Wendrona.

Holywell Bay. Two holy wells of St Cubert exist here. The first, in a fourteenth-century well-house, is at SW 7758, whilst the other, at SW 7660, is a rock-basin in a cave at the east end of the beach, accessible only at low tide.

Lewannick, SX 2780. Lewannick church has an ogham stone, but is better known for the font which, along with other esoteric sigils, bears a cross-containing labyrinth pattern.

Liskeard, SX 2564. At Liskeard is St Martin's Well, otherwise known as Pipewell. Once a well of healing, it is inaccessible now as the water is polluted and deemed undrinkable.

Maresk, SW 8443. Fragments of the Cornish forest of Morrois exist here as woodland in the parish of St Clement near Truro.

Morvah, SW 4035. Close to Morvah is the prehistoric structure of Men-an-Tol. Whatever its original purpose, and there is no shortage of theory, this stone was used at some time for healing. One had to crawl – or be passed – through the hole as a cure for infertility, or to bring good luck.

Mount Edgecumbe, SX 4452. Next to the Cremyll road is the well-house of St Julian.

Mylor, SW 8235. The churchyard contains St Mylor's holy well and the tallest cross in Cornwall, with solar carvings.

Pelynt, SX 2256. St Nun's (or Non's) Well is located in a grove of thorn and oak. The water collects in a stone basin protected by the local Piskies, who punish anyone who does not leave an offering.

Pendeen Vau, SW 3835. At Pendeen Manor Farm, off the B3306 between Morvah and St Just, is a fogou within a 'great wall'. It has a Y-shaped passage. It is on private property, and access must be requested.

Penzance, SW 4730. Outside the Penlee Museum is a notable wheel-head cross which once stood at another site, serving as a market cross. Its shaft is divided into panels, some of which bear peck-marks.

Perranzabuloe, SW 7752. A sacred place of the Cornish patron, St Piran, with a holy well.

Polperro, SX 2051. A cave called Willy Wilcock's Hole, on the western side of the harbour below Chapel Hill, is the haunt of a fisherman, who, entering, was taken into the fairy kingdom and still wanders, seeking his way back into this world.

Porthcurno, near Treen, SW 3923. On the headland east of here is the rocking stone called the Logan Stone, overthrown by

naval hooligans in 1824 and later re-erected.

Porthmeor, SW 4337. The remains of a fogou can be seen here. It is above ground and now roofless.

Roche, SW 9860. A fifteenth-century chapel dedicated to St Michael, solar saint of holy mountains, is integral with the higher pinnacles of a striking granite outcrop here, located south of the village on the road to Bugle. At SW 9861 is St Gundred's Well, visited at sunrise on Maundy Thursday and the following two Thursdays for the cure of eye ailments.

St Buryan. At Boskenna, at SW 4324 on the B3315 to the south-east of St Buryan, is a truncated phalloid wheel-head cross set into a cider-press stone. Another interesting cross is to the north of it at Vellansagia, SW 4325. To the north-west of St Buryan at SW 3927 is Crows-an-Wra, 'The Cross of the Witch', after which the hamlet is named.

St Cleer, north of Liskeard, SX 2468. Accompanied by a stone cross of Latin form, the fifteenth-century well-house of St Cleer is close to the church. A mile (1.6 km) from the village on the road to Redgate are the remains of a tenth-century inscribed memorial stone commemorating the Cornish King Doniert, drowned in the River Fowey in 875.

St Clether, SX 2084. The holy well and chapel of St Clederus, 8 miles (13 km) west of Launceston, to the north-west of the church. Water from the well flows beneath the chapel, which was restored in 1895 by the Reverend Sabine Baring-Gould, the antiquary.

St Levan's, near Land's End, SW 3821. Located on the cliff-top, the holy well of St Levan is accessible by a footpath opposite St Levan's Church. In former times, patients would incubate upon the saint's bed next to the well. On the south side of the church is the cracked stone called St Levan's Seat, which bears an end-of-the-world prophecy: 'When with panniers astride, A pack-horse one can ride, Through St Levan's Stone, The world will be done.'

St Michael's Mount, near Marazion, SW 5130. A holy mountain reputed to have been built by the giant Cormoran. Formerly inland, its Cornish name *Carreck los en cos* means 'the grey rock in the wood'. A solar holy mountain, it was dedicated after Christians interpreted an apparition seen there as St Michael.

Sancreed, south-east of St Just, SW 4129. The churchyard at Sancreed contains two notable Celtic unpierced wheel-head monolithic crosses. West of the church is the holy well, access to which is by a flight of stone steps into a cavern that contains the waters.

Tintagel, SX 0588. Many elements of the Celtic sacred landscape are present here. The castle on a rock promontory to the west of the town, associated in medieval legend with the birth of King Arthur, is the site of a former Celtic monastic settlement. The axis of the monks' garden here is orientated on Beltane (May Day) at sunrise. St Julitta's Well is one of three on this promontory. Beneath the neck of the castle peninsula runs Merlin's Cave. In the town is King Arthur's Hall, built in the 1920s to commemorate chivalry and the quest for the Grail. A mile away (1.6 km) in Rocky Valley at SX 0789 on a rockface are two carved classical labyrinths, perhaps a stopping-place on the route to the Celtic religious settlement further up the valley. Other stopping-places are St Piran's Well (SX 0788) and St Nectan's Kieve, a waterfall beneath the site of the saint's hermitage.

Whitstone, SX 2698. One of the many St Anne's Wells is in Whitstone churchyard,

a small well-house in the side of a bank. An archaic-looking Celtic head of Ana guards the entrance.

The Isle of Man

The Isle of Man is a holy island in its own right, being dedicated to the Celtic divinity of the sea, Manannan MacLir.

Millennium Way. Renamed in 1988, the trackway called 'Raad mooar ree Goree', the royal road of the Isle of Man, runs from Crosby (SC 3729) to Churchtown (SC 4294). It is identified with the mythic King Orry and links stopping-places of ancient sanctity.

Onchan, near Douglas, SC 4078. Onchan Church (Kirk Conchan) has an image depicting the Manx deity, Conchem, as a dog-headed man. Conchem was later assimilated with St Christopher, and his fair was celebrated on St Christopher's Day.

St Maughold's Head, SC 4993. St Maughold's Well is located east of the church at St Maughold, to the north of the headland. Legend tells how it appeared when the saint was flying across the Irish sea by horse, and its knee touched the ground. Its waters are a remedy for sick eyes and infertility. There is an important collection of Celtic crosses in the churchyard at Maughold.

Tynwald Hill, St John's, SC 2883. This is the last traditional meeting-hill still in serious use. Each 5 July the assembly of the Manx Parliament sits to enact their ancient ceremonies and proclaim new laws to the people.

France outside Brittany

Aix-en-Provence, Provence. Two and a half miles (4 km) north of Aix-en-Provence are the remains of the oppidum of Entremont, capital and national shrine of the Celto-Ligurian Saluvii. Sculptures, Celtic heads and sacred objects from Entremont are displayed in Aix at the Musée Granet.

Bourbon l'Archambault, Allier. The springs of the spa here were the focus of a sacred place of the Celtic god Burmanus (Borvo).

Cléry-Saint-André, Loire. In the basilica of Notre-Dame-de-Cléry are the tombs of King Louis XI (1461–83) and Queen Charlotte of Savoy. Whilst their bodies lie in the tomb, their mummified heads are kept, following Celtic tradition, in a glass shrine.

Dax, Landes. One of the most important spa towns in France. The Fontaine Chaude in the centre of the town is a hot spring that was the focus of the local cultus of the Celtic deity Gallicized as Néhé.

Douvres-la-Délivrande, Normandy, is reputed to be the oldest pilgrimage to the Celtic goddess La Delle Yv-Rande, an image replaced in the fourth century, it is said, by a Madonna image. The present image is a black Madonna, probably dating from the sixteenth century. The present nineteenth-century church building attracts votive offerings.

Groseau, Vaucluse. Connected with Mont Ventoux is the holy spring of the Celtic deity Groselos, the Source du Groseau which pours from a cliff-face on the D974 road that links it with the summit of the holy mountain.

Les Andelys, Eure, Normandy. The fountain of St Clothilde at Le Grand Andely, on the D125 road, was formerly the site of relic-washing, when the waters were empowered to heal. It is now a wishing well.

Les Fontaines Salées, near the River Cure, Burgundy. An ancient Celtic water-shrine, where mineral springs issue from the ground.

Les-Saintes-Maries-de-la-Mer, Bouches-du-Rhône. The most sacred shrine in Provence is this church in the Camargue, built over a spring sacred to a Celtic threefold water-goddess at a place once called Oppidum Priscum Ra. The church, which superseded a Celto-Roman temple, contains a Mithraic stone, but is dedicated to the Christian versions of the Celtic threefold goddess – the two Marys and St Sarah. Today, it is the most sacred shrine of the Romani, who flock there to venerate their divinity, Sarah-la-Kâli, at the Gypsy Pilgrimage on 24–25 May.

Lyons, Rhône. The Musée Gallo-Romaine de Fourvière (Rue Cléberg) in this former Celtic city of Lugdunum contains the Coligny Calendar, the most valuable document of Celtic druidism.

Mont Blanc, between Chamonix (France) and Cormayeur (Cormaggiore in Italy). Like Mont Pilatus, Mont Blanc is one of the forbidden holy mountains; it was formerly called 'la Montagne Maudite', 'the cursed mountain'.

Mont-Saint-Michel, Manche, Normandy. Said to be France's most visited place, Mont-Saint-Michel stands on the boundary between Normandy and Brittany. A Celtic holy mountain of the sun, like its Cornish counterpart near Penzance, it was rededicated by Christian priests to St Michael. Accessed by a causeway that is covered by high tide (as is the car park!), the monastery is reached by Grande Rue, which is lined with shops that sell the usual touristic kitsch that reinforces spectacle whilst demeaning the sacred.

Mont-Sainte-Odile, near Otrott, Bas-Rhin. Around the summit of the holy mountain of Alsace (2325 ft, 763 m) is the Pagan Wall, a Celtic stone wall 6¼ miles (10 km) long, bound with bronze joints, which has no parallel. The Chapel of the Angels in the monastery of Hohenbourg is located over a Pagan sanctuary, whilst the eye-curing holy well of Ste Odile springs from the rock on the road below.

Mont Ventoux, Vaucluse. Near Carpentras, on the northern border of Provence, is the Celtic holy mountain of the winds, 5760 feet (1890 m) high. The summit, 'The Home of the Winds', is accessible by the D974 road. Excavations here have revealed hundreds of small terracotta ex-voto trumpets.

Nîmes, Gard. Nîmes is named after the Celtic god Nemausus, whose holy spring at the foot of Mont Cavalier was the focus of a Celto-Roman water-shrine, of which the ruins of one temple dedicated to Diana remain. The source is the focus of the Jardin de la Fontaine, an eighteenth-century Nymphaeum. At the Place d'Assas is another fountain, with modern images of the Nemausus and his consort.

Saint-Honorat, in the Îles de Lérins, Côte d'Azur. Saint-Honorat reflects the Celtic tradition of the sacred island. The saint's monastic settlement (*c.* 375) is said to have played host to St Patrick. Since 1869 it has held a Cistercian monastery, which only men are permitted to visit. Saint-Honorat's relationship to its subsidiary women's island, Sainte-Marguerite, parallels exactly that of the monastic island of Caldey in Wales to St Margaret's Island.

Saint-Maure-de-Touraine, Indre-et-Loire. The Celtic sacred place of Ariacum, where in the mid-fifth century the 'graves'

of the holy women (or Celtic goddesses) St Maure and St Brigid were discovered miraculously. The twelfth-century church inside the castle walls is their shrine.

Saint-Rémy-de-Provence, Bouches-du-Rhône. At the Plateau des Antiques, south of the town centre, are Celto-Ligurian and Celto-Roman remains, including the Nymphaeum, marking the original holy well around which the complex grew up.

Vienne, Isère. In the Musée Lapidaire in the former church of Saint-Pierre at the capital of the Celtic Allobroges is a sculpture of the tutelary goddess, Tutela, found in a pool of the water-shrine of St Colombe nearby. The sacred complex contains a temple of Augustus and Livia, a temple of Cybele, baths and churches.

Brittany

Brocéliande Forest. Its remains are the Forêt de Huelgoat in the Montagnes d'Arrée, east of Brest; the Forêt de Paimpont, 12½ miles (20 km) west of Rennes; and the two sacred woods Coat-an-Hay (The Day Wood) and Coat-an-Noz (The Night Wood), 6 miles (10 km) west of Guingamp.

Carnac, Morbihan. Carnac means 'piles of stones', and it is rightfully famed for its plentiful megalithic structures, around three thousand stones in all. Most were never touched by Christian priests, though the tumulus of Saint-Michel is a notable exception.

Châteaubriant, Loire-Atlantique. On the N171 road to Pouancé, 1 mile (1.6 km) from the church of St-Jean-de-Béré, is the Carrière des Fusillés. Commemorating hostages murdered by the Nazis in 1941, the concrete base of this war memorial continues the Celtic tradition of transporting sacred earth by containing soil taken from all of the places where the atrocities took place.

Folle-Pensée, Morbihan. La Fontaine de Barenton: local lore tells that if a libation of water from this healing holy well is poured onto the rock called Merlin's Step, then a storm will be produced. The last recorded example of this was during a drought in the 1930s.

Forêt de Paimpont, between Rennes and Ploërmel. Off the N24, this is the remnant of the great Breton forest of Brocéliande, now expanding again after centuries of destruction. At the Château de Comper, 4 miles (6.4 km) north of Paimpont, is a lake claimed to be that where the Arthurian Lady of the Lake manifested herself.

Hameau de Rungleo, Finistère, near Daoulas, 28 miles (45 km) south-west of Morlais, 11 miles (18 km) east-south-east of Brest, is the Croix des Douze Apôtres.

Huelgoat, Finistère. Roche Tremblante, granite rocking stone.

Herm, Channel Islands. On a reef near Jethou between Herm and Crevichon Rock is the chapel of St Magloire, a typical seashore island-chapel in the Celtic tradition. In the eleventh century it belonged to the abbey of Mont-Saint-Michel.

Île de Sein, off the southern coast of Finistère, is accessible by boat from Audierne. This former Pagan holy island may be the famous 'Island of Women' of classical authors.

Josselin, east Morbihan. On the N24, this shrine, Notre-Dame-du-Roncier, is the site of a miraculous discovery of Our Lady's sacred image in a bramble bush. The pardon is held on the second Sunday in September.

Kerégard-Vraz, Plumeur, Finistère, 14 miles (23 km) south-west of Quimper, 4 miles (6.4 km) west of Pont l'Abbé. A narrow, rounded granite megalith cross.

Lampaul-Guimiliau, Finistère, has a seventeenth-century Calvary and ossuary.

Lanrivoaré, Finistère. Close to the church is the Moaning-Place, eight megalithic boulders with a stone cross marking, it is said, a massacre in the fifth century — clearly a place of ancestral memory.

La Roche aux Fées, south-east of Rennes, Ille-et-Vilaine. Megalithic remains mark an ancient place for lovers.

La Roche-Maurice, Finistère. This hilltop church has a seventeenth-century ossuary with a carving of Ankou, the king of the dead.

Le Folgoët, 1¼ miles (2 km) from Lesneven, Finistère. A pardon is held here each 8 September, commemorating the miraculous lily bearing the words 'Ave Maria' that grew on the grave of Salaün ar Foll.

Locronan, Finistère. St Ronan's Church. La Trôménie, second Sunday in July. The forty-four local shrines, decked with flowers during the pardon, include the Fontaine Saint-Eutrope. The annual Trôménie is 4 miles (6.4 km) long, whilst every six years (2001 being the next) the Grande Trôménie of 9 miles (14 km) is processed. At the summit of Locronan mountain (950 ft, 290 m), 1¼ miles (2 km) above the town, is the pilgrimage Chapelle Plach-Ar with the rock called Kador St-Ronan (St Ronan's Chair).

Menez-Bré, west of Guingamp, Côtes d'Armor. To the north of the N12 is the holy hill of Menez-Bré, visited by practitioners of earth religions, and sacred to the contemporary Odinist Church of Brittany.

Menez-Hom, Rumengol, west of Châteaulin, Finistère. Off the D887, the holy hill of Brittany where each year the venerable Midsummer festival is celebrated in addition to a Trinity Sunday pardon of Notre-Dame-de-Tout-Remède.

Moëlan-sur-Mer, Finistère. The church has a menhir next to its north-east corner.

Néant-sur-Yvel, Porhoët, between Mauron and Ploërmel, east Morbihan. The site of a Breton nemeton exists in the Forêt de Lanouée at Pont-Aven. The Pardon and Festival of Golden Gorse are held on the first Sunday in August.

Penvern, Côte-du-Nord, 5½ miles (9 km) north-west of Lannion, 2 miles (3.2 km) north-north-east of Trébeurden. The cross of St Duzec, 25 feet (8.1 m) high.

Plozévet, near Quimper. The Church of St Démet (Christianized version of Demeter), built over a holy well, whose water bubbles up on each side of the south porch.

Pluvigner, Morbihan. The Chapel of St Mériadek, 3 miles (5 km) east of Pluvigner, is the site of pardons in March and August and has a holy well, which is resorted to for the cure of sick cattle. Also at Pluvigner is the holy well of St Guignér, which has a stag legend associated with its discovery. A pardon is held here on the third Sunday in May.

Rochefort-en-Terre, east Morbihan. Notre-Dame-de-la-Tronchaye, where a black Madonna was discovered in a hollow tree in the twelfth century, is on the D774. The pardon is held there on the third Sunday in August.

Sainte-Anne d'Auray, Morbihan. The primary sacred place of Brittany is a perfect example of the evolution of shrines. From the place where Yves Nicolazic found the Pagan image of Bona Dea, interpreted as St Anne, a major pilgrimage shrine has evolved. There is the Fountain of Miracles, a treasury with relics of St Anne, a nineteenth-century basilica, a Calvary-way, and an enormous memorial to the fallen of the Great War. Nicolazic's house is preserved as a museum. The Grand Pardon is held every year on 25–26 July.

Sainte-Anne-la-Palud, overlooking the Bay of Douarnanez, pardon on the last Sunday in August, frequented by fishermen, as the shrine originated when an image of St Anne was dredged up from the sea in a fishing net.

Saint-Cado, north of Erdeven, Morbihan. On a former island in the Rivière d'Etel, now linked to the mainland by a causeway, is the church and holy well of Saint-Cado. The holy well is 325 feet (100 m) from the church, reached by steps. The small stone well-house is surmounted by an Irish-style Celtic cross finial.

Saint-Jean-du-Doigt, north of Morlaix. The Pardon of the Fire is held here; also home of the relic of the finger of St John.

Stival, Morbihan. St Mériadek's shrine contains his bell, the Bonnet of St Mériadek, used at the pardon (held the day before Trinity Sunday). One hundred yards (91 m) south-west of the church, in a wooded valley, is the holy well of St Mériadek.

Trédaniel, east of Moncontour, Côtes d'Armour. On a hill at Trédaniel is the seventeenth-century Chapel of Notre Dame du Haut, a shrine of the Sept Saints Guérisseurs (Seven Healing Saints) of Brittany. They are: St Yvertin, who cures persistent headaches; St Hervé (Houarniaule), who eliminates irrational fears; St Eugénie, who eases childbirth; St Lubin, who relieves rheumatism and eye troubles; St Hubert, who heals wounds; and St Mamert, who alleviates digestive problems. The identity of the seventh, sometimes given as St Corentin, sometimes as St Samson, sometimes as yet others, seems to vary from place to place. Their pardon is held on 15 August.

Tréguier, west of Paimpol, 15 miles (24 km) north of Guingamp. The Pardon of St Yves, patron of Brittany, is held on the nearest Sunday to 19 May, at the Cathedral of St Tugdual here.

Germany

Aachen, Rhineland-Palatinate. The Cathedral and Chapel Palatine stand over a Celtic shrine of water-healing, called Aquis Granum by the Romans. In the entrance is a bronze Celto-Roman she-wolf of circa 160, said to be the beast of the Celtic *anima loci*. The place called Quellenhof marks another of Aachen's water-shrines.

Altheim-Heiligkreuztal, Baden-Württemberg. In this area are two ritual enclosures and several groups of Celtic burial-mounds, including the tumulus of Hohmichele, the largest in central Europe, surmounted by a modern memorial.

Amöneburg, Niedersachsen. A Celtic hill-fort with a Pagan temple where a church to St Michael was erected in 721.

Belsen, Tübingen, Baden-Württemberg. A place of solar worship. The west front of the Romanesque church, standing on a high point, bears two images of the Celtic god Béél (Belenos), accompanied by heads of cattle, sheep and swine, and a cross. The tympanum of the south door is carved with solar symbols, and in former times a 'light funnel' projected sunlight into the church at certain times. To the south is a notable linden tree, and, south of this, a square *Viereckschanze*.

Blaubeuren-Asch, Baden-Württemberg. In the Attenlauh woodland, 1½ miles (2.4 km) east-south-west of Asch, is a group of sixty-two Celtic tumuli.

Bopfingen, Baden-Württemberg. The Ipf is a major Celtic hill-fort, with the remains of sacred places, access to which is by a serpentine avenue of linden trees.

Büdingen, Hesse. The Glauberg contains an 'archaeological footpath' that takes in sacred springs, stone walls and other interesting features.

Constance, Baden-Württemberg. The cathedral contains skulls preserved in the Celtic tradition, visible behind glass in the gilded Baroque high altar.

Dornburg, Hesse. Close to an early La Tène settlement on the Dornburg, a conical basalt peak which is 1286 feet (396 m) high, where the compass is deflected by a strong magnetic field. On the eastern slope is a gallery-like cavity. The snow lies here all year round in a miniature glacier called Ewiges Eis (Eternal Ice). Once a Celtic sacred place, it was profaned in the nineteenth century by the local brewer who used it as a natural refrigerator for storing beer.

Eberdingen-Hochdorf, Baden-Württemberg. At Hochdorf is the restored burial mound from which the grave-goods of the so-called *Keltenfürst* or Celtic prince, which are now in the Württembergisches Landesmuseum in Stuttgart, were removed. It is surmounted by a modern standing stone, and surrounded by posts. Nearby is the Keltenmuseum Hochdorf/Enz, with reconstructions and explanations of the site.

Externsteine, near Horn, North Rhine-Westphalia. An eleventh-century carving of the world tree Irminsul on a remarkable rock-outcrop recognized as a sacred place by every religion and sect from antiquity to the present day.

Göppingen-Bartenbach, Baden-Württemberg. In the Oberholz woodland, to the south-east of Bartenbach, is a group of thirty-three Celtic burial mounds.

Heckenmünster, Rhineland-Palatinate. The Victoria-Quelle and the Wallenborn here are two holy wells still flowing and used on the site of a Celtic water-shrine. The Victoria-Quelle is situated on the path to Erlenbach, whilst the Wallenborn is housed in a well-house which is 3 feet (1 m) high. In Celto-Roman times, there was a temple, baths, accommodation for pilgrims and a theatre.

Heidelberg, Baden-Württemberg. The wooded Heiligenberg, best reached by the Philosophenweg (the Philosophers' Path), is a Celtic holy mountain upon which a monastery and basilica dedicated to St Michael were built in the eleventh century. Roman temples of Mercury and Mithras once stood here. The castle contains the holy well of the wise woman or *anima loci*, Jutta.

Heidenheim-Grosskuchen, Baden-Württemberg. In the woodland called Badhäule, east of Grosskuchen, is a Celtic grave-field with sixty-eight tumuli.

Hirschlanden (Stadt Dinzingen), Baden-Württemberg. A Hallstatt-period grave-hill, once surmounted by a Celtic warrior hero-figure, now in the Württembergisches Landesmuseum, Stuttgart.

Holzgerlingen, Baden-Württemberg. A La Tène-period figure of a 'Janus-headed' deity, now in the Württembergisches Landesmuseum, Stuttgart.

Homburg-Schwarzenacker, Saarland. A full-size reconstruction of a Gallo-Roman temple at the Freilichtmuseum, a sacred locus of the goddess Epona.

Hörselberg, Thuringia. The holy mountain known in the medieval period as 'Venusberg', seat of 'the Lady Venus' and visited by bards.

Karlsruhe, Baden-Württemberg. Jupiter Column (another stands outside the former Lapidarium in Stuttgart).

Kempten, Bavaria. The Archäologischer Park Cambodunum contains the remains of a Celtic city mentioned by Strabo, along with the remains of a grid of streets and over a dozen temples.

Kilchberg, Tübingen, Baden-Württemberg. Full-size reconstruction of a later Hallstatt grave mound with standing stones and a sacred stone image.

Lauingen-Faimingen, Baden-Württemberg. A *Viereckschanze* here, west of Dillingen an der Donau, contains the remains of a temple of Apollo Grannos.

Leinfelden-Echterdingen, Baden-Württemberg. In the woodland called Federlesmahd, under the flight-path of Stuttgart Airport, are a *Viereckschanze* and tumulus-field. Close to one tumulus are stone replicas of Celtic memorials.

Münsingen-Dottingen, Baden-Württemberg. On the road to the Glendwald, south of Dottingen, are Celtic tumuli, formerly numbering twenty-four, but reduced by archaeology and agriculture.

Mürrhardt, Baden-Württemberg. The church is built on a high point, on the site of a Roman temple of Mithras, which itself occupied a Celtic holy high place.

Nagold, Calw, Baden-Württemberg. The Celtic tumulus known as 'Krautbühl' or 'Heidenbühl' is north-west of Schlossberg, south-west of the confluence of the Waldach and Nagold rivers. Dating from the seventh century BCE, it was used in medieval times as a judgment-hill.

Nettersheim-Pesch, south of Euskirchen, Rhineland-Palatinate. In the Hornbachtal towards Gilsdorf-Nothen is the signposted 'Heidentempel' on the Addis, the remains of a Celto-Roman temple dedicated to the Matronae. The local deities of Pesch are Matronae Vocallinehae.

Obermarchtal, Baden-Württemberg. A mile (1.6 km) south-west of Obermar-

217

Germany

chtal is a *Viereckschanze* and around seventy Celtic burial mounds.

Reichenau, Lake Constance, Baden-Württemberg. Ancient Celtic-founded churches and orchards on a former holy island with a remarkably favourable climate, now accessed by a road causeway.

Römerstein-Zainingen, Baden-Württemberg. A mile (1.6 km) north-east of Zainingen and north of Breiter Weg in woodland is a Celtic 'gravefield' containing sixty-two tumuli.

Schwäbisch Hall, Baden-Württemberg. The ancient Celtic salt well is still visible, surrounded by an octagonal well-head, though it is sadly neglected. In 1939, the remains of the Celtic salt settlement were discovered beneath the Kreissparkasse, and the museum contains the findings.

Speyer, Rhineland-Palatinate. The cathedral here is built on the site of a temple of Nantosuelta and the threefold goddess.

Teck, near Owen, Baden-Württemberg. The holy mountain called Teck is marked by a smaller hill, the Bölle, which bears a grove of pine trees uncannily similar to the mark-woods in Herefordshire noted by Alfred Watkins. It guards the Sybillenloch, a Celtic oracular cave. A double straight line across the valley, only visible as crop-marks, is aligned upon the pine-grove and cave.

Werbach, Baden-Württemberg. A Catholic chapel of Our Lady, built in 1902 over a stream and incorporating a Celtic holy well, is resorted to for cures, as attested by the ex-votos inside the door to the right. A Hallstatt-period cemetery was excavated nearby in 1977.

Würzburg, Franken. Founded by Irish monks Kilian, Kolonat and Totnan in the seventh century, the Romanesque church called the Neumünster is the shrine of St Kilian, to whom the cathedral to the south is dedicated.

Austria

Bregenz, Vorarlberg. The upper town of Bregenz is built over the Celtic oppidum of Brigantium. It stands on the delta of the Rhine at the eastern end of the holy Brigantinus Lacus (Lake Constance, the Bodensee). The Vorarlberger Landesmuseum in Kornmarkt contains many Celtic finds from Brigantium.

Georgenberg, near Kirchdorf an der Krems, Upper Austria. On the Georgenberg (Kalvarienberg) is the pilgrimage church of St-Georg, which stands on the site of a Celto-Roman temple.

Hallein, Salzburg. Ten and a half miles (17 km) south of Salzburg was a major centre of salt-extraction in Celtic times. The Keltenmuseum, in the old administrative building of the saltworks by the river, holds one of the most important collections of Celtic artifacts in Europe.

Hallstatt, Salzkammergut. South of Bad Ischl on the B166 road at the side of the Hallstätter See is Hallstatt. Archaeological finds here gave their name to the Hallstatt epoch (*c.* 1000–600 BCE).

Karnburg, Kärnten. On the B94 road close to the Ulrichsberg is the former Celtic holy mountain, Mons Carantanus, on which a temple of Isis Noraia stood in Roman times. Karnburg once held the inauguration-stone of the dukes of Carinthia, now in the Klagenfurt museum.

Klagenfurt, Kärnten. The name of Klagenfurt perpetuates the Celtic tradition of 'the washer at the ford', *Klaga* being Old Bavarian for a woman guardian of the dead at a ford. The church of St Peter am Bichl here has late ninth-century Celtic interlace carvings.

Leibnitz, Steiermark. South-west of Graz on the road to Maribor, close to Leibnitz, is the former Celtic holy hill of Frauenberg. Adjacent to the Baroque pilgrimage church is the site of a Roman temple of Isis.

Magdalensberg, near Klagenfurt, Kärnten. The Filialskirche St Helena und Magdalena stands on the peak of this Celtic holy mountain (3345 ft, 1059 m), the successor of a Romanesque church erected on the foundations of a temple of the Celto-Roman god Mars Katobius. There is a pre-Christian stone with three heads in the nave. The *Vierbergelauf* (the 'four mountains' run'), a sacred passage with Pagan origins, is held after Easter each year and begins at this peak.

Sonntagberg, Rosenau, Lower Austria. The pilgrimage church of Sonntagberg (Mount Sunday) is built on the site of a reputed miracle where a shepherd boy found a loaf on a mysterious Pagan inscribed stone on the former Celtic solar mountain. In 1614, an image of the Trinity was set up above the stone to allay Protestant accusations of Paganism.

Vienna. Austria's capital is the successor of the Celtic settlement of Vindobona. South of Stefansdom (the cathedral), at the junction of Kärntnerstrasse and Graben, is Stock-im-Eisenplatz, where the trunk of the hammermen's tree is preserved. Like Zurich, Vienna has a street called Rennweg, recalling an ancient ceremonial alignment.

Switzerland

Baden, 12½ miles (20 km) north-west of Zurich. The Kursaal here (1875) continues the use of the Celtic-venerated hot springs called Aquae Helveticae by the Romans. Legend tells of the miracles wrought here by St Verena, the Christian

aspect of the water, or the lake-goddess Verena.

Beatenberg. Beside Lake Thun near Interlaken, beneath Beatenberg on a major fault line, are the Beatushöhlen caves, once the hermitage of the Irish monk, Beatus, who drove a dragon from them. The Beatenbach issues from the rockface nearby.

Bern. This capital city was founded in 1191 by Berchtold V, duke of Zähringen, after an apparition of a bear indicated the importance of the site. Since 1480, bears have been kept at municipal expense at the Bärengraben, the bear-pit that continues the remembrance of the Celtic bear-goddess Artio, whose sacred land this is.

Geneva. Geneva was the last oppidum of the Allobroges. A life-sized wooden figure, the Hooded Man, dating from around 80 BCE, was found in the lake here, and is on show in the Schweizerische Landesmuseum in Zurich.

Lake Constance. Lake Constance, which contains the holy island of Reichenau, was a Celtic sacred lake, called Brigantinus Lacus by the Romans.

La Tène, Lake Neuchâtel. Beyond Saint Blaise on the road from Neuchâtel is the hamlet of La Tène, the ritual water-deposit site, where the La Tène style was defined from objects recovered from the holy lake in 1856.

Lucerne. In former times, Mount Pilatus, close to Lucerne, was, like Mont Blanc, one of the forbidden holy mountains of Europe. Until the fifteenth century it was called Frackimünd, and the connection with Pontius Pilate appears to explain its former forbidden status.

St Bernard Pass. The Grand St Bernard Pass is on the road between Martigny and Aosta. Now bypassed by a tunnel, it was a Celtic stopping-place sacred to

Poeninus. Its ancient name, from Roman times, was Mons Jovis. A temple of Jupiter Poeninus formerly stood at the Plan de Jupiter. Only in the twelfth century was the place taken over by the Christian Church and renamed after St Bernard of Menthon, founder of the nearby hospice of the Col du Grand St Bernard, which may be on the site of Pagan collegiate buildings.

St Gallen. The town is named after the monastery founded by the eponymous 'Gallic' (Irish) monk, St Gall. It was a major centre of Celtic Christianity, renowned for its learning. The cathedral library contains many treasures, including eighth-century Irish gospels, an eighth-century Virgil and a plan of the abbey dating from around 820.

St Maurice. South of Monthey on the Martigny road is the Abbey of St Maurice at the northern end of the town of the same name. The treasury preserves the skull of St Candidus in a fine reliquary.

St Petersinsel, Bieler See, between Neuchâtel and Biel. Connected to Lake Neuchâtel by the canalized River Zihl, the Bieler See contains a wooded former Celtic holy island dedicated to St Peter. The Cluniac abbey there is connected to the shore by a causeway called the Heidenweg (Pagan Way).

Italy

Cervo, east of Imperia, Liguria. Around Cervo and inland is the *Lucus Burmani*, the sacred area of the Celtic god Burmanus (Borvo). Two churches in Cervo show Burmanus's influence. The front of the Baroque church of St John the Baptist has images of a stag and crossed antlers, Burmanus's sacred animal. Another church, dedicated to St George, stands over a Celto-Roman temple of the god. A church dedicated to Our Lady in an olive grove at nearby Rovere has, on the west end beneath an image of the Madonna, a tree and head of Burmanus.

St Pierre, west of Aosta, Piedmont. In the castle here are the rich findings from the sanctuary of Jupiter Poeninus on the St Bernard Pass. They include a silver head of the god and numerous votive offerings left by travellers crossing the dangerous pass.

Varallo, Piedmont. The Sacro Monte at Varallo, the Sanctuary of the New Jerusalem, founded by Bernardo Caimi, is the model from which all other Calvary mountains were copied.

Bibliography

All books published in London unless otherwise stated

Adamnan: *The Life of Saint Columba*. Trans. Wentworth Huyshe. n.d.
Andrews, E.: *Ulster Folklore*. Belfast, 1913.
Anwyl, Edward: *Celtic Religion*. 1906.
Atkinson, Robert: *The Book of Ballymote*. Dublin, 1887.
Ayres, James: *British Folk Art*. 1977.
Bächtold-Stäubli, Hans (ed.): *Handwörterbuch des deutschen Aberglaubens*. 9 vols. Berlin, 1927–42.
Bain, Robert: *The Clans and Tartans of Scotland*. Glasgow, 1990.
Bamford, Christopher, and William Price Marsh: *Celtic Christianity*. Edinburgh, 1986.
Baring-Gould, Sabine, and John Fisher: *The Lives of the British Saints*. 4 vols. 1908.
Benoit, F.: 'Le Symbolisme dans les sanctuaires de la Gaule', *Coll Latomus* 105 (1970).
Bernheimer, Richard: *Wild Men in the Middle Ages*. Cambridge, MA, 1952.
Berresford-Ellis, Peter: *The Celtic Empire: The First Millennium of Celtic History, 1000 BC–51 AD*. 1990.
—: *Dictionary of Celtic Mythology*. 1992.
Best, R.I.: 'The Settling of the Manor of Tara', *Eriu* 4 (1910).
Bieler, L.: *The Life and Legend of St Patrick*. Dublin, 1949.
Bittel, Kurt, Wolfgang Kimmig, and Siegwalt Schiek (eds): *Die Kelten in Baden-Württemberg*. Stuttgart, 1981.
Bonwick, James: *Irish Druids and the Old Religions*. New York, NY, 1986.
Bowen, Dewi: *Ancient Siluria, its Old Stones and Ceremonial Sites*. Felinfach, 1992.
Bowen, E.G.: *The Settlements of the Celtic Saints in Wales*. Cardiff, 1956.
Brand, J.: *Observations on the Popular Antiquities of Great Britain*. 3 vols. 1890.
Briggs, K.M.: *The Personnel of Fairyland*. Oxford, 1969.
Bromwich, R.: *Trioedd Ynys Prydein*. Cardiff, 1979.
Burgstaller, E.: *Felsbilder in Österreich*. Linz, 1972.
Bush, J.: *Hibernia Curiosa*. 1769.
Campbell, D.F.: *The Celtic Dragon Myth*. 1911.
Campbell, J.G.: *Superstitions of the Highlands and Islands of Scotland*. Edinburgh, 1900.
Chadwick, H.M.: *The Heroic Age*. 1912.
Chadwick, Nora K.: *The Age of the Saints in the Early Celtic Church*. 1963.
Clemen, Carl: *Die Reste der primitiven Religion im ältesten Christentum*. Giessen, 1916.
Coleman, J.C.: *The Caves of Ireland*. Tralee, 1965.
Cornish, V.: *Historic Thorn Trees of the British Isles*. n.d.
Croker, T. Crofton: *Fairy Legends and Traditions of the South of Ireland*. 1825.
Crossing, William: *The Ancient Stone Crosses of Dartmoor and its Borderland*. Exeter, 1902.
Cubbon, M.: *The Art of Manx Crosses*. Douglas, 1971.
De Vries, Jan: *Keltische Religion*. Stuttgart, 1961.
Dexter, T.H.: *Old Cornish Crosses*. 1896.
Dickins, B.: *Runic and Heroic Poems of the Old Teutonic Peoples*. 1915.
Dillon, M. (ed.): *Irish Sagas*. Dublin, 1959.
—, and N.K. Chadwick: *The Celtic Realms*. 1967.
Edwards, N., and A. Lane: *Early Medieval Settlements in Wales, A.D. 400–1100*. Cardiff, 1988.
Ellis-Davidson, H. R.: *Myths and Symbols in Pagan Europe*. Manchester, 1988.

Éluère, Christiane: *The Celts: First Masters of Europe*. 1993.
Evans, E. Estyn: *Irish Folk Ways*. 1957.
Evans-Wentz, W.Y.: *The Fairy Faith in Celtic Countries*. Oxford, 1911.
Filip, J.: *Die Keltische Zivilization und ihr Erbe*. Prague, 1961.
Fillipetti, Hervé, and Janine Trotereau: *Symboles et pratiques rituelles dans la maison paysanne traditionelle*. Paris, 1978.
Fitzpatrick, Jim: *Érinsaga*. Dublin, 1985.
Friers, Rowel: *Ulster Folklore*. Belfast, 1951.
Gantz, J.: *Early Irish Myths and Sagas*. Harmondsworth, 1981.
Göttner-Abendroth, H.: *Die Göttin und ihr Heros*. Munich, 1982.
Green, Miranda J.: *The Gods of the Celts*. Gloucester, 1986.
—: *Dictionary of Celtic Myth and Legend*. 1992.
Halliday, W.R.: *The Pagan Background of Early Christianity*. Liverpool, 1925.
Hanson, R.P.C.: *Life and Writings of the Historical Saint Patrick*. New York, NY, 1983.
Hardings, Leslie: *The Celtic Church in Britain*. 1972.
Hélias, Per Jakez: *Dictionnaire des saints bretons*. Paris, 1985.
Hemery, Eric: *Walking Dartmoor's Ancient Tracks*. 1986.
Henderson, G.: *Survivals in Belief among the Celts*. Glasgow, 1911.
Henken, Elissa R.: *Tradition of the Welsh Saints*. Cambridge, 1987.
Henry, Françoise: *Irish High Crosses*. Dublin, 1964.
Herrmann, Paul: *Das altgermanische Priesterwesen*. Jena, 1929.
Houston, J.M.: 'The Scottish *Burgh*', *Town Planning Review* 25 (1954–55), pp. 114–47.
Jackson, K.H.: *Language and History in Early Britain*. Edinburgh, 1953.
Jacobsthal, P.: *Early Celtic Art*. Oxford, 1944.
Johnson, Walter: *Byways in British Archaeology*. Cambridge, 1912.
Jones, David: *Epoch and Artist*. 1959.
Jones, Edward: *The Bardic Museum*. Cardiff, 1802.
Jones, Francis: *The Holy Wells of Wales*. Cardiff, 1954.
Jones, O. (ed.): *The Myvyrian Archaeology of Wales*. Denbigh, 1870.
Jones, Prudence: *Eight and Nine: Sacred Numbers of Sun and Moon in the Pagan North*. Bar Hill, 1982.
—: *Sundial and Compass Rose: Eight-fold Time Division in Northern Europe*. Bar Hill, 1982.
—, and Nigel Pennick: *A History of Pagan Europe*. 1995.
Jung, Erich: *Germanische Götter und Helden in Christlicher Zeit*. Munich, 1922.
Kaul, Flemming, Ivan Marazov, Jan Best, and Nanny De Vries: *Thracian Tales on the Gundestrup Cauldron*. Amsterdam, 1991.
Kennedy, Patrick: *Legendary Fictions of the Irish Celts*. 1866.
Kermode, P.M.C., and W.A. Herdmans: *Manks Antiquities*. Liverpool, 1914.
Keysler, J.G.: *Antiquitates Selectae Septentrionales et Celticae*. 1720.
Krahe, H.: *Unsere ältesten Flussnamen*. Wiesbaden, 1964.
Kruta, V. (ed.): *The Celts*. 1983.
Laing, Gordon J.: *Survivals of Roman Religion*. 1931.
Langdon, A.G.: *Old Cornish Crosses*. Truro, 1896.
Leask, H.G.: *Irish Churches and Monastic Buildings*. Dundalk, 1955.
Le Fanu, W.R.: *Seventy Years of Irish Life*. 1893.

Le Roux, Françoise, and Christian-J. Guyonvarc'h: *Les druides*. Rennes, 1978.

Lewis, F.R.: *Gwerin Ffristal a Thawlbwrdd*. Y Cymmrodorion, 1941.

Levis, Howard C.: *Bladud of Bath*. Bath, 1973.

Lindenschmit, L.: *Die Altherthümer unserer heidnischen Vorzeit*. Mainz, 1874–77.

Logan, Patrick: *The Holy Wells of Ireland*. Gerrard's Cross, 1980.

MacAlister, R.A.S.: *The Archaeology of Ireland*. 1928.

—: *Tara: A Pagan Sanctuary of Ancient Ireland*. 1931.

—: *Corpus Inscriptionum Insularum Celticarum*. Dublin, 1945.

McAnally, D.R.: *Irish Wonders*. 1888.

MacCana, Proinsias: *Celtic Mythology*. 1970.

MacCulloch, J.A.: *Celtic Mythology*. 1992.

Mackenzie, W.M.: *The Burghs of Scotland*. Edinburgh, 1948.

Mackey, James P. (ed.): *An Introduction to Celtic Christianity*. Edinburgh, 1989.

MacManus, Dermot: *The Middle Kingdom*. Gerrard's Cross, 1959.

McNeill, F. Marian: *Iona: A History of the Island*. Glasgow, 1920.

MacNeill, Maire: *The Festival of Lughnasa*. Oxford, 1962.

McParlane, J.: *Statistical Survey of the County of Donegal*. Dublin, 1802.

MacWhite, E.: 'Early Irish Board Games', *Eisge* 5 (1945).

Mahé, Canon: *Essai sur les antiquités du département du Morbihan*. Vannes, 1825.

Maringer, J.: 'Priests and Priestesses in Prehistoric Europe', *History of Religions* 17, 2 (1977), pp. 101–20.

Marstrander, C.: 'Thor en Irlande', *Revue celtique* 36 (1915–16).

Martin, Martin: *A Description of the Western Isles of Scotland*. 1703.

Marwick, E.W.: *The Folklore of Orkney and Shetland*. 1975.

Matthews, Caitlín: *The Elements of the Celtic Tradition*. Shaftesbury, 1989.

Mauny, Raymond: 'The Exhibition on "The World of Souterrains" at Vezelay (Burgundy, France) (1977)', *Subterranea Britannica Bulletin* 7 (1978), pp. 12–15.

Megaw, Ruth, and Vincent Megaw: *Celtic Art*. 1990.

Meirion-Jones, Gwyn I.: *The Vernacular Architecture of Brittany*. Edinburgh, 1982.

Michell, John: *The Old Stones of Land's End*. 1974.

—: *At the Centre of the World: Polar Symbolism Discovered in Celtic, Norse and Other Ritualized Landscapes*. 1994.

Mould, D.D.C. Pochin: *The Mountains of Ireland*. 1955.

—: *Irish Pilgrimage*. Dublin, 1955.

Munro, R.: *Ancient Scottish Lake-Dwellings*. Edinburgh, 1882.

Murray, Liz and Colin: *The Celtic Tree Oracle*. 1988.

Nance, R.M.: 'The Plen an Gwary', *Journal of the Royal Institute of Cornwall* 24 (1935), pp. 190–211.

Nash-Williams, V.E.: *The Early Christian Monuments of Wales*. Cardiff, 1950.

Nichols, Ross: *The Book of Druidry*. 1990.

Owen, Trefor: *Welsh Folk Customs*. Llandysul, 1987.

O hUginn, Tadg Dall: *The Bardic Poems*. Trans. E. Knott. 1926.

O'Rahilly, T.F.: *Early Irish History and Mythology*. Institute for Advanced Studies. Dublin, 1946.

O'Riordain, S.P.: 'The Genesis of the Celtic Cross', in W. Penders (ed.), *Feilscribhinn Torna*. Cork, 1947.

Pauli, L.: *Keltischer Volksglaube: Amulette und Sonderbestattungen am Dürrnberg*. Munich, 1975.

Pennick, Nigel: *The Ancient Science of Geomancy*. 1979.

—: *The Subterranean Kingdom: A Survey of Man-Made Structures beneath the Earth*. Wellingborough, 1981.

—: *Einst war uns die Erde heilig*. Waldeck-Dehringhausen, 1987.

—: *Earth Harmony*. 1987.

—: *Mazes and Labyrinths*. 1990.

—: *Secret Games of the Gods*. York Beach, 1992.

—: *Anima Loci*. Bar Hill, 1993.

Piggott, Stuart: *The Druids*. 1968.

Powell, T.G.E.: *The Celts*. 1980.

Radford, C.A.R.: *Margam Stones Museum*. 1949.

Redknap, Mark: *The Christian Celts: Treasures of Late Celtic Wales*. Cardiff, 1991.

Rees, Alwyn, and Brinley Rees: *Celtic Heritage*. 1967.

Rhys, John: *Lectures on Religion as Illustrated by Celtic Heathendom*. 1888.

—: *Celtic Folklore*. Oxford, 1901.

Rochholz, E.L.: *Drei Gaugöttinen: Walburg, Verena und Gertrud als deutsche Kirchenheilige*. Leipzig, 1870.

Ross, Anne: *Pagan Celtic Britain*. 1992.

Rowe, Samuel: *A Perambulation of the Antient and Royal Forest of Dartmoor and the Venville Precincts*. Plymouth, 1848.

Rowlands, Henry: *Mona Antiqua Restaurata*. 1723.

Rutherford, Ward: *The Druids*. Wellingborough, 1985.

—: *Celtic Mythology*. Wellingborough, 1987.

Ryan, J.: *Irish Monasticism*. Dublin, 1931.

Sammes, Aylett: *Britannia Antiqua Illustrata*. 1673.

Schwarzfischer, Karl: 'A Study of Erdställe in the Danubian Area of Germany', *Subterranea Britannica Bulletin* 2 (1975).

Sharkey, John: *Celtic Mysteries*. 1975.

Sikes, Wirt: *British Goblins: Welsh Folk-lore, Fairy Mythology, Legends and Traditions*, 1880.

Simpson, W. Douglas: *The Ancient Stones of Scotland*. 1973.

Spence, Lewis: *The Mysteries of Britain*. 1928.

Stokes, W.: *Three Irish Glossaries*, 1862.

Thevenot, E.: *Divinités et sanctuaires de la Gaule*. Paris, 1968.

Thomas, Patrick: *The Opened Door: A Celtic Spirituality*. Brechfa, 1990.

—: *A Candle in the Darkness: Celtic Spirituality from Wales*. Llandysul, 1993.

Trede, T.: *Das Heidentum in der römischen Kirche*. Gotha, 1901.

Tuke, J.H.: *A Visit to Donegal and Connaught in the Spring of 1880*. 1888.

Twiss, R.: *A Tour in Ireland in 1755*. 1776.

Vernaliken, Theodor: *Völksüberlieferungen aus der Schweiz*. Vienna, 1858.

Watkins, Alfred: *Early British Trackways, Moats, Mounds, Camps and Sites*. Hereford, 1922.

Wellcome, Henry S.: *Hen Feddegyaeth Cymric (Antient Cymric Medicine)*. Swansea, 1903.

Wilde, Lady Jane Francesca Speranza: *Ancient Legends, Mystic Charms and Superstitions of Ireland*. 1888.

Wilks, J.H.: *Trees of the British Isles in History and Legend*. 1972.

Williams, Edward (ed.): *Barddas*. Llandovery, 1862.

Wood-Martin, W.G.: *Pagan Ireland*. 1895.

—: *Traces of the Elder Faiths of Ireland*. 1902.

Wright, Dudley: *Druidism: The Ancient Faith of Britain*. 1924.

222

Index

223

224